ANGUAGE PR⌷⌷⌷⌷R

HE DISADV⌷⌷⌷AGED

The Report of the NCTE Task Force on Teaching English to the Disadvantaged

Richard Corbin

Muriel Crosby

COCHAIRMEN

NATIONAL COUNCIL OF TEACHERS OF ENGLISH

BOOK DESIGNED BY IRENE SLOTTOW

PHOTO CREDITS

The photographs in this book are used through the courtesy of the following persons, schools, and organizations:

Front Cover: Gordon McAndrew, North Carolina Advancement School, Winston-Salem, North Carolina.

Frontispiece of Book: New York City Board of Education, Brooklyn, New York.

Part I: Frontispiece, William Dallam, State Department of Public Instruction, Harrisburg, Pennsylvania; page 5, Charles Calitri, Hofstra University, Hempstead, New York; page 10, Bureau of Publications, Baltimore City Schools, Baltimore, Maryland; page 14, Charles Calitri, Hofstra University, Hempstead, New York; page 15, Audio-Visual Section, Los Angeles City School Districts, Los Angeles, California; page 18, Hildegard Thompson, United States Bureau of Indian Affairs; page 22, Will Kyselka, University of Hawaii, Honolulu, Hawaii; page 27, Robert Bennett, San Diego City Schools, San Diego, California; page 33, Gordon McAndrew, North Carolina Advancement School, Winston-Salem, North Carolina; page 35, Mary McDonald, New York City Board of Education, Brooklyn, New York.

Page II: Frontispiece, William Dallam, State Department of Public Instruction, Harrisburg, Pennsylvania; page 41, John Sheehan, Department of Education, Honolulu, Hawaii; page 45, Ruth Baylor, New York City Board of Education, Brooklyn, New York; page 48, Virginia Reid, Oakland Public Schools, Oakland, California; page 53, Verda Evans, Cleveland Public Schools, Cleveland, Ohio; page 57, Ruth Baylor, New York City Board of Education, Brooklyn, New York; page 60, Virginia Reid, Oakland Public Schools, Oakland, California; page 72, Audio-Visual Section, Los Angeles City School Districts, Los Angeles, California; page 75, Hildegard Thompson, United States Bureau of Indian Affairs; page 79, William Dallam, State Department of Public Instruction, Harrisburg, Pennsylvania; page 82, Helen Lloyd, New York City Board of Education, Brooklyn, New York; page 85, Hildegard Thompson, United States Bureau of Indian Affairs; page 90, Robert Bennett, San Diego City Schools, San Diego, California; page 95, Virginia Reid, Oakland Public Schools, Oakland, California; page 100, Verda Evans, Cleveland Public Schools, Cleveland, Ohio; page 106, Gordon McAndrew, North Carolina Advancement School, Winston-Salem, North Carolina; page 114, Ruth Reeves, Houston Public Schools, Houston, Texas; page 129, Gilbert Johnson, Dade County Public Schools, Miami, Florida; page 136, Gilbert Johnson, Dade County Public Schools, Miami, Florida; page 141, Mary McDonald, New York City Board of Education, Brooklyn, New York; page 155, Mary McDonald, New York City Board of Education, Brooklyn, New York; page 167, William Hoth, Wayne State University, Detroit, Michigan; page 175, Charles Calitri, Hofstra University, Hempstead, New York; page 178, William Hoth, Wayne State University, Detroit, Michigan; page 182, *Washington Post*, Washington, D.C.; page 189, Virginia Reid, Oakland Public Schools, Oakland, California.

Page III: Frontispiece, Charles Calitri, Hofstra University, Hempstead, New York; page 196, Bureau of Publications, Baltimore City Public Schools, Baltimore, Maryland; page 200, Audio-Visual Section, Los Angeles City School Districts,

Continued on vi

BLIND MAN'S BLUFF

by ELSIE CORREA, age 11
Public School 87
New York City
Art Teacher: MRS. F. P. COHEN

THE TASK FORCE

Members

RICHARD CORBIN, Hunter College High School, *Cochairman*

MURIEL CROSBY, Wilmington, Delaware, Public Schools, *Cochairman*

PAUL D. ALLEN, Wayne State University

ROGER K. APPLEBEE, University of Illinois

BERNICE M. CHRISTENSON, Los Angeles Public Schools

WILLIAM M. DALLAM, Pennsylvania State Department of Public Instruction

ROGER D. GEHLBACH, National Council of Teachers of English

ROBERT F. HOGAN, National Council of Teachers of English

TOM R. HOPKINS, United States Bureau of Indian Affairs

ROBERT J. LACAMPAGNE, National Council of Teachers of English

SAN-SU C. LIN, Southern University

ALLAN MUSKOPF, Wisconsin State University, Eau Claire

VIRGINIA M. REID, Oakland Public Schools, Oakland, California

FRANK E. ROSS, Oakland County Schools, Pontiac, Michigan

WILLIAM M. SEE, Jefferson High School, Portland, Oregon

ROGER W. SHUY, Michigan State University

MARJORIE B. SMILEY, Hunter College

JAMES R. SQUIRE, University of Illinois, National Council of Teachers of English

ETHEL C. TINCHER, Detroit Public Schools

DARWIN T. TURNER, North Carolina Agricultural and Technical College

ANDREW J. VISCOVICH, Interagency Project, Oakland, California

MARY YORK, St. Louis Public Schools

Consultants

ROBERT F. BARNES, University of California, Davis

CARL E. BEREITER, University of Illinois

ARNO JEWETT, United States Office of Education

SAMUEL A. KIRK, University of Illinois

WALTER LOBAN, University of California, Berkeley

LEE A. PEDERSON, University of Minnesota

JANET SAWYER, Long Beach State College

SOL TAX, University of Chicago

National Council of Teachers of English

COMMITTEE ON PUBLICATIONS

JAMES R. SQUIRE, NCTE Executive Secretary, *Chairman*

GLENN LEGGETT, Grinnell College

VIRGINIA M. REID, Oakland Public Schools, Oakland, California

FRANK E. ROSS, Oakland County Schools, Pontiac, Michigan

ACKNOWLEDGMENTS

The NCTE Task Force thanks all authors and publishers who granted permission to quote copyrighted material, school districts which furnished curriculum guides for reference, and persons who furnished photographs. Credits for quoted material appear in accompanying footnotes. Photo credits are on page ii.

iv

PREFACE

When Congress and the President committed the nation less than two years ago to unprecedented war upon poverty, the basic importance of education in every sector was at once clear. Without the skills, the knowledge, the understandings that only training of the mind provides, there can be no durable solutions to the age-old human problems of vocational incompetence, slum housing, social disjuncture, and intellectual atrophy that are the fated products of poverty. Without literacy and without the experience of literature, the individual is denied the very dignity that makes him human and a contributing member of our free society.

The National Council of Teachers of English, aware of its unique position of leadership in the nation's effort to rid itself of the curse of poverty, responded quickly to the call. Meeting in February 1965, the Executive Committee of the Council concluded that the great need of the moment was for information about the hundreds of independent and uncoordinated programs in language and reading for the disadvantaged that had sprung up in every part of the country. So compelling was this need that the Committee determined to establish a National Task Force which would survey and report upon individual programs throughout the nation.

So urgent, indeed, did the Committee judge this need that rather than wait upon the delay and the uncertain possibility of government or foundation support, it decided to underwrite the not inconsiderable cost of the Task Force from the Council's own funds .

From schools, universities, and related educational agencies, it enlisted a force of twenty-two experts and three consultants who met in Chicago in March for briefing. Within two months, visiting in teams, the Task Force had observed and reported in detail upon 190 programs for the disadvantaged, both rural and urban, in all sections of the United States. They visited 115 districts and agencies in 64 cities and towns. By the end of June—but three months after the project began—the members of the Task Force with five consultants met at French Lick, Indiana, to review their findings and to plan this report.

That so massive a project was completed in so short a time can be attributed only to the willing cooperation and often personal sacrifice on the part of many individuals. The Executive Committee, on behalf of the Council and the profession, is deeply grateful to these people:

—to the administrators, teachers, and other personnel of the programs surveyed

—to the members of the Task Force who interrupted already busy professional lives to travel tens of thousands of miles to carry on their investigations

—to their school and college administrators who made possible the release of Task Force members from regular teaching and administrative assignments

—to members of the NCTE headquarters staff for their tireless work, and especially to Robert Lacampagne and Roger Gehlbach for their able coordination and round-the-clock efforts in behalf of the project.

We release this report to the profession and to the nation, well aware of its shortcomings, but confident that it is a major contribution to our knowledge of the special problems of the disadvantaged.

November 1965   RICHARD CORBIN
                       President
                       National Council of Teachers of English

Continued from ii

Los Angeles, California; page 210, Hildegard Thompson, United States Bureau of Indian Affairs; page 218, *Ebony* Magazine, Johnson Publishing Company, Chicago, Illinois; page 221, Audio-Visual Section, Los Angeles City School Districts, Los Angeles, California; page 227, Division of Elementary Schools, Los Angeles City Schools, Los Angeles, California.

Part IV: Frontispiece, Virginia Reid, Oakland Public Schools, Oakland, California; page 243, Gilbert Johnson, Dade County Public Schools, Miami, Florida; page 263, Will Kyselka, University of Hawaii, Honolulu, Hawaii; page 268, William Hoth, Wayne State University, Detroit, Michigan.

Part V: Frontispiece, Helen Mackintosh, United States Office of Education, Washington, D.C.; page 274, *Ebony* Magazine, Johnson Publishing Company, Chicago, Illinois.

Part VI: Frontispiece, Gordon McAndrew, North Carolina Advancement School, Winston-Salem, North Carolina.

Rear Cover: Ford Foundation, Roy Stevens, Photographer; Courtesy of Helen K. Mackintosh, United States Office of Education.

CONTENTS

CONTENTS—continued

Part I

THE TASK FORCE AND THE PROBLEM

Literacy, Literature, and the Disadvantaged
RICHARD CORBIN

**The NCTE Task Force: Its Organization,
Operation, and Major Findings**

Literacy, Literature, and the Disadvantaged

RICHARD CORBIN

How will you ever straighten up this shape;
Touch it again with immortality;
Give back the upward looking and the light;
Rebuild in it the music and the dream?

Edwin Markham

The caricature of a well-meaning citizen shutting the door of his house against a ragged, alcoholic vagrant and then returning to his desk to finish writing a generous bank cheque payable to the order of the Salvation Army is not uncommon in our literature. He is genuinely disturbed at the idea of human poverty and suffering. He is willing to give unselfishly of his hard-earned money to help relieve it. But, ironically, he does not recognize poverty and suffering when he meets it face to face on his own doorstep.

That his charity is not entirely unselfish does not detract from his essential goodness and laudable desire to do what is seemly and right. In an abstract way he realizes that undernourished, undereducated, unemployed human beings are potentially a hazard to his own security and well-being, though as he drives comfortably in his last year's car through Harlem and Harlan County he fails somehow to perceive the hunger and the spiritual dismemberment which he dimly knows and subconsciously fears, and which he would be very glad, indeed, to help eradicate if he thought he could.

Granted that this cartoon oversimplifies and at the same time distorts its subject, nonetheless there is in it an essential truth. There has never been on earth, so far as history discloses, a people more sympathetic to human suffering and more willing to give of its earnings to help alleviate that suffering than the American people as a nation. Yet as individuals the vast majority of us prefer agencies to personal charity. We prefer making a donation to the Society of the Blind, Inc., to dropping a quarter in a blind man's cup. We would rather contribute to ''Disabled War Veterans'' than push wheelchairs two hours a week in a nearby Veterans' Hospital.

In this preference for "letting George do it," we may possibly be wiser than we know, for George, whoever he is, may be more knowledgeable in such matters than we. In an increasingly complex civilization, unavoidably he becomes our agent and intermediary. And he is, we hope, an expert. He knows which man is the true sufferer and which is the faker. He will see that our quarters buy soup and not beer, or beer instead of soup, if that seems the indicated therapy. Paradoxically, as we grow more compulsive in our sharing and more determined to wipe out human suffering, we are in effect putting greater distance between the sufferer and ourselves, until, at last, he becomes an abstraction—and thus it is that we abruptly shut the door in his face when he knocks, not seeing him for what he is, a part of poverty itself.

But poverty is not the subject of this paper, though it is inescapably a related theme to which we will, and must, return. The caricature with which I began was only partly intended to make this relationship clear. The purpose of this paper is to suggest that the ancient stalemate in mankind's war against poverty has at last begun to resolve itself, that the decisive and determining force responsible is education, and that the heart's core of this force is, or should be, or must be, the teaching of English. For the armory of our profession contains two of the most powerful of all social weapons, skill with language and meaningful familiarity with literature. In a most realistic sense, we cannot save the fifty million economically and culturally disadvantaged human beings who are drowning in the sea of our national affluence until we have taught them, beginning in their earliest childhood, to speak, to read, and in some measure, to write the words and forms of English that are acceptable to our society. We cannot effectively impart these skills until, through the help of literature, we have struck some spark of self-illumination, a flash of that inner light which informs the human spirit as to what it is and what it can become, and without which we are but vegetables.

From our distant vantage points, however, we cannot, we must not, delude ourselves into the belief that helping the disadvantaged to find their way up from the fenways of illiteracy is merely a matter of acquainting them with the "great poets." There are many mansions in the house of literature, too, but most of them, as we well know, are securely locked against the mind that does not possess the key of literacy. The white teacher of an underachieving eighth grade class of inner city Negro children who began their study of poetry with Wordsworth's "Daffodils" is a case in point. Yet the house of literature is as varied as human experience, and somewhere among its uncounted chambers are those that disadvantaged can and might enter, if and when these chambers are identified and if their doors are flung wide.

At this point, let me draw you another caricature, this time of a well-trained, dedicated teacher of English. From the department meeting where he has just spoken out passionately against the suggestion of a special, "ungraded" program of appropriate (that it, "meaningful") literature for the disadvantaged pupils in the school ("We cannot lower our standards!"), he is returning to his home where he will write a bank cheque in favor of Youth Saved, Inc., an agency that works in the less privileged neighborhoods of his community to save dropouts and "pushed-outs" from an all too certain life of vocational, social, and cultural unfulfillment.

This teacher knows his subject and, to the extent that he can, he knows his students. He knows that some are superior in ability, most are average, and too many are "slow learners." These categories are, perhaps have always been, common stereotypes in the profession. He is vaguely disturbed by the self-knowledge that he is giving the best of

Students in a Demonstration Class at Summer Institute at Hofstra University

5

himself to the superior, is managing to bear rather nobly with the average, but is impatient with and neglectful of the slow. "But what's the use?" he says in self-justification. "They can't learn anyway!" And he is at least partly right. Some of the group called "slow learners" are indeed slow in the most hopeless sense and, for their own and society's good, should have special, separate handling. They are nature's mistakes who depend for their survival upon our common humanity. They can and do come from all levels of the community, although for reasons that have little or nothing to do with genetics, they come into the common schools more often from the "wrong" side than from the economically and socially more advantaged side of the tracks. But trained though he has been in the semantics of the generalization, our teacher somehow fails to recognize the fallacy in his rationalization. Though he has come unquestioningly to accept "superior" and "gifted" as useful labels for distinguishing a degree of difference among pupils in the upper range of ability, he is not yet prepared to see, or if he sees, to acknowledge the sharp, in a sense the sharper, division among the pupils in the lowest track, or band, or stream, or whatever it is called, in his school.

For submerged in the generalization "slow learners" is a large and definable group, newly discovered, in a sense, and known by various labels—the "culturally different," the "educationally deprived," the "underprivileged," or, more commonly of late, the "disadvantaged," (which is the designation that I will use hereafter). These are the children from America's slums, both rural and urban. These are Puerto Ricans, migrant whites from Appalachia and other economically depressed areas, Mexican "wetbacks," and American Indians, but mostly they are Negroes.

Whatever the racial or ethnic background of these disadvantaged, their circumstances are much the same. They come from families that exist on annual incomes which fall below the established national minimum subsistence level, that have known little or no schooling, that have no job security. More than half have only one parent (generally the mother), and many have never known either parent. They come from families who seldom aspire, or when they do, aspire unrealistically, who are often idle because few jobs are open to them. They are the people who exist—one can hardly say "live"—on the wretched rim of an otherwise affluent world. And they number not fewer than one quarter of our total national population.

We have our lower track students, indeed, but camouflaged among them, and thus largely unattended, is this larger group of children from "different" and sometimes foreign-speaking cultures, refugees from our

6

infamous poverty pockets, or, increasingly, the offspring of the ghetto itself. They appear one day at the principal's door, are given verbal intelligence tests, reading tests of to them meaningless content, and on the basis of these gross and misleading measures are assigned either to classes dedicated to the reading of "Dick and Jane" or *Silas Marner* and the conjugation of the English verb, or to "special" classes resentfully supervised by professional "baby sitters."

A crucial fact that must be understood about this group is that proportionately as many of them are slow, average, superior, and gifted as for the school population as a whole—proportionately as many of them are, potentially, "college entrance" material or, at the least, contributing members of society. But this the conventional tests do not disclose. The tests and other standard sources of data condemn the majority of these children to failure before they enter their first classroom. They are trapped and helpless in the deep fissure of economic and educational impoverishment. Nor is much that happens to them in the ghetto school likely to free them from this cruel trap. In fact, the standard curriculum to which they are committed hastens the decay of their egos and reduces, rather than strengthens, their ability to deal successfully with books, ideas, and language. Instead of growing, their measured I.Q.'s decline as they advance from grade to grade, though we know, in general, that growth is the normal pattern of the human intellect. Few of these children ever come to know what our magic word *college* means, however high their real, but unrealized, intelligence level may be.

I have tried to evoke an understanding of the nature and character of the so-called "disadvantaged" student. This image is not entirely accurate, however, for I have presented him in the context of an atypical, heterogeneous setting. More commonly he is segregated. More commonly he is a sociological statistic among those thousands of other similarly disadvantaged, deprived, different—or what you will—statistics who populate the slum or ghetto schools in our great urban centers. But I have seen him and I have taught him, and I can report to you that he is an educable human being and not a statistic. Unfortunately, this kind of child is becoming less and less the exception in our expanding, mobile, and increasingly urban and industrialized society.

He is multiplying at a disproportionate rate as science and automation force upward the minimal educational requirements for every kind of labor (the human ditch digger has long since disappeared from our technically proficient culture), and consequently increasing numbers of the unskilled and semiskilled sink below the subsistence level. This condition is so threatening, so real and, indeed, so nationally reprehensible, that it demands of us more sleeplessness than any nebulous threat of a nuclear holocaust.

Since it is no secret that somewhat over half of the disadvantaged share two special characteristics—they are Negro and they are prisoners of the urban slum—I shall in the remainder of this paper focus attention upon the educational problems of this group as they relate to the teaching of English, subtle as this relationship may at times seem. I shall, moreover, speak mainly of Harlem, which has become a generally recognized symbol for the minority ghettos in all of our great cities. This is not to minimize the importance of dealing nationally, in small town and large, with the problem of the "disadvantaged American," be he white or black or red. But this is the group that I know best and whose hopelessness poses, in my opinion, the greatest challenge to our national conscience and to our will to be that which we claim to be—the most advanced of all nations economically, socially, technically, and culturally on this shrinking, but still sizeable, planet.

Harlem, viewed through the eyes of the mass media, and judged only according to the value standards of middle and upper class America, is a fearsome jungle of crime, antisocial behavior, sexuality, dope addiction, domestic irresponsibility—and all of the other characteristics that are ever associated with the word *slum*. The trained and impartial observer, however, though he would not dismiss these reports as entirely false, reminds us that evil behavior is always more conspicuous than good. To counterbalance the tabloid picture, he would remind us that there are many churches and religious cults in Harlem, and many hardworking PTA's, and parents who live their lives out together and who love their children and try, within their pitifully restricted limits, to give them more than they themselves have had. In other words, it must be remembered that Harlem is a community of 233,000 human beings, saddled with all of the problems that any other community of comparable size endures. But in Harlem these problems are larger and seemingly less soluble; they are aggravated and intensified by the complication of "color."

I once heard Puerto Rico described as a country with a rhythmic pattern of wealth and poverty. Traveling through the country, my informant noted, one passes hovels and mansions almost evenly interspersed. In the great cities of the United States (and even in the small), in contrast, the dwellings of the poor and of the wealthy tend to cluster like iron filings about the separate poles of a magnet. But the density at the slum pole is normally the thicker. One statistician has noted that if the population density of one particular Harlem block were extended

8

throughout the borough, the entire population of the United States could be housed on Manhattan Island.

In the community of Harlem there are twenty elementary schools and four junior high schools. For the purposes of this paper, we may assume that whatever conditions hold for these schools in general hold also for the teaching of English. Yet actually, the statistics look better on paper than they probably are in fact. For the last study was in 1955, and it reported that 50 percent of the elementary teachers in Harlem schools at that time were on tenure as contrasted with 78 percent for the rest of the City. In the junior high schools, it was only 47 percent as contrasted with 62 percent. One can assume that the situation today, almost a decade later, is no better, if it is as good. But this is only part of the picture, for looking further we find that 18 percent of the Harlem elementary teachers and 37 percent of the junior high school teachers had been appointed with only permanent substitute status as compared with 8 percent and 25 percent respectively for the elementary and junior high schools outside of Harlem.

If these percentages are roughly true for the teachers of English in the junior high schools, then the condition revealed nationally in the recent *The National Interest and the Teaching of English* report is substantiated, but more grimly in Harlem. There the shortage of trained, capable teachers is aggravated by the fact that the great majority of such teachers appear to feel no personal or professional involvement in the problem. Assigned to a disadvantaged school, they waste no time applying for transfers to more desirable schools. Compounding the problem, large numbers of teachers are assigned to classes outside their major field of interest or training.

Of six junior high school teachers who tried out the Hunter College Project English materials in several Harlem schools, two were social studies teachers and one a business education teacher. Of the remaining three, two were relatively inexperienced teachers. These two, however, though young, were particularly effective teachers who could at any time obtain appointments in less demanding suburban schools, but who chose to remain among the urban disadvantaged. Their decision to stay with the job can be attributed in no small measure to two factors: they had some special training for this work, and they had the support of new and specially developed materials provided by the Project Center. Even this small help, there is good reason to believe, has enabled them to experience that sense of accomplishment which the true teacher craves. They are a demonstration that the situation is not hopeless, that teaching the disadvantaged can be richly rewarding if it is approached positively, with

9

understanding, with relevant materials, and with common sense. Here and there in the disadvantaged schools are other teachers who underscore the truth of this observation. Unfortunately, they are few in number.

If we believe that well-prepared, interested teachers are essential to an effective educational program under normal conditions, how are we to continue to rationalize this almost impossible situation in the disadvantaged school, where good teachers are even more essential, yet sometimes almost impossible to attract? For in such schools, teachers need to be not only good in the usual sense, but "good" also in very special ways. Or perhaps it would be more accurate to say that a "good" teacher is a good teacher anywhere but, for the purposes of the ghetto school, must be better in ways different from those that spell success in the typically rural or suburban school.

This is especially true of the teacher of English. He must not only understand and believe in the culture of his own, more privileged, background and be sensitive to the methods most practicable for transmitting its values to others, but he must also be a working sociologist, psychologist, and anthropologist, able to understand in depth the structure of the

Investigating a Starfish in Baltimore, Maryland

different culture of which his students are a part. Like his rural and suburban colleagues, he must, of course, be able also to understand and sympathize with the child as a distinctly human being. But where the suburban teacher and his pupils are part of the same world, the teacher in the disadvantaged school is essentially a stranger. If he behaves like a "tourist," he will make little headway as a teacher. He must not only know that daffodils do not grow in the window boxes of Harlem, but why there are few window boxes at all. He must realize that many of the people of Harlem do not lie serene upon couches in vacant or in pensive mood, but toss frantically upon "hot beds." He must understand that when a Harlem resident *is* found in vacant or in pensive mood, "pot" more likely than poetry was the magic casement through which he fled to faery lands forlorn. Upon such alien images, with their socially violent implications, the teacher must look with compassion and an understanding that this way of life for the disadvantaged was not of their choosing, but is the only way they have or know. That final word "know" provides, at least, a toehold for the alert and agile teacher.

Now, for a moment, let us hypothesize that by some magic we have staffed at least the English classes of our substandard school with trained and reasonably competent teachers who are determined to raise the sights and the achievement levels of their disadvantaged pupils. What are some of the obstacles they must surmount? Typically, first of all, fewer than 10 percent of their students will be reading at or above grade level; most of the rest will be reading from two to four years below. And the charts show clearly that the gap between the median for these pupils and the national median grows wider with each year of schooling. The textbooks available for teaching reading or for literary study (a euphemistic term!) will be taken from a Board of Education approved list. For the lower grades there will be the usual reading texts that are found in classrooms the country over—readers generously illustrated with well-fed, pink-cheeked, honey-haired boys and girls playing against backdrops of white picket fences. In these books the strangely pale children in their strange, white world talk about the strange activities of their Anglo-Saxon fathers and mothers in a strange, childish dialect that one might even hesitate to describe as good Scarsdalian. Advancing through the grades, there will be other books with still other foreign dialects— the London and Midland dialects, perhaps, of a *Great Expectations*. With these materials the upper 10 percent will progress, but never to the same degree as the upper 10 per cent of readers in non-ghetto schools. As we have already noted, the great majority will fall further and further below the achievement levels of their counterparts in the schools "outside."

Yet, reading, we are assured by almost every reputable authority, must be the main focus of our program, if we hope ever to raise the general educational level of these children.

But reading, we are also told, leans inescapably upon the skills of speaking and listening. Can a child—a nonmotivated slum child—learn to read a dialect that he seldom hears used and does not use himself in speaking? And if it is not a dialect that spells survival at home or in the streets, what motivation is there for him to learn it at all? The perceptive teacher very quickly discovers that his problem is more complex than his courses in reading methods made it appear. He discovers, for one thing, that he and his pupils do not speak the same language and, furthermore, that they see very little reason for adopting his. Their families, their streetmates, after all, speak theirs, not his. What is he to do now, Miss Landers?

When the teacher attacks the problem of the pupils' spoken English, as he certainly must, which dialect is he to offer for a model? Shall he begin, for instance, with the seemingly missing *g* on *ing*? (He himself was educated at Brooklyn College and Columbia University, yet in his unguarded speech, commonly says "Wotaya doin?") Or should he concentrate upon the qualities of vowels? Will insistence upon *sir* for *suh* or *sah* increase the vocational competence of children to whom most vocations, in spite of all the laws, still are closed? Will it contribute to their achievement as readers? Or will it, possibly, add to the number of classroom clams—the children who not only do not speak voluntarily or when spoken to, but do not speak at all?

And the skill of listening! By most accounts, audiodiscrimination is essential to success in beginning reading. Put another and simpler way, the surest road to beginning reading success is the opportunity to hear stories told at the earliest possible age. Yet the teacher of the primary grades in the disadvantaged school discovers that hardly a child in his class has enjoyed this experience. Shall he begin naively to fill this vacuum by reading to his pupils "Goldilocks and the Three Bears" or "Little Black Sambo"? What will be the silent impact of either of these innocent stories upon his largely Negro audience? Is there an easy answer?

And what of the skill of writing, what is to be his approach? Shall it be intensive drill upon subject-verb agreement (yo' *are*, not yo' *is*) or shall the teacher overlook dialectal differences, hoping that some few in the class writing on the time-dishonored topic "My Summer Vacation" will move beyond stickball on 138th Street to the question of "why?" Should each slight effort be read and marked minutely for grammatical "correctness," or should the teacher be encouraged by even single instances of eloquence, such as these sentences, with their sad overtones, culled from a set of seventh grade papers, in which the writers are giving a "free" response to a "still" shot of the courtroom trial in the motion picture *To Kill a Mockingbird*:

"One calm quite [sic] day in a small town in Missouri, Tom Robinson decided he had enough."

"Knowing that he was a Negro, he knew that something bad would happen."

"He walked slowly to the door and sat down in the electric chair."

"My life is common labor every day.
"Nothing by [sic] trouble comes the easy way."

"But she will get up enough nerve to tell the truth."

"He was white lawyer who believed in Negroes."

"And then the jury looking to her—Mayella Ewell, Atticus Finch, and Judge Taylor, like they say with the eyes you lier [sic], and he say no I did not kill her and that was the story. He did not kill her."

" She felt sorry for Tom because he was a thief like her father."

If these isolated bits and pieces of rhetoric do not add up to composition, they are at least disturbing revelation. Could these disadvantaged children possibly be written off as uneducable? By the tens of thousands, every school day, all over the nation, they are.

Though distorted by oversimplification, these are the kinds of perplexities that present themselves to the teacher. What line of action shall he follow? Even if he has been born and brought up and educated in the city, his home is likely a thousand miles away, by subway and socioeconomic level, from the realities of Harlem. He was well trained in the city college to teach (the very designation *city college* has a strange connotation for historical America), yet even there he was not prepared to teach in a ghetto school. He gained his initial experience, with some exceptions, in a predominantly white, middle class school, with pupils who *did* know a daffodil from a handsaw. Where do teachers in this uncommon and perilous situation turn for help?

This is perhaps the focal question of this paper. And although I fervently wish I did, I do not know the answer. I do not, in fact, think at the present time that there is an answer. Though at least one quarter of the nation is directly affected, only a small part of the federal effort in the form of Project English and NDEA institute grants is directed at this problem. In recent years, some of the great cities and universities of the nation have initiated projects on their own. But in the main we have sat by and watched the problem grow unchallenged for too long.

Students in Demonstration Teaching Class at Hofstra University

It has moved beyond the power of local agencies to control it. Whether Democrats or Republicans inhabit the White House is irrelevant; this is not a political problem—it is a real, a degrading, an immediate national problem that confronts us all. I have focused on Harlem, but I might as well have been speaking of Cleveland, Rochester, Chicago, Phoenix, Newburg, Atlanta, or a hundred other cities—or the bean fields of central New York State, the orchards of Oregon, or of a Navajo Reservation. The problems of the very poor vary in degree but negligibly in kind. Only by putting our national wits together can we solve this problem. The words, perhaps, sound hackneyed; the conviction underlying them is not. Being the nation that we are, I am convinced that we can.

What is to be the role of NCTE and other comparable professional organizations in this mushrooming national problem? Are we to engage it, or is this essentially a peripheral, not a central, problem in our society, and therefore not a compelling responsibility of the Council? The latter position seems hardly tenable in view of the opinions expressed, by leaders in every area of our public life, from President Johnson to James Conant, that education is the chief weapon in the currently pending all-out war on poverty and illiteracy. Even if the politicians withdraw their forces from the fight, the teachers can not, for we have always been and must continue to be dedicated to any cause that promises, by the application of our skills and talents, to improve the human condition.

By training and by nature I am not a "city" teacher, though that is where chance has finally brought me. Most of my life has been lived in rural and suburban communities, closely associated with their English needs. This fact of background guarantees that I am no expert on urban problems, though it has, I believe, served to broaden my perspective as an observer. In the past four years, I have seen enough of the disparity

Learning about a Holiday in a Los Angeles Preschool

15

between a great city's excellent "special" and its "disadvantaged" schools to become deeply disturbed. The gap is too large and is growing steadily. As the middle class continues to fly to the suburbs, the essential neutral zone, with all of its regrettable inadequacies, is disappearing. By 1970, we are told, more than one half of the population of Manhattan will fall under the label of disadvantaged, if the present trend continues unchallenged. But let me remind you again that while I am speaking here mainly of the disadvantaged as a nationwide problem, and of New York's Harlem only as a convenient and obvious symbol, this condition is a reality in all of our great cities. In every sense, it is a national problem, affecting rich and poor, rural and urban citizens alike.

I have seen the disadvantaged in their schools, have observed inept teaching, have examined inappropriate materials and, in the face of all of these adverse factors, have yet been tremendously impressed by the promise of the central fact, the children themselves. Either we must learn to live with and eventually succumb to ignorance and illiteracy or we put our minds to the project of its control and eventual obliteration. For myself, I favor the latter course, though I dearly love to teach the "Ode on a Grecian Urn."

The NCTE Task Force:
Its Organization, Operation and
Major Findings

Concern for the disadvantaged among the American people has assumed much significance since the 1954 Supreme Court decision on the desegregation of public schools. Of corresponding significance, however, are more recent attacks upon the problems of the disadvantaged to find the means not only to guarantee civil rights but to overcome social and economic handicaps. Although neither problem is new, there is currently a new urgency to find solutions to these problems. During the past two years, the American people through their representatives in the United States Congress have clearly assigned a high priority to educational and social programs designed to improve the living conditions of the disadvantaged. Again and again, the educational legislation of the past year provided support and encouragement for this movement. The Economic Opportunity Act of 1964 (and its Job Corps program), the National Defense Education Act of 1964, the Civil Rights Act of 1964 with its provision for assisting desegregating districts, and the Elementary and Secondary Education Act of 1965—these testify to the growing concern.

In the new programs, teachers of English at every level have a special stake. Language is the primary vehicle for learning and for communicating ideas. On language more than almost anything else depends not only acquisition of knowledge and skill, but also one's role in society, the scope of his influence in his own regional or social group, and his mobility in the face of new opportunities. Teachers of English thus have a profound contribution to make to the education of the disadvantaged. The strength of the English component will largely determine whether students will some day be able to surmount the social, economic, and educational barriers which have given rise to the present conditions.

Teachers of English cannot restrict their attention to a single language problem or an easily identified area or group. Rather, they must be concerned with the many dialects of disadvantaged learners from all parts of the United States: the Southern dialects still spoken by Negroes in inner cities of the North, the Midland tongue of middle Tennessee, the

English of the Cajun in Louisiana and Spanish-speaking child of the Southwest, the pidgin English of the Hawaiian child, the linguistic habits of the North American Indian. Whatever the ethnic group, however different the dialect, whatever the social conditions, whatever the age of the learner—the teacher of the English language faces a special responsibility. At a time when new educational programs for the disadvantaged are forming in virtually every region, those who specialize in the learning of language can assess important leadership.

This report is an attempt to determine the effectiveness of language learning in special projects and programs for the disadvantaged across the country. It seeks to identify desirable educational practice and to suggest guidelines for other programs. Above all it is intended to stimulate further effort toward resolving the problems of language learning among the disadvantaged.

Question Games in Oral Language Work with Navajo Children (Donald J. Morrow, Photographer)

Appointment of the Task Force

Concerned about the lack of reliable information on the burgeoning programs for teaching language to the disadvantaged, the Executive Committee of the National Council of Teachers of English in February

18

1965 appointed a special Task Force to study and describe current programs throughout the nation. The Committee directed the Task Force to concern itself with the teaching of language in any of its dimensions—with reading and basic literacy; with literature; with spelling, writing, and speaking; with preschool language programs and postschool opportunities for adults.

Despite years of special programs in the great cities, little was generally known about how school programs were approaching language instruction. Surely a report on what experienced teachers had discovered about the problems, possibilities, disappointments, and opportunities for using new content and approaches in teaching basic skills of literacy was needed by the profession at a time when many other programs seemed prepared to embrace similar approaches. Moreover, new field studies and new research in dialectology, sociology, psychology of language learning, among other fields, offered promising new insights for school programs. But were these new findings reaching directors and teachers in many of the projects for teaching the disadvantaged? Leaders in the National Council of Teachers of English thought not.

Indeed, fearful lest new programs do little more than concentrate on content and approaches long since proven inappropriate for teaching language to the disadvantaged, the NCTE began to consider ways of exercising needed leadership. A special Committee on Adolescent and Adult Illiteracy had just recommended that the Council prepare new materials for teaching reading to disadvantaged adults. Incoming President Richard Corbin, whose paper precedes this chapter, reminded all teachers of English of their stake in programs for the disadvantaged. The Executive Committee responded by appointing a twenty-two member Task Force to survey programs for teaching language and literacy to the disadvantaged and to prepare a report to the profession for distribution no later than the annual November convention in 1965.

The NCTE Task Force on Teaching English to the Disadvantaged is broadly representative of those persons in the profession directly concerned with such programs: professors of English and of education participated in the group, some with special training in linguistics and dialectology, others with background in sociology and social education; directors of two special projects for educating the disadvantaged; supervisors and administrators from large cities already extensively involved in such instruction; a specialist from a field center of the Bureau of Indian Affairs; another from a state department of education. Two classroom teachers participated, their districts generously releasing them for time to make extensive field visits. All educational levels were represented (elementary, secondary, college), as were various geographic regions. In their interest in English, Task Force members were equally varied, some concerned with the structure of language or with reading, others with oral English, literature, or writing. In short, Task Force members represented the varied strands of the profession concerned about teaching English to the disadvantaged. This was the group which accepted the charge to visit programs throughout the country and prepare a descriptive report of current practices.

Operation of the Task Force

During late March, the Task Force met in Chicago to clarify procedures and prepare instruments to guide field visits. Three consultants presented background papers to provide discussion and point of view. Samuel Kirk reviewed research in psychology, indicating the potential success of concentrated educational programs for disadvantaged children. Lee Pederson reviewed the study of social dialects and language learning and reported results of a conference of linguists and educators cosponsored by NCTE and Illinois Institute of Technology.[1] Robert Barnes, having just completed a study of programs for teaching language to disadvantaged adults, not only summarized some of his findings but discussed methods for observing field programs. These background papers appear in this report.

During the ninety days which followed, members of the NCTE Task Force visited and reported in detail on 190 programs, administered by 115 separate districts and agencies, located in 64 different cities. Twenty-eight programs concentrated on preschool education; 60, on elementary; 54, secondary; 6, adult; and 28, teacher education. Fourteen administrative offices were visited largely for the purpose of considering overall administrative organization. Visits normally lasted one or two days and involved two observers, although on some occasions a single member of the Task Force visited for a slightly shorter or longer period. The programs selected for review were those which had received sufficient national attention to be known to leaders of NCTE, as well as programs which were recommended by members of the Task Force, directors of the NDEA institute programs for teachers of the disadvantaged, specialists in the United States Office of Education and in state departments of education, and directors of major projects in urban centers. No claim can be made that the Task Force visited all important programs for teaching English to the disadvantaged, but it can be asserted that the

---

[1] Roger W. Shuy (ed.), *Social Dialects and Language Learning* (Champaign, Ill., National Council of Teachers of English, 1965).

visits encompassed as many programs as possible within the ninety day limit and are probably the most extensive field review of such programs yet undertaken by the profession. Members secured information on other programs and projects from written reports.

In selecting and visiting projects, Task Force observers attempted to gain a comprehensive picture of current developments. They visited every section of the country and every type of institution; if schools of the inner cities offered one focus, programs in rural areas and small towns gave another. Visiting teams sampled programs for teaching English to speakers of other languages including North American Indians and Spanish-speaking youngsters. They visited preschool and adult projects along with programs for elementary and secondary school; they observed teacher education programs because new patterns seem to be emerging in this area. For each program or project visited, a member of the Task Force prepared a separate report. In addition, five members of the Task Force spent several days in June reviewing and studying accumulated materials for teaching the disadvantaged. A summary of the reports on individual visits and of the analysis of teaching materials appears in Part II of the report.

The Task Force did not concern itself extensively with the teaching of college and university students. With the exception of visits to teacher education programs, observers concentrated on preschool, elementary, secondary, and adult programs. The most important reason for this exclusion, perhaps, is that information concerning many such programs is already available to the profession through a newsletter published by the American Council on Education.[2] The great foundations, especially Ford, Rockefeller, Carnegie, and Danforth, have invested millions of dollars in college-level programs and have made possible intercommunication and consultant help not yet widely available or used in the schools.

Still this leadership coming from institutions of higher learning deserves recognition and commendation. For example, precollege summer programs for able disadvantaged youth are being developed on such campuses as Oberlin, Dartmouth, Mout Holyoke, Franklin and Marshall, Dillard, Princeton, Yale, Georgetown, Chicago, Illinois, St. Louis, Pittsburgh, Georgia Tech, Alaska, and Harvard, among others.

Brown University, working with Tougaloo College in Mississippi, is only one of several northern institutions assisting predominantly Negro colleges to strengthen their academic offerings. Cornell University is in

---

[2] *Expanding Opportunities,* Newsletter on the Negro and Higher Education (Washington, D. C.: American Council on Education).

the fifth year of a reciprocal enrichment program with Hampton Institute. The University of Wisconsin has a faculty exchange program with North Carolina College, North Carolina Agricultural and Technical College, and Texas Southern University in Houston. New fellowships are also becoming available to disadvantaged youth. Last year, for instance, the Ford Foundation granted $7 million to the National Merit Scholarship Corporation to provide 200 "National Achievement Scholarships" each year for five years. The Bureau of Indian Affairs has an extensive program of scholarships and grants-in-aid for Indians who are college students. The broadest single effort by far is the educational improvement program launched by the Southern Association of Colleges and Schools and the College Entrance Examination Board, a project that seeks to establish centers in several cities in the South for the purpose of bringing together predominantly Negro and predominantly white colleges and selected public schools for a concentrated attack on the

Indoor Play in a Honolulu Preschool

22

conditions that retard Negro progress. In addition to strengthening their overall educational efforts, about eighteen colleges and eleven school districts are identifying promising Negro youth in the seventh and eighth grades and working with them through the high school years toward the goal of college entrance.

These university programs are an important dimension of the total effort of our society to provide greater educational opportunities for our total citizenry. In this report they receive less attention than preschool, school, and adult programs only because of the greater present need to concentrate on those programs and projects about which so little is now known.

The French Lick Conference

On June 24–27, 1965, the Task Force met for a final three-day study conference at the Sheraton-French Lick Hotel in Indiana. Visits to school programs were completed; final cumulative reactions had been prepared in advance. The purpose of the session was to compare impressions, determine the nature of the final report, and discuss overall observations and recommendations. Almost immediately the conferees discovered that the diversity of what they had observed throughout the country exploded popular fallacies held by teachers concerning the disadvantaged. They asked that their observations be reported as they are later in this chapter. More difficult, however, was the task of agreeing on general observations. The various conditions under which instruction occurs, whether in public and independent schools or in outside agencies, clearly militates against too easy generalizations. Still it seemed possible to identify certain overall impressions reported here and even more desirable to prepare recommendations and suggestions for programs at the various age levels as discussed in Part II of this report.

Participating in the French Lick Conference were five consultants, each of whom brought a unique background and experience to the meeting. Carl Bereiter, Associate Professor of Experimental Psychology, University of Illinois, has been directing an academically oriented preschool for disadvantaged children. Arno Jewett, Specialist in English, United States Office of Education, was director of a national conference on improving the English skills of the disadvantaged.[3] Walter Loban, Professor of Education, University of California, Berkeley, is conducting a twelve-year longitudinal study of language development, including

---

[3] Arno Jewett, Joseph Mersand, and Doris Gunderson (eds.), *Improving the English Skills of Culturally Different Youth* (Washington, D. C.: U. S. Department of Health, Education, and Welfare, Office of Education, 1964).

children who are clearly disadvantaged. Janet Sawyer, Professor of English and Linguistics, Long Beach State College, is a specialist on linguistics and the teaching of English to speakers of other languages. Sol Tax, Professor of Anthropology, University of Chicago, with much experience in studying the cultural concomitants of disadvantaged groups, has begun direction of a project designed to strengthen the education of the Cherokee Indians of eastern Oklahoma. At the conclusion of the French Lick Conference, each consultant presented his observations concerning problems discussed by the Task Force, as well as his suggestions for teachers and educators. The recorded comments of the consultants, with a summary of the discussion which followed, is presented in Part III of the report.

Fallacies to Be Dispelled

Seven widespread beliefs affecting the education of the disadvantaged, pervading and often limiting the thinking and practice of teachers, were found fallacious. Central to the improvement of language programs for the disadvantaged is the exposure of such misconceptions. Consequently, each fallacy identified here is followed by a discussion of what Task Force members actually found in school rooms and programs throughout the country.

FALLACY No. 1: A SINGLE SET OF SUBCULTURAL MORES GUIDES THE BEHAVIOR OF DISADVANTAGED MEMBERS OF OUR SOCIETY.

Despite the fact that school programs often seemed oriented to a single set of subcultural values, Task Force members report great variation in the attitudes of various ethnic and social groups toward such matters as the family, violence, school achievement, honesty, and language habits. Failure to recognize that several attitudes may be represented even in a single classroom results often in oversimplification of content and approach. Within every Negro group or every Spanish-speaking group, for example, subcultural patterns vary considerably. Certainly the habits of these groups will differ significantly from those of the Cajuns of Louisiana or the Oriental subcultures of the Pacific Coast. To understand subcultural mores better, teachers need frequent contact with sociologists and anthropologists who have studied the individual communities. Programs which involve not only educators but also social workers, nurses, and doctors from public health agencies, and consultants from neighboring universities, reveal progress in understanding cultural patterns.

FALLACY No. 2: LANGUAGE PROGRAMS NEED TO INVOLVE ONLY
INSTRUCTION IN USING STANDARD ENGLISH.

That one important aspect of language instruction for the disadvantaged is developing mastery of standard informal English, no one will deny. Yet members of the Task Force often found programs limited to concern for the superficialities of standard formal English. A rigorous, almost exclusive, emphasis on reading workbook passages of nonfiction prose; a concentration on spelling selected words; an oral program limited to drills in formal English usages—these emphases dominate many classrooms. In other programs, however, Task Force members report that concern for language is far more basic and profound. The major task of the language teacher is to assist the pupil to learn to think through language and to communicate with others through language. Oral language experiences in sharing and telling, often conducted in the child's own dialect, thus become important, as do experiences in the logical and effective presentation of ideas. Literature needs to be introduced both for the richness of the esthetic experience and for the insight it can offer about the human condition. The assumption that the teacher of the disadvantaged can concern himself only with the superficial aspects of language threatens the ultimate success of far too many programs.

FALLACY No. 3: ALL DISADVANTAGED CHILDREN ARE APATHETIC
OR DULL AND THEIR CLASSES ARE SELDOM EXCITING.

Task Force members report little evidence to indicate that disadvantaged children are generally less responsive than other children when teachers know how to proceed in the classroom. Some apathy was found, of course, but less than could be expected. A great many such children are warm and appreciative; some appear exceptionally creative when their inner resources are tapped; more than a few were reported as alert and intelligent. The potential for learning is present; teachers need to discover how to develop it. In some schools, disadvantaged children were making important contributions in art, drawing, creative writing, and other cultural and intellectual pursuits.

FALLACY No. 4: DISCIPLINE IS A RADICALLY DIFFERENT PROBLEM IN INNER CITY CLASSROOMS.

The NCTE Task Force reports no extensive difference in the nature of class control in inner city schools for the disadvantaged from those observed elsewhere. The fear of discipline problems prevents many teachers from teaching the disadvantaged, yet class after class visited by Task Force members seemed orderly and responsive. To most members, discipline in the inner city as well as elsewhere seemed largely a matter of teacher expectation.

FALLACY NO. 5: DISADVANTAGED LEARNERS CANNOT ENGAGE IN INDUCTIVE, INQUIRY-CENTERED LEARNING.

Is telling teaching? Too many teachers of the disadvantaged seem to think so. Believing that pupils cannot engage in a variety of thinking processes, especially those involving inquiry, exploration, and generalization, many teachers seem to waste much classroom time trying to present information to children. Disadvantaged children, like any others, must learn to seek information and draw inferences on their own. Task Force members reported numerous classroom activities in which children and young people are thinking inductively—viewing incidents first hand, for instance, and describing and generalizing about them. Since much of the instruction for the disadvantaged must be specific and focused on those deficiencies which most need to be remedied, the inquiry approach with stress on generalizing from specifics may be more important for disadvantaged than for other learners.

FALLACY NO. 6: TEACHING POSITIONS IN SCHOOLS FOR THE DISADVANTAGED DO NOT ATTRACT ABLE TEACHERS.

Task Force members reported that districts, schools, and projects differ considerably in their ability to recruit able teachers of English. Despite widely publicized reports of difficulties in two or three large cities, many administrators throughout the country reported a substantial increase during recent years in the number of highly qualified teachers—some young teachers, some experienced—interested in teaching the disadvantaged. And the teachers seemed genuinely committed, optimistic, and altruistic. In some instances, districtwide recruitment policies requiring prospective teachers to accept a teaching contract with the district without prior information on the assignment apparently interfere with recruitment of teachers for inner city schools. Out of fear that teachers may not accept assignment to the inner city, some districts do not permit school principals to recruit staff members directly. Certain others have virtually abandoned any recruitment program and arbitrarily require every teacher to spend a two-year term in the inner city, a "sentence" which seems based on the asumption that no teacher would ever elect to teach in such schools. Yet according to Task Force members, many principals believe that new teachers can readily be attracted to programs for the disadvantaged if allowed to see existing classroom conditions, to meet fellow staff members, and to consider in advance the purposes of the program. Arbitrary assignment of teachers who would not elect such assignments only creates problems in morale. Apparently, the rising social consciousness in this country, reflected in the response of youth to Job Corps and Peace Corps programs, is stimulating an increasing number of teachers to volunteer for inner city appointments. More well-qualified teachers are needed, of course, but recent recruitment efforts are showing tangible results.

Speech in a San Diego, California, High School

FALLACY NO. 7: SPECIAL TRAINING IS NOT REQUIRED FOR TEACH-ING ENGLISH TO THE DISADVANTAGED.

Perhaps because the profession has been unclear about both content and method in teaching language and literacy to the disadvantaged, a belief has grown that virtually any teacher can successfully direct the learning of English in such a program. Indeed Task Force members reported schools in which stated administrative policy actually *required* principals to fill schedules for all teachers with classes in English, re-gardless of the academic preparation of the teachers. Yet members of the NCTE Task Force report instance after instance of programs floundering because of the shortage of personnel trained in English. Some understanding of the nature of the language appears to be crucial, especially in programs which deal with differences in dialect. Important, too, is study of the sociological influences on language learning, of the interrelationship of reading and language growth, of patterns of thinking and expression. Where teachers without background in English had been assigned to disadvantaged children, Task Force members too often found language instruction to be mechanistic in content and method—concentrating on the niceties of English expression or on superficial problems of spelling or punctuation, while overlooking important basic problems.

Understanding of the psychological characteristics of the pupils is important too. Graphic evidence is reported from several high school programs that imported successful elementary teachers to direct instruction for adolescents, teachers who had mastered techniques for teaching elementary language skills but who did not always understand adolescent psychology. Their instruction was therefore hampered not by a lack of technical knowledge, but by their inability to understand their pupils.

The Learning and Teaching of Language

Charged with the responsibility of describing the teaching of language and literacy in programs for the disadvantaged, the Task Force concentrated much of its attention on programs with this special purpose. A detailed summary of their observations at every level occurs in Part II of the report; however, certain overall impressions demand special stress.

One basic and encouraging observation reported by several Task Force members was the genuine willingness of most teachers to accept the child and his language, even when his language departed severely from standard English. Though not all observers could report such willingness (indeed too many found the opposite to be true), all agreed that instruction in language must begin with this acceptance.

The important need for developing programs in oral language at almost every educational level was repeatedly stressed by the Task Force. Everything known about language suggests that the improvement of writing and reading must be built upon instruction in oral English. Even more obvious is the fact that if children are to develop skill in using English dialects other than their own, they need oral instruction. Among a few hopeful developments, Task Force members reported the use of the Language Master with its programed series of taped oral-aural drills, but most members felt that far more needs to be attempted.

The teaching of reading and the teaching of English as a second language have long been recognized as specialized fields. College courses are offered in these areas, and trained specialists are available. Perhaps for this reason project administrators seem more likely to employ special teachers or consultants in reading or in English as a second language than in other areas. Extensive materials for teaching these specialties also are available. Unfortunately, neither appropriate materials nor special consultants seem extensively involved or available in oral language, in usage and grammar, in literature, and in composition. An occasional Task Force member reported some use of literary materials—perhaps in a story reading situation—but such reports were in the minority. Pattern practice in the use of verb forms, for example, was occasionally found, but in general program directors gave far more attention to reading. Some Task Force members found the emphasis on reading to be appropriate and well planned; others expressed concern that, at times —especially in the junior high school and beyond—instruction in reading was overorganized, stressing mechanical aspects of the reading process rather than the purposes of reading. All members of the Task Force felt that strong programs of oral discussion are needed to support reading programs and to lead toward writing and the reading of literature.

One problem to be faced in programs for teaching English as a second dialect is the extent to which teachers are justified in using procedures and approaches which work successfully in teaching English as a second language. In many ways the problems are similar. Practice of sentence and intonation patterns may be provided through planned use of oral-aural experiences, through language laboratories, through the use of tape recorders and the Language Master. But the demands are different as well, and the difference stems in many ways from the cultural differences of the learners. "What we are trying to do," explained linguist W. Nelson Francis, discussing instruction for speakers of nonstandard English, "is much like what is done in those countries like Switzerland or Norway where there are many regional dialects of local usefulness and acceptance, but where the educated person must acquire command of the standard language in order to go ahead with his education and take a position in professional or other educated circles."[4]

Teachers' lack of awareness about the nature of language did not surprise Task Force members familiar with recent studies of teacher

---

[4] Quoted in *The Wall Street Journal*, July 15, 1965.

preparation in this area. What did seem surprising was the discovery that so few supervisors and project directors were adequately informed about modern studies of regional and social dialects and how these can affect language learning. Many had only the vaguest notions about modern English grammars. Few seemed even aware of recent progress in language learning, such as emerging from the use of transformational analysis in studying the language of preschool children. Many directors had not even considered the fact that linguistic constructs might be employed, and a few were almost defensive about their ignorance in this area. In too few areas, also, had teachers and supervisors even discussed the possible adaptation of the oral-aural approach used successfully in teaching English dialects to young people.

To be sure, what is known about the language of children is still relatively modest. One consultant to the Task Force likened modern understandings of the language of young people to the tribal medicine man's knowledge of disease. Yet even the limitations on present information offer no justification for the project directors' not attempting to inform themselves of the very real advances in knowledge which have occurred during the past decade. Just as teachers of the disadvantaged must attempt to learn as much as posible about their students, their backgrounds, mores, and attitudes toward instruction, so they are obligated to inform themselves about the English language. Surely most teachers should know something about the history of the English language and the development of several modern grammars; about the social and regional variations in language and how these are related to social and cultural factors; about such special linguistic problems as lexicography; about language and thinking; and about the psychology of language learning.

In view of the strength of conventional and frequently erroneous concepts about language learning, the Task Force unanimously agrees on the importance to each program of inservice education programs on the teaching of standard English as a second dialect.

Emphasis on Specific Approaches

As reports on individual projects were analyzed, certain emphases in the programs visited became apparent. Most schools devoted more attention to reading, for example, than to oral language or composition. Literature received little attention. Audiovisual aids were popular, especially the traditional filmstrips and recordings. At the conclusion of a visit, each Task Force member completed a brief questionnaire to indicate the degree of emphasis on particular approaches which he observed. The following table gives the raw totals from responses to these questionnaires.

EMPHASES IN INSTRUCTION REPORTED BY THE TASK FORCE
(Based on 263 reports by 21 observers*)

Approaches to the Teaching of English	Emphasis Is on Approach in Each Program	Level of Instruction				
		Preschool	Elementary School	Secondary School	Adult	Teacher Education
Oral Language	stressed	50	46	32	2	7
	observed	1	25	36	3	0
	not observed	0	11	19	13	0
	no report	2	9	3	1	3
Oral reading of literature by the teacher	stressed	46	24	12	0	8
	observed	5	38	27	1	0
	not observed	2	24	45	18	0
	no report	0	5	6	0	2
Practice in the use of standard English dialects	stressed	14	35	22	3	1
	observed	11	30	33	0	5
	not observed	21	22	32	14	3
	no report	7	4	3	2	1
Linguistically based teaching programs	stressed	1	11	2	1	2
	observed	11	15	11	0	4
	not observed	37	53	60	17	4
	no report	4	12	17	1	0
Traditional schoolroom grammar	stressed	0	23	38	12	1
	observed	7	30	21	0	6
	not observed	39	31	26	6	3
	no report	7	7	5	1	0
Teaching of reading	stressed	2	80	58	14	4
	observed	3	6	22	2	1
	not observed	41	5	10	2	4
	no report	7	0	0	1	1
Use of imaginative literature	stressed	25	31	17	1	8
	observed	11	40	30	1	0
	not observed	10	16	32	16	1
	no report	7	4	11	1	1
Use of machines in the teaching of English	stressed	6	20	20	0	0
	observed	3	20	22	1	1
	not observed	37	47	45	16	9
	no report	7	4	3	2	0
Programs to encourage individual reading	stressed	0	27	32	2	4
	observed	1	45	38	3	1
	not observed	45	18	10	13	5
	no report	7	1	10	1	0

EMPHASES IN INSTRUCTION REPORTED BY THE TASK FORCE
(Based on 263 reports by 21 observers*)

Approaches to the Teaching of English	Emphasis Is on Approach in Each Program	Level of Instruction				
			Elementary	Secondary		Teacher
		Preschool	School	School	Adult	Education
Teaching of	stressed	0	16	19	2	2
composition	observed	0	25	48	3	1
	not observed	45	48	14	12	7
	no report	8	2	9	2	0
Teaching of	stressed	45	38	24	3	8
listening skills	observed	3	39	39	3	2
	not observed	4	13	23	12	0
	no report	1	1	4	1	0
Ungraded	stressed	3	12	14	6	2
grouping	observed	0	27	18	7	0
	not observed	41	44	47	4	7
	no report	9	8	11	2	1
Reduction	stressed	38	44	40	6	6
in class size	observed	5	23	15	2	1
	not observed	2	16	25	9	2
	no report	8	8	10	2	1
Audiovisual aids	stressed	33	27	21	3	3
(excluding tele-	observed	8	47	41	2	6
vision and teach-	not observed	10	13	24	13	1
ing machines)	no report	2	4	4	1	0
Educational	stressed	7	5	1	0	0
television	observed	2	9	15	1	1
	not observed	42	72	63	17	8
	no report	2	5	11	1	1
Programed	stressed	0	10	13	4	1
material	observed	0	12	7	3	1
	not observed	41	65	66	11	8
	no report	12	4	4	1	0
Adequate	stressed	13	21	12	1	2
classroom	observed	14	34	15	0	4
library	not observed	20	33	56	17	2
	no report	6	3	7	1	2

* The Task Force visited 190 programs of 115 separate administrations divided as follows: preschool, 28; elementary, 60; secondary, 54; adult, 6; project offices, 14; teacher education, 28. Totals vary from those in the table because most programs were observed by more than one individual.

General Impressions of Programs

In addition to their agreements about language instruction and program emphases, Task Force members concurred in several other

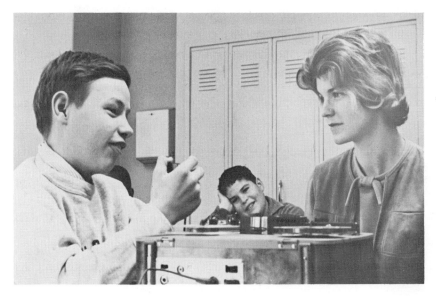

North Carolina Students Study with a Tape Recorder

reactions. Without question the single, overriding impression of the Task Force was the widespread interest and concern about education of the disadvantaged in schools, agencies, and colleges throughout the country. Many schools seem willing to reexamine curriculum and methods, to direct new attention to groups needing assistance, and to expend more funds. They are devising a variety of materials, approaches, and programs, often in imaginative ways, to reach disadvantaged pupils on a magnitude far greater than ever before. Although the source of this newly found concern and the nature of its motivation are not always apparent, the effect is clearly an acceleration in effort which augurs well for American education.

Diversity in content and method was also reported by Task Force members. Although too many programs still seem limited to fixed notions concerning method and content, an increasing number of projects and programs are experimenting with new ideas. At present, however, no single new approach seems predominant. Ideas and methods reported successful with one group receive scant attention elsewhere; a unit proved effective in one seventh grade is rejected by another. The success of a program often depends upon one person, but what one teacher can do well will not necessarily be done well by another. For this reason, no one program at any level yet seems applicable to a significant number of other classes at the respective level. Another problem is that a great many trial programs have been introduced without first devising suitable methods of evaluation.

For all of the confusion among diversified approaches, most Task Force members felt them justified because recent educational history has lacked experimentation to provide an extensive backlog of experiences on which today's teachers might build.

In addition to diversity, visited programs shared certain other characteristics. Many, for example, are striving to reduce the size of classes in which pupils are taught, recognizing that the teacher of disadvantaged learners must come to know intimately the individual learner.

Most programs used as wide a variety of materials as possible. Although one or two kinds of commercial publications tend to dominate reading classes, about twenty-six different kinds of workbooks or skill-oriented readers were used in the classes visited. In addition, classroom collections of paperback books, a variety of audiovisual aids, and a number of self-contained boxes, units, and kits are being introduced. In only a few cases did teachers complain about shortage of materials and of the funds to purchase materials, perhaps because the financing of these programs is often more generous than for conventional classrooms. This does not mean, however, that Task Force members reported no need for additional funds. One real shortage seems to be in specialized materials for particular instructional concerns—oral language skills, for example, or appropriate literary selections.

Again and again, Task Force members reported differences in approach, attitude, flexibility, and sometimes success in programs offered at different levels. Invariably the preschool programs attracted the most favorable attention. Preschool children seemed the most responsive; preschool teachers the most flexible; preschool projects the most experimental. Some observers felt that programs at this level were less hampered by tradition; others noted that parents of the preschool child tend to be more interested and more supportive than, for example, the parents of the junior high school youth. (Perhaps for this reason programs seem to make few efforts to involve the parents of older boys and girls.) To some observers preschool programs seemed more profitable and more economical than remedial teaching later. Whatever the reason, the preschool experiments attracted almost universal commendation, which also extended to a considerable degree to programs organized for the primary grades. However, beginning with intermediate level classes and extending into junior high school and senior high school, projects and programs seemed generally more structured and formal, more variable in quality and in responses of pupils, and more closely related to traditional school programs. Perhaps because the efforts in the upper grades and in secondary school often emphasize silent reading, sometimes to the exclusion of work on oral expression or communication, student learners in many reading programs seemed unresponsive and disinterested. The lack of creativity and experimentation in the high school programs, and in most adult programs, bothered observers almost as much as the reliance of these teachers on traditional methods and approaches.

One characteristic common to programs and projects at all levels and in all sections of the country is the absence of information on what is happening elsewhere. Because of a lack of professional leadership in project administration, local colleges and universities, or regional affiliates of the NCTE, few attempts are being made to disseminate what is known about the teaching of English to the disadvantaged. Indeed, often within the same large city, Task Force members discovered staffs of projects similar in organization and intent almost unacquainted with what the other was doing. Many project administrators and teachers expressed grave concern over this absence of information and desperately sought reports, suggestions, and advice from visiting Task Force members. This report of the Task Force will help to supply the information sorely needed by teachers throughout the country, but it will not elimi-

An Adult in New York City Learns to Read

35

nate the basic problem. The profession at large must also find continuing ways to keep its local and regional leaders informed about the latest developments in language teaching, about new programs and possibilities for teaching language to the disadvantaged, about new projects across the city and across the country. The present report, then, is only a first analysis. On the continuing exchange of new insights and new scholarship depends the future of language programs for the disadvantaged.

Part II

PROGRAMS FOR TEACHING ENGLISH TO THE DISADVANTAGED

Preschool

Elementary

Secondary

Adult Basic Education

Problems in Adult Basic Education
ROBERT F. BARNES

Observations of the Task Force

Teacher Education

Program Administration

Preschool[*]

Introduction

The preschool has a special role in the education of the disadvantaged child. It is no new discovery that our system of education has been geared to the needs and abilities of the middle class child. The child of poverty has entered this system with little of the knowledge and experience which have traditionally been assumed for all students. Despite changes being made at all levels of education to accommodate the disadvantaged child, a wholesale revision of the elementary-secondary curricula is not possible within the time allotted by educators and the general American public for his meaningful inclusion. The current preschool effort is an attempt to bring the disadvantaged child to a level of readiness for the primary school instruction equal to that of the middle class child.

Modern research in human development indicates that early childhood experiences set the stage, so to speak, for all later development, that the early years of a child's life are formative ones which influence crucially the limitations which act on later growth and achievement. Among the most important findings of recent years are those which relate early childhood experience to the development of intelligence. Research indicates that intelligence is not a constant "birth-to-death" phenomenon as was once thought, that a child does not have an entirely predetermined, inherited I.Q. Rather, "a child has an I.Q.—not of 80 or 120—but of 80 to 120 or 120 to 160, and how the individual develops after birth depends on his interaction with his environment. So this individual may have an I.Q. of 80 with a poor environment or 120 with a good environment." [1] Thus, the I.Q. is not constant throughout life, and at no other time is it more variable than during preschool years.

Discussion of intellectual development must consider complex issues in measurements of intelligence. Variability in I.Q. can grow from the nature of any one test and the population on which it was standardized; from the changing nature of tests from one age level to the next; from situational factors at the time of testing.

One study, for example, shows that a Negro child, when tested with

* The observations in this chapter are based on 53 reports from observers of 28 separate programs.
[1] See "Language, Intelligence, and the Educability of the Disadvantaged," by Samuel A. Kirk, Consultant to the NCTE Task Force, in Part IV of this report.

an individual I.Q. test by a highly trained, competent Negro examiner, scores on the average six points higher than when tested on the same test by a Caucasian examiner with equivalent training. It is widely recognized that group tests of verbal intelligence rely heavily on the vocabulary and on problem situations that characterize the dominant middle class culture.

Not all of the variability rests with the nature of intelligence testing, however. To be sure, genetic determinants of intelligence are revealed in comparative studies of identical and nonidentical twins, of correlation between a child's intelligence and that of the intelligence of foster and natural parents. Nevertheless, changes in environment tend to show far more influence on measured intelligence than they do on physical size.

So long as I.Q. tests were regarded as measures of individual *attainment* within the limits of whatever skills the tests measured, rather than as measures of *human potential,* they served the schools in many ways. For all their weaknesses, they still served middle class schools as useful predictors of success in school. But abuses and misinterpretation have been widepread, particularly with disadvantaged children. Single scores blurred differences which profile analyses would have revealed. Low scores were taken not as restricted measures of attainment by middle class standards, but as predictors of certain failure. Rigid tracking systems developed and, for children with the lowest I.Q. scores, curricula were built on despair, on the expectation of children's failure. Consequently, certain large city school districts have abandoned I.Q. tests. At the same time, it is important to know that some of these same school systems have not abandoned the idea of measuring intelligence and intellectual development. Rather, with the resources of a national testing organization, they have undertaken to devise a series of measures of intellectual abilities that will result not in a single score based exclusively on the culture of social class and relying heavily on the vocabulary of that class, but in a profile of scores based on problem-solving abilities that disadvantaged children, among others, can reasonably be expected to possess.

In the meantime, it is clear that preschool programs which use measures of intelligence either to place students initially or to assess the outcomes of the programs will have to approach with caution any of the conventionally used intelligence tests that rely more heavily on such devices as skilled observation in problem-solving situations.

The task of the preschool, therefore, is to do more than to provide the disadvantaged child with this or that experience, or to acquaint him with this or that fact. The task of the preschool is to lay the foundation on which it is hoped can be built later school success, something which statistics normally deny the disadvantaged child.

Objectives of Preschool Programs

Neither the objectives, the curricula, nor the practices and methods described in following pages differ greatly from those of a conventional nursery school for middle class children. It is, however, difficult to determine whether the implicit assumption has been made that the conventional preschool curriculum is the best possible, regardless of the student, or whether there has been insufficient time to develop programs concerned with the special needs of disadvantaged students. Inasmuch as the greatest need is for accelerated development in language, those purposes contributing to this goal should surely receive the greatest emphasis. Perhaps more than anything else this emphasis should set apart from regular preschools those programs organized especially for the disadvantaged.

The stated objectives of a preschool program for the disadvantaged should be more than neat generalities taken from a textbook on child development. If the objectives are to mean anything at all, they will be based especially upon those needs resulting from linguistic impoverish-

Children in Honolulu, during Outdoor Play

ment which lies central to the children's educational handicap and to their later failure in school.

Language Objectives

Although the disadvantaged child is often retarded in most areas of language development, it is not adequate to recognize "language" as a basic educational deficit of the disadvantaged child and to stop there. If one is to design a program which emphasizes language development, one must begin by breaking down language into its basic functions.

The inability of the disadvantaged child to express himself is one of the first noticeable facts about him. His first days of preschool may be silent ones. When he finally begins to open up and talk, it becomes apparent that he lacks not only a wide variety of experiences but also a vocabulary with which to describe those experiences that he *has* had. The middle class child typically has parents who speak to him in sentences, read to him, take him places and explain them to him, and urge him to talk. Often the disadvantagd child has parents whose verbal contact with their children may be mostly commands of only a few words, who may not read well themselves and thus cannot read to their children, who may not have the money or the desire to spend a day at the zoo or museum. So one of the most important tasks undertaken by virtually every preschool across the nation is that of giving disadvantaged children some of these experiences and, more important, the words to talk about them. Judging from reports of Task Force observers and many written reports and curriculum guides studied, preschools are filling this void in language development. Commonly teachers report that students who cannot or will not speak at all during the early weeks or months of their preschool experience begin to speak after an interval of time as they gain a stock of experiences and the words and self-confidence to talk about them.

Of course, language is used to talk about more than what happened in the park yesterday or to describe the colors in a finger painting. It is also used to communicate feelings and emotions, but in this use of language the disadvantaged child seems equally unskilled. Preschool teachers note that the disadvantaged child typically does not have the words to express emotions such as displeasure or love and that he relies on physical means of expressing them. He hits, spits, or kicks when he is angry and, similarly, hugs or kindly touches when he is pleased or gratified. Negative reactions are more prominent than the positive ones because, once again, disadvantaged children seem to have more direct experience with anger and negative behavior than positive emotional and social expression, physical or verbal.

The middle class child gets much opportunity to tell about his feelings and to hear other people talk about theirs: "What's the matter, Johnny, don't you feel well?" "You be nice to Mrs. Jones today because she has been sick and may not be feeling well." Or in a storybook, "The little black and white puppy was *very unhappy*." Most of these things are absent from the disadvantaged home, where "What'sa matter, you sick? or "Leave Jones alone today, you hear?" may be typical. In such homes there may not even be a newspaper, to say nothing of a storybook. So once again, the preschool staff has felt the need to function in the role of middle class parents to the children. During periods of undirected play, the classroom adults normally pay close attention to the children's feelings and emotions. By patiently conversing with the children about why "we should let Billy finger paint for a while" and why "you hit Susie when she wanted to play with the blocks too," teachers attempt to replace physical with verbal expression. Preschool teachers consider it progress when, instead of hitting Susie, Johnny tells her in no uncertain terms that "she's s'posed to go play with the dolls."

If it is true that the disadvantaged child's lack of language is partially responsible for his tendency to express himself physically, then perhaps some of the current concern for "social adjustment" could be translated profitably into concern for language development.

Teachers already emphasize the importance of firsthand experiences for preschool children; they need to remember also that the basic purposes for these concrete experiences are to make the need for language real and necessary to the child and to create an environment in which he can develop concepts. Members of the Task Force, through interviews with personnel involved in programs and through a review of available guides, reports, and materials, have noted these language objectives for the preschool child:

—Learning to use skills of listening,
—Learning that all things have names and that things that appear different may have the same names,
—Learning to speak in complete sentences,
—Learning to use the vocabulary that is within his level of understanding as he listens,
—Developing the use of vocabulary needed for successful communication with others.

43

A major function of language is its role in the process of thought, in the assimilation of specific pieces of information into meaningful concepts. The disadvantaged child has an even less adequate grasp of this use of language than he has of language as a means of expression.[2]

Basic statement patterns in even the most casual language serve to "carry" logical thought. The basic pattern, "This is *hot*," for example, is the base on which can be built a whole network of related statements, as, "If this is *hot*, then it is *not cold*," or "If this is *not cold*, then it is *hot*." The point is, without going into an exhaustive listing of the patterns, that all of the operations of logical thought needed by a primary grade child are covered by a few basic sentence patterns.

The ability to form concepts, considered in its broad sense, is more than merely a knowledge that "This is hot." It is also the ability to ask, "Given that this is *hot*, what *else* is it? What is it *not*?" To be fully understood, a concept must be put into perspective with related concepts, smoke into proper relation with fire, or cause with effect.

How does one teach conceptual language? More is involved than merely presenting *or, and, if, then,* and *only* as vocabulary. Can children be expected to "pick up" the basic logic of language through informal conversation and frequent experience in manipulating toys? Or are there ways of teaching these basic concepts of language directly?

The preschools visited by the Task Force develop conceptual skills through providing structured experiences usually involving manipulative skills. Throughout the activities, children are urged to talk about what they are doing, to use their existent verbal skills with concepts to work through experiences to new verbal skills. Teachers explain that the middle class child arrives at his level of concept development through experience of much the same type that the preschool provides, that in a preschool situation, where the child has adequate opportunity to express himself, the verbal skills related to concept development will develop naturally. In addition, teachers generally feel that the "experience approach" permits the development of other, nonlanguage skills in which the disadvantaged child needs improvement.

---

[2] Only a brief, working discussion of this aspect of language is presented in this section. For more complete discussions, see the comments by Carl Bereiter in Part III of the report and the manuscript by Siegfried Engelmann listed in Appendix B.

Preschool Children in New York City ''Read'' Favorite Storybooks

Nonlanguage Objectives

Nearly all preschool programs in operation for disadvantaged children place important emphasis on the obtaining of nonlanguage objectives. Interviews with preschool teachers and studies of reports, proposals, and curriculum guides reveal that specific nonlanguage objectives for a disadvantaged child include the development of

. . . a positive self-image,

. . . an interest in his environment,

. . . a wide background of information from firsthand experience,

. . . the ability to work and play individually and with other children,

. . . the ability to use skillfully both large and small muscles,

. . . the ability to use various materials (books, puzzles) and equipment (phonographs, tape recorders),

. . . a sense of respect for others and their property,

. . . the ability to be independent and self-sufficient,

. . . an appreciation of music,

. . . an increasing attention span,

. . . the experience of success,

. . . a recognition of bodily needs and desirable health habits,

. . . a sense of balance,

. . . a feeling of physical adequacy,

. . . the ability to sing songs both alone and with others,

. . . the ability to give and receive affection,

. . . the ability to identify in male or female adult roles,
. . . the ability to recognize qualities (long, short, hot, cold),
. . . the ability to recognize basic shapes (circles, squares),
. . . wholesome attitudes toward school,
. . . adequate habits of conduct,
. . . hand-eye coordination,
. . . creativity in different media.

Many preschool teachers and reports become much more specific, but nearly every activity carried on in the preschools observed fits into one or more of the above categories.

Observation of preschool classes, interviews with teachers, and studies of reports and curriculum guides indicate that the bulk of classroom activities in many districts are built around nonlanguage objectives. Undirected play period activities are nearly all visual-motor and kinesthetic activities. The development of language and its usage takes place in these essentially nonlanguage experiences through conversation among the children and adults around a puzzle, in the "doll corner," or at the sand or clay table.

All programs include teacher-directed activities such as discussing, singing, word games, and storytelling. These activities are felt to result in language growth, usually in vocabulary, verbal-visual (stories) and verbal-motor (finger plays) and repetition skills.

The Preschool Curriculum

A curriculum guide, of course, is little more than a plan which outlines the means by which stated objectives are to be attained. Nearly all the preschools visited by the Task Force have well-planned curricular organization and definite daily scheduling of selected classroom activities. The same schedule is normally followed each day, and the children become accustomed to the sequence of activities. Although every program contains teacher-directed activities, most of the activities are child-centered, and the child is allowed considerable freedom to determine what he does and the manner and speed in which he does it. Capable teachers are able to distinguish between unguided disorder and a departure from plan which allows the child spontaneous learning.

One preschool schedule is presented below.

45 minutes   Conference. Provision of this time period before the children arrive each day gives the teacher and her aides an opportunity to review in detail the day's activities and to set up the environment and materials as planned for and prepared following the previous morning session.

50 minutes	Children's arrival and guided activities. During t⁻is period, children are allowed to engage in one of several activities as they wish, with minimal direction from the adults present.
15 or 20 minutes	Nutrition or snack time. This time is spent in small groups of five or seven children (depending on whether one or two aides are in the classroom) around a table with the teacher. This time is used to discuss and eat the food and drink the juice. Children compare foods and develop understandings at this time.
	Toileting. Toilet needs are taken care of following the nutrition time. If facilities are adjoining the classroom, the child is taught to care for his needs at any time during the morning.
15 or 20 minutes	Rest. Usually appropriate rest music is played to help children relax.
30 minutes	Teacher-directed activity. Included in this period are such activities as music, games, dramatizations, puppetry, storytelling, and records. The children may be gathered into one or several groups, depending on the ability of the staff to conduct such activities. Rhythms and puppetry would be examples of active and quiet activities for this block of time.
45 minutes	Outdoor play. If weather prohibits this activity, children are usually allowed undirected play indoors.
10 minutes	Storytelling, or poetry and nursery rhymes.
10 minutes	Preparation for dismissal.

Although the above program represents most of the preschool programs observed, there are, of course, variations. Most programs, however, use the general sequence of experience which alternates active and passive activities and outlines time allotments. Programs in which a noon lunch is included frequently allow another period of undirected play before afternoon dismissal. Only a few of the programs observed operate for an entire day.

Play guided by the teacher is claimed to foster the achievement of more of the usual preschool objectives than any other. In every case, the period of play is a time during which the adult staff of the preschool mingles with the students, talking to them, asking and answering questions, focusing attention on otherwise unnoticed objects and phenomena. Some programs attempt to keep the children in small groups around several different activities, providing group social situations which are small enough to allow children to do things individually. Generally, the children are free to move from group to group so long as no single group becomes too large to permit constructive activity. Nearly all preschool programs that were observed are structured loosely within the daily scheduling with no intensive academic instruction in either large or small groups. The teachers feel that disadvantaged students need many varied experiences, and to spend valuable preschool time teaching only to certain specific needs is undesirable.

The Task Force observers were frequently impressed with the careful selection and organization of classroom facilities and learning situations. And in this one respect many of the preschools observed can be said to be highly structured. For example, teachers of preschool normally select from the hundreds of toys, games, and activities available for children those which best foster the development of the skills in which they judge the children to be deficient. Many teachers observed and interviewed seem to be well aware of the need for high quality materials rather than mere quantities of them.

Virtually every preschool visited emphasized the importance of personal child-adult interaction at all times. Preschool teachers stressed that the root problem of most, if not all, the developmental deficits of disadvantaged children is the absence of a home environment which fosters

Small Group Activity in an Oakland, California, Preschool

the social and emotional growth that characterizes middle class children of the same age. Regardless of specific curricular organization, successful programs attempt to surround all preschool activities with close, affectionate child-adult relationships, which are normally not encouraged so much in a preschool for middle class children. Classroom adults generally make special efforts to hold the children, praise them for accomplishments, redirect rather than punish them, help them patiently with difficult or unfamiliar tasks, and give other similar attention which the middle class mother typically does. The disadvantaged child accepts this treatment readily, and the problem is usually one of holding this kind of activity down rather than having to encourage it.

Recognizing that virtually all preschool classroom personnel are women, one is reminded of the fact that nearly every disadvantaged child has in his family unit at least a mother. It may be that he is not in as much need of such "mothering" as he is of "fathering." For this reason, school districts may well consider hiring male teachers or teacher aides for the preschool.

Organization and Staffing

Most preschools are administered through local boards of education. The administrative supervisor, depending on the size of the system, may be the superintendent or assistant superintendent of schools or the head of a division of early childhood education. Preschool programs observed depend on a variety of sources for classroom personnel, who are usually classified into several major types.

Head Teacher. Almost every preschool classroom is under the direct supervision of a head teacher trained either in child development or elementary education. In many cases, preschool teachers have been drawn from kindergarten classrooms because of demonstrated competence in work with small children. In city programs involving many preschool centers, the teachers often participate in an orientation or workshop session to disseminate policy information and establish some continuity of purpose. (See Teacher Education later in the report.)

Student Leaders. A number of programs are able to use college students in the classrooms. One school system, where funds are very short, has hired junior college freshmen to staff its preschools. The students, who work three and one half hours a day are paid $6.50 per preschool day plus their tuition at the local junior college. The board of education has hired one highly qualified consultant for every twenty student leaders. This particular system has been able to find students who seem to take a great interest in the children. They demonstrate a willingness to listen to and follow the suggestions of trained preschool consultants and go far beyond their contracts in the time spent to devise games, activities, and classroom improvements.

Teacher Aides. Since maximum attention to individual children is desirable at the preschool level, virtually every program has obtained the services of nonprofessional classroom aides. These aides work under the supervision of the head teacher and, besides helping with many routine tasks in the classroom such as preparing the snack, toileting the children, or cleaning up, function as "interested adults" who give as much attention as possible to each child. Programs usually choose teacher aides on the basis of their education, clear speech, and past experience with children, as in church, summer camp, or YMCA work.

In districts where sufficient funds are available, teacher aides are hired who have relatively good educational backgrounds and experience in work with children. In some systems, these aides are working toward certification. They are occasionally required to increase their effectiveness as classroom personnel by reading in the field of child development and education or by participating in workshops.

Many programs are in communities where there are active volunteers, interested women's civic or religious groups who provide one or two volunteer teacher aides for each classroom. Each aide usually works from one to three days a week. In many communities, it is reported that such aides participate in workshops and orientation programs to improve their classroom effectiveness. Generally, these women are from middle and upper middle class neighborhoods, and for many, preschool work is regarded as a constructive use of free time or to satisfy a community service obligation of their organization.

Some preschool programs attempt to combine several purposes and goals by using women from the neighborhood of the children as teacher aides. In nearly every case, these persons are paid employees and normally receive between $1.50 and $2.00 an hour. This wage is usually higher than the people could normally earn in nonschool employment. In the programs which follow this practice, such an arrangement has the simultaneous effects of providing classroom personnel who are familiar with the lives of these children beyond a mere home visit or conversation with a parent and of establishing school-community liaisons.

In most preschools, nonstandard dialect is dealt with indirectly by the encouragment of good standard English speech by classroom adults. The point might be made that the use of classroom personnel who speak a nonstandard dialect may counteract the effectiveness of such a practice. On the other hand, this practice might aid attempts to equip children with the ability to use their own dialect effectively.

Consultants. Most large city programs, which include a number of preschool classrooms located in various parts of the city, have the services of consultants who serve principally as classroom advisors and liaisons between individual teachers and central administrators. Generally, consultants are highly trained and experienced people with additional important qualifications in human relations. The consultant can also be an important carrier of ideas from classroom to classroom, helping all teachers benefit from the experience of each. In addition, the consultant is able to hold inservice training meetings which bring all of the teachers of preschool children together for general information, training in the use of materials, and for an exchange of ideas.

The Preschool and the Community

Preschool programs are severely limited in their total effectiveness by the low socioeconomic home environments of the children. Children who spend three productive hours a day in preschool may spend ten hours of that day in a home or neighborhood environment that is the very antithesis of what the preschool represents. Thus, many preschools have instituted programs which involve parents in the school's work in an effort to influence the nonschool environment of the children. All of the personnel of preschools that operate parent programs report that the task of gaining active parent interest and support is long and difficult. Parents in disadvantaged areas are often not accustomed to having the school actively interested in them and their children. Many mothers have several younger children to care for and, therefore, are unable to participate although they may wish to do so. Many parents have ugly memories of their own unsuccessful schooldays and are not therefore disposed to new involvement with education or with the people in it.

One promising point mentioned to Task Force members by preschool teachers and community workers is that most parents in disadvantaged areas *do care* about their children. Parents want their children to succeed in school, to succeed in escaping from the poverty that they, as adults, have always known. Teachers report the greatest problem to be that parents, however concerned they are, do not know *how to care* for many of the needs of their children. They do not know the many things about hygiene, child care, or child development, which are common knowledge to the middle class parent. A parent who has never known the value of a book is not to be expected to realize the importance of providing books for his children, assuming that he could even afford it. The severity of disadvantaged children's deficits then is only compounded by the parents' ignorance of the existence and nature of the deficits. Parents of disadvantaged children were themselves disadvantaged children and grew up in a school system and society which did not take the compensastory measures that are finally being taken.

Those teachers who work with established community parent programs iterated time after time to Task Force members the importance of these programs to the total effectiveness of the preschool. Regardless of how carefully planned and how effective a preschool curriculum may be, the fact remains that the children still spend most of their day in the home. Thus, any home conditions which can be improved or changed to support and reinforce rather than counteract and weaken what is taught in preschool are considered desirable and worthy of the school system's attention.

A number of preschool programs visited by the Task Force require participation in a parent program as a requisite to the children's attendance in preschool. By taking advantage of most parents' desire to do anything they can to help their children (which includes, of course, sending the children to preschool), the preschool program has a lever with which to influence parents as well as the children. One program visited requires the children's mothers to attend a weekly ninety minute workshop which stresses such topics as hygiene, child care, budgeting, and menu planning. In another preschool-parent education project, the purpose of the parent meetings is to teach parents about language and ways in which they can help to improve their children's language. The parent classes reported are taught by community workers, teachers (in some cases on their own time), and even program administrators. The task, as many preschool people see it, is to get the parents involved and active in the work of the program and thus increase their total interest in the school's work.

Most preschool programs visited by the NCTE Task Force use definite criteria, such as the income per family member, in selecting children for preschool participation. However, preschool teachers and administrators say that the problem of defining *disadvantaged* is not as great as the initial problem of getting into the homes and locating individual children who need preschool experience. A preschool program cannot use merely a newspaper, radio, or a parent group meeting announcement to publicize that it is seeking students and then expect the parents of the disadvantaged children to respond. Generally, parents of disadvantaged students do not read a newspaper and are not active in parent group organizations. Even if they hear about the preschool program on the radio or television, their unwillingness to be classed as poor or disadvantaged may prohibit any actual attempt to send their children to the school.

Preschool teachers and administrators report that the only really effective way to get disadvantaged children into a program is to *go out after them.* Social workers, ministers and priests, school principals and nurses, community relations workers, along with welfare lists, are reported to be the best sources of names of disadvantaged families who have children of preschool age.

Several of the preschools visited by the Task Force hire teachers and aides two or three weeks in advance of the first day of class for the purpose of finding names of families and then visiting the homes to invite parents to enroll their children.

Children Engrossed in a Story in Cleveland, Ohio

Practices and Methods

If, on the basis of Task Force observations, any single language activity is singled out as the major teaching method, it must be conversation. Most teachers and teacher aides attempt to inject every preschool experience with conversation, to give the children every opportunity to have questions answered, to be listened to attentively, and to be challenged themselves by questions.

Most preschool programs are characterized by an orderly but permissive classroom atmosphere. Children are rarely forced to do or participate in anything against their will. If a child does not wish to take part in music, for example, most preschool teachers allow him to sit and listen quietly or to leave the group and play quietly in another part of the room.

For purposes of organization, practices and methods observed are broken down into three principal types: audiovisual activities, undirected activities, and teacher-directed activities. No attempt is made to provide an exhaustive listing of all the activities and materials used for preschoolers. Rather, the attempt is to present those which teachers and Task Force members consider important to language learning in preschool children.

Audiovisual Activities

Record Player. Task Force members noted that many teachers consider the single-play record player to be the most useful piece of equipment, since it can be operated easily by preschool children. When a record player is used, teachers emphasize the importance of careful record selection. Records with which children can sing along permit them the experience of learning to sing as well as the more passive pleasure of listening to music. Teachers who include story records usually select those which feature material not duplicated in regular storytelling periods.

Special "listening center" record players are available which provide for the use of six or more earphone headsets. Here, children can play their own record choices and listen to them without disturbing the rest of the class. Some teachers use the listening center in conjunction with a filmstrip viewer, which can be operated by a child. A number of record-filmstrip story sets are commercially available. However, this practice, which involves the coordination of more than one piece of equipment, may lead to difficulties unless children are carefully trained in the operation of the equipment and have learned to listen for the signal to turn the next picture frame. Teachers generally find that greater supervision is needed as the number or complexity of equipment pieces is increased.

The record player in many schools gets considerable use in teacher-directed activities. It can be used for music when there is no piano or pianist, for small children generally have difficulty singing without some accompaniment to help them maintain the rhythm and melody.

Tape Recorder. Although not suitable for operation by children, a tape recorder is made available for individual child use in at least one preschool visited. An ideal recorder for this activity is fitted with circulating tape cartridges as children are not able to rewind and thread the tape. This is also an important consideration for the teacher's use, because children's attention can be lost while the teacher is rewinding a tape.

One teacher cautioned that the cost of a tape recorder equals that of many books, puzzles, or other materials. She feels it does not have enough classroom uses to justify its purchase. There are idle tape recorders in many storage closets simply because constructive uses have not been devised or because the machine is too cumbersome to operate in a classroom situation. Teachers also reported that considerable practice is often needed to operate these machines without distraction.

Since there is normally only one trained teacher in a preschool classroom, it is necessary, if direct instruction is to be done, to work with children in groups of four and five. Teachers report that the tape recorder is a great aid in this kind of teaching, for by equipping the recorder with earphone headsets, one third to one half of a class (of fifteen or twenty children) can listen to a prerecorded story while the teacher takes the remainder for the small group instruction. Usually a teacher aide can operate the tape recorder and supervise the children. Teachers in some programs have compiled libraries of taped stories they recorded originally for this use.

The tape recorder can be applied to the ''experience chart'' idea for following up a field trip or class activity. Instead of or in addition to writing the story, the account of the class activity can be recorded sentence by sentence and then played back for the children at will.

Language Master. A unique form of the tape recorder observed in several classrooms is the Bell and Howell Language Master. The machine is built to play back and record from a strip of recording tape which is fastened to a special card on which can also be put words, sentences, and pictures. The tape has two tracks, one normally prerecorded by the teacher and the other used to record and play back student responses. The machine controls are designed so that a four-year-old can operate them and so that the prerecorded track cannot be erased except by special hidden switches known only to the teacher. For example, the machine may be used for sentence pattern drill in the following manner: The teacher prerecords a particular sentence which is written on the upper part of the card. The child operates the machine by placing the card in the provided slot; the card then moves across the top of the machine, playing the prerecorded sentence. Next, the child reinserts the card, repeats the sentence as he heard it, inserts the card once again and hears what he has said.

Although the Language Master has many uses for language work in the preschool classroom, some teachers interviewed felt that a skilled teacher can accomplish many of the same things without it, especially if her group total is no more than fifteen and she has at least one aide. The cost of the machine exceeds $200, and "that amount of money will provide a substantial quantity of books and blackboard chalk."

Teletrainer. One of the most interesting and practical pieces of equipment observed by Task Force members is the Teletrainer, which the Bell Telephone Company makes available free of charge to schools. It consists of two battery-powered telephone units which children can use to practice conversation. Normally, the Teletrainer units are simply set out on a table for children's voluntary use. Teachers who use it report often that the Teletrainer is most effective for encouraging children to communicate without the extensive gestures on which they typically rely.

A number of programs make considerable use of different cameras to take pictures of the children for display and discussion. Almost any kind of camera is suitable, although in most preschools visited, simple box cameras are used because film and film processing for them are inexpensive. Other preschools take movies or use cameras which internally process the film so that children can see finished photos immediately. Children enjoy seeing pictures of themselves on field trips and in class, and teachers report that most children's verbalization increases severalfold when they discuss pictures posted around the classroom or presented by the teacher during group activities.

Educational Television. One large city school system, lacking the funds to staff its preschools with certified teachers, uses educational television to take some of the planning and teaching burden off its inexperienced, untrained teachers.

Planned in detail before the school year, three telecasts are presented each morning of the school week. One is designed for the "culturally different," and one is designed for average preschool children (in this case, five-year-olds), and a third telecast is designed for all students. Every classroom teacher has a copy of the overall preschool guide, containing suggestions for home activities and abstracts of the teaching units to be presented. Each teacher is also given a monthly supplement presenting a detailed outline of the month's televised lessons with suggestions for follow-up classroom activities to reinforce and enlarge upon the televised lesson.

In addition to the outlines of the telecasts, the monthly supplement also includes suggested finger plays, nursery rhymes, poems, stunts, games, or songs which are appropriate to the theme of the teaching unit. For example, in a unit on farm animals, nursery rhymes such as "Little Bo-Peep," "I Had a Little Pony," and "Hey, Diddle-Diddle" are suggested.

The coordination of classroom work with the television presentations is handled by consultants (one for every twenty classrooms) who meet with the television teacher and staff each week and regularly visit individual classrooms.

Playing with Blocks in a New York City Preschool

Guided Play Activities

Most preschool programs try to include language experiences in guided play activities, since the latter consume the major portion of preschool time. Many curriculum guides and preschool teachers have stated that guided play activities can be major learning experiences. The educational value of guided play is determined by the quality of the activities from which the child may choose. Careful selection of materials for the classroom contributes to learning also.

Task Force visits to preschool classrooms revealed that most teachers try to localize the several types of learning situations by establishing "interest centers" in distinct parts of the classroom. For example, materials such as puzzles, blocks, or matching games are placed in one corner of the classroom, music and reading materials in another, the "doll house" in another. The idea is to provide situations with a number of specific activities which help to foster essentially one type of development.

Most teachers select specific materials for each activity carefully, for materials should be not only attractive but also pertinent to the more serious deficits of the disadvantaged child. Since teachers work the development of language skills into essentially nonlanguage activities, they consider the conversational value of toys and games. They recommend that when a toy or puzzle or game does not prove useful in practice, it should either be removed or replaced.

Rather than putting all materials out at the beginning of the year or having many books and games available at any one time, preschool teachers suggest that a smaller stock of materials providing a range of difficulty is more useful. As students master the easier ones, the more difficult can be introduced, emphasizing progress in the desired skills. Similarly, the difficult materials should not be accessible before children are ready for them. Attempting to play a game that is too difficult may destroy the child's interest in that game even after he has the skill to master it.

Most teachers constantly search for objects and activities that will stimulate children to talk and take interest in things around them with a minimum of direct stimulus. One of the objectives of guided play is to create a situation where children will be relaxed enough to use whatever skills they may possess, to capitalize on previous or future teacher-directed and group experiences.

A number of preschool teachers make special efforts to use a "theme approach" to structuring guided play. Most often the emphasis will center on a major event, such as a field trip or class project. For example, for several days before a trip to a farm, the teacher may display books and devote story time to introductory books about the farm and post pictures of farm animals. Then, after the field trip, toys and puzzles related to the farm can be brought out of storage, and teachers and aides can informally bring children's attention to the posters which were put up earlier, comparing those pictures to what they actually saw on the trip. They can add recordings of songs about the farm to the record collection and introduce appropriate games. This kind of planning reinforces and enlarges upon the theme for a maximum total impression.

When many children begin preschool, they point to things they want to do or use, or merely watch and listen when something new is presented. Therefore, all preschool programs visited attempt to provide children with verbal labels for objects about them to encourage them to use names, rather than to point or touch. A number of teachers have laid even heavier emphasis on naming by attaching written labels to the piano, the windows, the door—to everything, including the children themselves. The teacher and her aides attempt, whenever possible, to refer frequently to the written label in order to familiarize children with written representation. When a child begins to use language for asking, "What is that?" or "Can I use the record player?" he has progressed in the effort to use language as a natural, spontaneous medium for communication.

A number of teachers say that because one of the greatest problems is getting children to *want* to express themselves, a large part of helping them acquire verbal skills is to provide something exciting to talk about: activities such as field trips, block building, finger painting, and creative work. A child then begins to talk about what he has *done*.

Teacher-Directed and Group Activities

Virtually all preschools visited include a period for teacher-directed activities, such as singing, dancing, storytelling, and direct instruction. Whether or not the class is divided into small groups for such activities varies from preschool to preschool.

Music. Music, of course, is an important part of the preschool experience. One of the most enjoyable language activities, singing also is important for its value as a language learning tool.

The type of music used is important in the education of the disadvantaged. Careful selection of songs can insure a maximum amount of language growth for the time spent. An excellent example of a "language" song observed by Task Force members is "Hokey Pokey":

> You put your left foot in.
> You put your left foot out.
> You put your left foot in
> And you shake it all about. . .
> You do the Hokey Pokey
> And you turn yourself about. . .

"Hokey Pokey," of course, has more language content than most children's songs—direction (left, right, in, out, etc.) ; parts of the body (foot, hand, etc.) ; pattern drill (you put your _____ in/out)—but many songs provide the same type of experience.

Interesting improvisation in music was observed. After the children have become familiar with a melody, some teachers ask the children to make up substitution words for songs like "Old McDonald" (Old Mc-Donald had a _____ . . .), or lines, retaining a refrain, as in "Go Tell Aunt Rhody" (I had a _____.; no _____ would it _____ . . .).

In one program, where music is used exclusively for furthering language development, children compose entirely new lyrics for a familiar melody. Teachers felt this *directed* verbal creativity to be an excellent exercise. In the same program, the teachers compose entire new songs which, because of deliberate selection of the rhythm and word patterns, provide practice in specific types of sentence patterns or word groups with which the children are having difficulty.

Some teachers visited by the Task Force believe they increase children's interest and experience with music by varying the live accompaniment. For example, children enjoy singing with a guitar or listening to someone play the trumpet or saxophone. One preschool teacher asks children from the upper elementary grades who play instruments to play for the preschool children.

Clapping to the Music of an Autoharp in Oakland, California

Literature. All preschool classrooms visited have some kind of "library corner" where, during play periods, children may browse through books. Some teachers place one of the aides in the library area to help children select and use the books. Teachers generally arrange classroom libraries so that books are freely accessible, with the covers facing out to attract the children.

Although every preschool had books available, the number and quality of books varied widely. At least one preschool visited had fewer than ten books and others had fifty to seventy-five. Some libraries had only limited selections of imaginative literature, the emphasis being on factual material. An encouraging number of preschools, however, had good, balanced libraries, according to the Task Force members.

Teachers report that one of the major reasons for having libraries in preschool programs is to establish familiarity with books among the children who do not have books in their homes. Any innovation or idea which will lead them to more time with books is considered important.

Storytelling is an important part of virtually every preschool program visited. Many variations on the activity were observed, but because of the general familiarity with the activity, only the significant storytelling innovations are discussed.

One storytime period was observed in which the teacher gives each student a laminated page from the book. As the story progresses (the teacher has memorized the story), the child whose page is read stands up and displays the page for the class.

Some teachers vary storytelling time by holding class in different parts of the room from day to day. One day the teacher might work with only part of the children (the others at play or with an aide) sitting on the floor. Other days, the teacher might read to the whole class in the traditional manner. Other teachers report problems with this practice, saying that it is a good idea to establish a special place for storytelling so that children become accustomed to sitting and listening in one place.

Role playing and dramatic activities may or may not be teacher-directed but involve much language participation. They provide experiences and words with which to describe them, and they provide situations in which children need to use those words in context. Many teachers regard dramatic and role playing activities as excellent verbal stimulation.

Children, in one preschool visited by observers, enjoy "Grocery Store." The materials consist of a cardboard facsimile of a storefront and some pretend packages, for which empty commercial food containers work very well. The provision of adult "dress-up" clothing leads quickly to "family" role play. The "doll corner" leads to "mother and family" role play as well as social conversation.

Puppets are used in a number of preschools for both undirected and directed activities. The teacher presents a story on Monday, using puppets as characters. On Tuesday after a second puppet storytelling, the class makes puppets from gloves, mittens, paper bags, or sticks. On Wednesday the children work on their own stories or on their own versions of familiar stories. Although these activities offer only partial experience with verbal expression, teachers normally consider them important language activities.

Poetry and nursery rhymes were considered by the teachers visited to be "musts" as part of the preschool curriculum. Through listening to poetry and nursery rhymes children are immediately able to enjoy and participate in many kinds of experiences they would not otherwise have. Through listening they are also given a pleasant introduction to a wealth of words. These words are organized in melodies which move rhythmically and are delightful for children to hear and use. As children listen to rhymes and poetry they begin to discriminate among sounds as well as learn to recognize rhyming words. These skills are basic to success in the reading program.

Verbal Motor Activities. Finger plays, involving the coordination of rhyming and rhythmic instructions with the proper movements of the parts of the body, are used by most teachers. In order to do finger plays, the child must be able to listen and interpret words and, because of the rhythm, to participate at a given rate of speed.

The flannel board is also used for language activities. In several preschools visited by the Task Force, the teacher used the flannel board for storytelling, moving the cutouts around as the story progressed. This practice, like the use of puppets, gets attention because it gives children something to look at while listening. Children find the simple flannel board easy to use. In a number of preschools the children are regularly asked to retell or to change the endings of familiar stories. Teachers find that because the flannel board gives children something to do while speaking to the class, it tends to reduce anxiety and frustration about "platform" performance. It also provides opportunities for children to use new vocabulary and to recall a sequence of ideas.

Some schools visited make the flannel board available for use during guided play. Here a shy child finds a wonderful opportunity to "try" a story or poem on the flannel board without an audience in evidence.

Experience Charts. Task Force members discovered many forms of story composition. "Experience chart" work normally consists in the teacher's asking the children for suggested sentences or in helping them to turn fragments into sentences ("before we can write it") and then writing them, usually with crayon or felt pen, on large newsprint or similar types of paper. Generally, teachers try to get a sentence or two from each student. Where experience charts are employed, the stories are normally taken from field trips or class projects such as cooking, recounting the sequence of events that occurred.

Other variations of content for experience charts are the weaving of a story around a familiar or interesting object or picture. One school district makes available a series of photographs of local sights for use in both preschool and elementary classes. Other teachers record on tape class rewritings of familiar stories.

Vocabulary. Teachers find that identification games provide vocabulary review. Several objects with differing qualities may be placed on a table. Children may be asked to "pick up the blue ones" or "the square ones," with "big," "little," and so on. An interesting variation of this game is to place objects before children, have them close their eyes, remove *one* of the objects, and ask them to name what was taken away.

Motor coordinating activities provide opportunities for extensive work with conceptual vocabulary. Teachers talk over puzzlework with such statements as "turn it around," "over the other piece," "into that space," and "too big." Many teachers also point out to their aides the importance of using these opportunities.

Perceptual Discrimination. The ability to perceive accurately is the ability to discriminate the sights and sounds of one's environment. To the extent that a child cannot discriminate perceptually, he cannot, of course, discriminate verbally. So the preschool must accompany its tasks in language development and concept formation with that of helping the children develop their basic discriminatory skills. This is a common objective of all preschool programs visited by the Task Force. Most of them work toward this objective primarily through provision of experiences and materials which require or give practice in perceptual discrimination. Careful selection of puzzles, records, books, indeed, all preschool activities, involves consideration of the value of individual selections in the development of perceptual discrimination.

Recommendations for Language Instruction

"We are trying to provide our children with important experiences that their parents are unable to provide, experiences which the middle class child typically has." Such statements were commonly heard on Task Force visits. Worthy as this objective may be, *it is not enough*. The preschool for disadvantaged children cannot stop at providing experiences that a middle class child normally has, for the disadvantaged child enters school one to two years behind the middle class child. As Carl Bereiter, consultant to the Task Force, pointed out, "If a child who starts out behind is to catch up, he has to progress at a faster than normal rate. . . . It follows, therefore, that any educational program that claims to be helping children overcome their environmental handicaps must be able to show not just a normal rate of progress, but a superior rate." It is not safe to assume that the conventional preschool program, designed for middle class children, will do this.

Far too many of the preschools visited by the Task Force seem little more than substitute middle class home environments for fifteen or twenty children. To be sure, the children in the preschools are making progress. But the children with whom the disadvantaged child must eventually expect to compete are also progressing in their suburban homes. Many preschool curriculum guides read like a text for college-level family living courses, stressing such objectives as the development of small and large muscle coordination, the learning of elementary rules of social etiquette, the development of an appreciation for music, the ability to identify in male or female roles, and so on. These objectives are important, but they are not sufficiently important to justify the attention that they receive in nearly all preschools for disadvantaged children.

In the preschool for middle class children, such all-inclusive programs can be justified because for these children the preschool experience is usually an effort to further or to reinforce experiences they already receive in their homes. The disadvantaged child, however, does not receive the same experience at home. In language and concept formation especially, the work of the preschool has to begin at the lowest levels. To hope to eliminate all deficits of the disadvantaged child during the short period of time spent in the preschool is unrealistic. Rather, preschool programs must be selective in what they set out to accomplish. The first step has been made, for virtually all preschool teachers visited by the Task Force recognize that in addition to lack of experience, language and conceptual skills are the most important deficits of disadvantaged children. But the second step—still to be taken in many programs—is to select for intensive work those objectives for preschool programs which attack the deficits which are the most crucial to school success. Schools must recognize, therefore, that skills in language and conceptualization are crucial to academic achievement and that disadvantaged children are normally retarded most severely in these skills.

The NCTE Task Force recommends that the development of skill in language and concept formation be the overriding concern of preschools for disadvantaged children and that emphasis on all other objectives be reduced accordingly.

Language and Expression

Expressive language is already receiving much attention in preschools across the nation. By means of storytelling and its associated activities, poetry and nursery rhymes, finger plays and other word games, music, and informal conversation—all reinforced and stimulated by field trips and special class projects—children gain much experience in expressing skills. However, increased efforts must be made to provide activities which involve oral language participation by children themselves. This means that such activities as the retelling of stories, the writing of experience charts, role playing, puppetry, and dramatization should take a larger place in preschool programs. The step from mere comprehension of expressive language to its spontaneous production is a large and important one. For example, as soon as the children understand the plot of a story, its characters, and its action sequence, a teacher should give them extensive practice in telling the story in their own words. For children at this age, oral language is their only language. Teachers must help children to answer specific questions, to tell particular stories, to play specific roles—to organize and discipline their thought and expression.

All preschools visited by the Task Force made books available to the children, although the quantity and quality varied widely. Sometimes a wide selection of books is apparently not considered to be very important, for the classrooms appeared to be well equipped with many other kinds of materials. On the other hand, a number of preschools allocated money to books before they did to almost any other kind of materials.

The NCTE Task Force recommends that every preschool classroom for disadvantaged children contain a library with a wide selection of children's books.

The books should be of two types, factual and imaginative. The first of these receives much attention in preschools visited by the Task Force. Teachers typically have books on the zoo, the farm, the fireman, etc., in the classroom library; they read such books to the children before and after related field trips.

Imaginative literature, however, is also important, for it serves a unique purpose. Factual books about the zoo and the farm are essentially repetitions of other experience. For example, a story about the farm involves the same vocabulary and concepts as a trip to the farm. The material is presented as fact rather than fantasy, to be believed rather than merely enjoyed. But there is no counterpart in reality for a story about a tugboat that talks, a bean that grows as high as the clouds, or a boy who can fly, for the world of the imagination is a world apart from the world in which a child, particularly a disadvantaged child, lives. The development of children's imagination is important, in part because the imagination not only provides content for oral expression but also provides content which children typically enjoy telling to others.

Most important, good literature serves to extend the experience of a child beyond his daily life. Because of books a child does not have to visit or live near the sea to know something about it; he doesn't have to actually ride in an airplane to begin to love planes and imagine himself a pilot. This is especially important to disadvantaged children, who typically live within relatively narrow geographical limits, compared, say, to middle class children in a family that takes Sunday drives, yearly vacations, and trips to the local zoo.

Language and Concept Formation

Conceptual vocabulary also receives much attention in the preschools visited by the Task Force. Most preschools teach this vocabulary by coupling manipulative and kinesthetic experiences with conversation and group activities which deal with concepts individually, such as word games, songs, and stories. However, this remains descriptive language, descriptive of concepts, to be sure, but still not language extended to its fullest potential. As children develop a descriptive conceptual vocabulary, work with language can be expanded to include a third important use, that of manipulating and enlarging upon individual concepts. On this aspect of language, preschools need to place more emphasis.

A concept is "an idea, especially a generalized idea of a class of objects; a thought, general notion."[3] By this definition, virtually every word in the English language, except for the proper noun, is a concept. "Horse" represents a general idea; horses come in various shapes and sizes, and the simple, unmodified word does not necessarily call to mind a particular individual animal. Nonetheless, it does differ from the word, "big," for example. One can draw a picture which would be immediately recognized as that of a horse. "Big," however, is different; no picture can be drawn, it cannot be pointed to or seen. "Big" is a general idea,

---

[3] *Webster's New World Dictionary of the American Language* (Cleveland and New York: World Publishing Company, 1958).

but of a *relationship,* not of an object. Moreover, it is a relationship which depends upon language for its existence. Without language, "big," to continue with the example, is only a fuzzy image in the mind, incommunicable and, relative to its existence in language, useless.

In addition to individual concepts such as "big," "small," "long," and "short," still more general and complex concepts express relationships between individual ones. Such concepts have their existence only in language. The ideas that something is "big" and therefore not "small," that something is "either big or small," that something is "both big and long," are such concepts. Their existence depends upon certain basic words and statement patterns in language. Without them, no functional use of language is possible. For the child without an understanding of these basic elements of language, achievement in school is a virtual impossibility.

Individual, one-word concepts are often unformed or, at best, are at the "fuzzy image" stage of development when the disadvantaged child enters the preschool. The preschool has to begin at the beginning with concept development. The first step is that of developing individual concepts; of relationships between single things; of "big," "little," "long"; of "square," "green," and "round"; and of "over," "on," and "in," etc. The second step is that of developing a knowledge of the relationships between the individual concepts.

In language, certain words, word groups, and word patterns serve as carriers of thought or concepts. They are the bridge over which passes *meaning.* Three important single words are "not," "or," and "and." Important word groups are the comparatives, such as "big," bigger," and "biggest." An important statement pattern is the "if-then" construction. These words and word patterns are language "operators," for they are the means by which concepts are manipulated and put into relation with one another. They enable language to serve the function of enlarging upon already learned concepts. For example, once one knows that a box is *big,* he can know that the box is *not little* if he understands "big" and "little" individually as opposites and if he knows the proper use of "not." If he knows that "and" can be used to relate compatible concepts and "or" to relate incompatible ones, then he knows that he can say "the box is big and red," but not "the box is big and little," that he cannot say "the box is big or red" but he can say, "the box is big or little."[4] An additional use of language is in classification of indi-

---

[4] No attempt is made here to present a complete analysis of this aspect of language. A more complete discussion of conceptual language appears in the comments of Carl Bereiter later in the report.

vidual ideas into more general ones, of horses and cows into "animal," or houses and garages into "building."

Such concepts are not formed purely in the basis of sensory criteria. As Roger Brown points out in his book, *Words and Things*,[5] the categories used to group experiences are essentially *cultural,* only in part sensory. "Would we group Fords together and distinguish them from Chevrolets on the basis of. . . sensory attributes?" If such were the case, "we should be more likely to divide cars into classes defined by the color of the paint job. What of desks and tables, garages and barns, musical comedies and grand operas, Holsteins and Guernseys, schizophrenics and manic-depressives? . . . We need some sort of indication from those who participate in the culture of the things they treat as equivalents and those that are distinguished."[6]

Virtually every aspect of language is influenced by the culture of those who speak it. The disadvantaged child, reared on the margin of or apart from the dominant culture, must learn the language of that culture if he is to operate successfully in it. In the preschool, he must learn it from "those who participate in the culture"—the preschool teachers.

The NCTE Task Force recommends that the preschool curriculum for disadvantaged children include planned small-group instruction in basic vocabulary and statement patterns of conceptual language.

The teaching of this aspect of language must occur within the context of experiences to which the language can refer. For in the absence of experience to make meaningful the language which is taught, young children can learn little. One of the strongest points of the preschools visited by the Task Force is their emphasis on providing important experiences for children. However, experience alone will not teach the great amount of language skill needed to begin primary school, language skill almost totally undeveloped in the disadvantaged child. Nor can attempts to engage children in conversation guarantee that children will "pick up" the needed skill, for there is too much to be learned. Just as the teacher does not expect to teach mathematics only through casual experience or to teach reading by allowing the child to look over an adult's shoulder at the page being read, he cannot expect to develop necessary skill in language without some direct instruction.

Instruction in language is most effectively presented in small groups. Nearly all preschools have at least one teacher aide who can assist in

---

[5] Roger Brown, *Words and Things* (New York: Macmillan Company, Free Press of Glencoe, 1958).
[6] *Ibid.,* p. 208.

such work. In classrooms of fifteen children, staffed by a teacher and one aide, two twenty minute classes can be arranged in a forty minute time allotment. During the first twenty minutes, the teacher and aide can each take half the group, switching groups for the second twenty minute period. In a preschool classroom of fifteen to twenty children, staffed by a teacher and two aides, the children can be divided into three groups, alloting a total of sixty minutes for the period of instruction, one group participating in instruction and the other two under supervision of the aides.

The choice of activity for the children who are not under the supervision of the teacher is important, for untrained aides are usually limited in the activities which they are able to lead. The more capable aides can conduct such activities as storytelling or can present informal instruction in counting and general vocabulary. Less capable aides can supervise such activities as undirected play in a particular area of the classroom. The important consideration is that the noninstructional activities be reasonably quiet and not distracting for those undergoing instruction.

Whenever possible, approaches to instruction should not stress only the comprehension of conceptual language, but its use as well. Children must be encouraged to produce statements. Opinions differ today on the better methods of teaching language totally unfamiliar to the child for the purpose of enabling him to produce the language and to adapt it to later situations. However, the method of teaching foreign languages by pattern drill might show a way. The learner repeats a given pattern which involves the substitution of different words in a given sentence frame. This method establishes in the learner's mind the particular pattern itself, not any specific sentence or idea.

A teacher working with the pattern would show the children a large box and say, "This _____ is _____." She might have the children repeat, "This box is big." When all the children can repeat the sentence readily and can produce it when asked, "Now tell me about this box," the teacher can point to another box, "This box is little." Within a given instructional period, the content is varied ("This line is long," "This circle is red," etc.), although enough time must be spent with each pattern to allow the children to produce it readily. Perhaps only two or three patterns should be presented in a given period, but always with varying content and with appropriate gestures by the teacher to hold the interest of the children.

The individual concepts to which the introduced vocabulary refers can be varied with other activities. After a field trip to a farm, pictures or small figures may be used and the statements might be, "This cow is brown," or "This tractor is big," or "This pig is fat." In this way, the enthusiasm that field trips and special class projects generate in children can be used to advantage in instruction.

Clearly instruction in this aspect of language also serves a number of auxiliary objectives. First of all, introducing individual concepts in undirected activities at the same time as in the planned instruction mutually reinforces the concepts and their use in language.

Second, such small-group instruction insures that the silent or shy child has the opportunity to speak, for the teacher elicits responses from all the children. Often such children tend to be lost in the shuffle when the teacher is busy with more active children. In small-group instruction, the quiet child is one of five children in the teacher's attention, rather than one of fifteen or twenty.

Finally, direct instruction, especially if accompanied by visual aids, provides excellent practice in perceptual discrimination. The child must watch the teacher and listen to what she says in order to repeat it, as in pattern drill. The teacher, of course, must speak so that every word is important and must make the lessons interesting so that she holds the children's attention.

Language Development and Nonstandard Dialect

Most disadvantaged children come from homes in which a nonstandard English dialect is spoken. It may be pidgin, Cajun, Midland, or any one of a large number of regional or cultural dialects. Many preschool teachers are concerned about the dialect of their children and take measures to encourage standard pronunciation and usage.

The NCTE Task Force recommends that nonstandard English dialect be a concern at the preschool level only to the extent that it interferes with the acquisition of fundamental language learnings.

The crucial issue in the preschool is the relation of language to thinking. Whether a child thinks in standard or nonstandard dialect is not as important as the fact of his thinking. His ability to pronounce English "properly" is not as important as his ability to express himself, or to acquire a working vocabulary and skill with conceptual language. If the teacher and the student both know that "Zee leetel talafone" means "The little telephone," then they need spend little time in instruction to correct the former. A far more important concern is the child's ability to use language, to say, "Zee leetel talafone ees *not beeg.*"

This is not to say that adults should drop all concern with good speech in the preschool classroom. But the adult should continually remember

70

that his purpose is to help the child extend the ability to communicate through language, not merly to master superficial items of English usage.

Language and Nonlanguage Objectives

One of the common preschool objectives, not discussed directly so far in this report, is the development of a positive self-image in the children. Most preschools try to promote a favorable self-image by letting the child gain "success through experience." In preschools for middle class children, such experiences, related only indirectly to language through conversation practice, will stress such practices as art work; clay, sand, and wood work; and indoor play with toys. However, the inclusion of planned language instruction in the preschool curriculum need not work against developing a feeling of worth in children; rather, such small-group instruction helps to build the feeling through the individual attention it permits the teacher to give. Moreover, as the child's power in language grows, his confidence grows as well.

Every minute the teacher spends in the preschool classroom is expensive, and activities chosen must use teacher time to maximum advantage. In preschools for the disadvantaged, those activities which do not contribute directly to the concentration on language need to be carefully evaluated in terms of their contribution to the total program. Every decision to add or subtract an activity or classroom facility is a matter of weighing what is being sacrificed against what is to be gained. Children enjoy playing with trucks and tractors, sawing wood, randomly stacking pieces of wood as high as possible, and putting paint onto paper; but when the same minutes could be spent working increasingly difficult puzzles, doing creative role play and dramatics, working under supervision with form boards, listening to literature read by the teacher, or looking at books, any estimate of the relative value of the former activities must change. Not all activities which contribute to language development need be formally structured, but all should have a clearcut purpose if learning time is to be used to advantage. If a child lacks a home environment which prepares him for school, the period he spends in preschool, whether it is eight weeks or one year, is too short. To spend that time in any but the most important activities developing any but the most important skills is expensive, undesirable, and unwise.

Summary

The preschool period may be the best time to educate the disadvantaged. Preschools for disadvantaged children are an established part of society's total educational effort in many parts of the country. The work that preschools are currently doing is laudable and wholly constructive. But it is a new effort and much is yet to be learned. Some things are known, however, and might be summarized as follows:

—The average disadvantaged child is probably doomed to failure in present elementary and secondary school if efforts are not made to overcome the results of his home and neighborhood environments.

—The disadvantaged child, if he is to be competitive when he enters school, must have developed to the highest level possible the basic skills of communication.

—The greatest deficit, and threat to academic achievement, of the disadvantaged child is his retardation in the development of language and conceptual skills.

—The preschool curriculum designed for average and gifted children is often too broad in its range of objectives and needs to be modified for a greater concentration on the essential skills of language and conceptualization.

Oral Language Play in a Los Angeles Preschool

—The preschool must offer disadvantaged children cultural experiences which the low socioeconomic environment of the children cannot provide. But such experiences must offer practice in perceptual discrimination, conceptualization, and expression.

—The preschool must provide for disadvantaged children direct instruction to bring them to the level of average middle class children in a very short time.

—Selected experiences provide practice in *existing* skills. Direct instruction introduces and provides practice in *new* skills.

Elementary*

According to scores in academic potential and reading readiness tests, the gap between disadvantaged and middle class children is at its smallest when both groups enter school. This gap, however, widens as the two groups progress in school. The basic problem in educating disadvantaged children of elementary school age is that schools have been unable to overcome this initial handicap and, as a result, the gap becomes more pronounced and the problem more difficult to solve each year the children are in school.

Teaching disadvantaged children would be easier and more consonant with the normal elementary school curriculum if they had the preschool experience envisioned in the previous chapter of this report. Despite encouraging signs, however, preschool programs are not yet geared to the intensive program that will place disadvantaged children coming to elementary school on an equal educational plane with disadvantaged children. Task Force members are aware of the enormity of the problem of effecting such a program; yet, they believe that to plan for less is a failure in educational commitment.

Another initial problem facing elementary schools is that many states do not have kindergartens, much less preschool programs. As a result, the burden of educating the disadvantaged child falls upon the elementary school and more specifically upon the primary levels of these schools. *Within the elementary schools then, it is clear that the most critical school years are on the primary (K–3 or 1–3) school level.*

Children entering the upper elementary grades already behind in reading, oral language, and writing start with an extreme handicap. Their situation becomes more desperate and more difficult to cope with on each succeeding grade level. In many areas a majority of students in secondary schools read on an elementary school level. With present knowledge and techniques of reading, schools find it extremely difficult to bring such students up to their potential grade level ability. This progression of difficulty and failure by so many disadvantaged students illustrates the importance of elementary school language programs.

Task Force observers were impressed with a number of elementary school programs. Nevertheless, social and technical pressures of our

---

* The observations in this chapter are based largely on 91 reports from observers of 60 different programs.

74

society dictate that far more be done. Elementary schools for disadvantaged children must concentrate on those skills most necessary for school and social success. Not because of parochial interest does this report of the NCTE recommend the basic skills of reading, oral language, and writing—such a recommendation is made because children can achieve little other academic success without these skills.

Evening Reading in the Dormitory of a Boarding School for Taos Indian Children (Donald J. Morrow, Photographer)

Goals and Objectives of Program

Children from areas of economic poverty come to school with many deficiencies. These seem to fall into three general areas: (1) Conceptual development, (2) Language facility, and (3) Self-concept. These deficiencies put the child of poverty at a disadvantage in a school curriculum designed for middle class children. In deciding on the overall objectives for their program, schools are faced with two alternatives. They can, through extensive preschool work, change the children before the children enter school, or they can change the school to teach the children they have—not the children they might like to have. Project visits reveal that most effective school systems are using a combination of the approaches. They are seeking to eliminate early as many problems which beset the the disadvantaged child as they can and to develop, at the same time, a school program which will make the most effective use of the positive academic potential the children possess.

One common goal of virtually every project visited was to reduce class size. When classes are small, problems of discipline diminish, each student receives greater attention, a creative environment is easier to achieve, and work can be flexible. Most teachers interviewed felt that fifteen students is a good class size; supervisors see twenty or twenty-five as a more realistic figure. The aim is to schedule enough students to allow for interaction and cross-stimulus, but not so many that individuality is drowned.

Another common goal of the programs visited was to improve reading and language skills. Full commitment to this objective will require that every student raise his skills to expectations based on his age, grade, and intelligence.

The objectives of at least one elementary program visited concentrate on the strengths of the students. Much attention is given to the usual reading, writing, and spelling skills, but on a creative, individual basis rather than in remedial drill or intensive instruction.

The stated objectives of other programs are often highly structured, with drill and repetition as the basic methods. Some teachers feel that overlearning is the only way to overcome such problems as poor speech patterns or poor usage. Because the problem of this approach seems to be that of student motivation, only an exceptional teacher can succeed.

What is the difference between the quantitative and qualitative aspects of drill and repitition? What types of material are suitable for over-learning?

Characteristics of Students

The following were named by teachers and administrators as some of the characteristics of elementary students from disadvantaged backgrounds:

. . . language retardation
. . . lack of experiences needed for academic learning
. . . inability to postpone immediate satisfaction for longer term goals
. . . aggressive behavior
. . . lack of time concept
. . . tendency to be slow in learning and a need to pursue one idea at a time
. . . lack of interest in academic achievement

. . . inability to generalize

. . . social dialects that strongly differ in structure, style, and vocabulary from informal, standard English

. . . lack of self-concept and feeling of being unable to succeed

. . . feeling of rejection by society

By no means did Task Force visits substantiate all of the above characteristics. Nevertheless, it is important that the objectives of a program be based on the characteristics typical of the students involved. The program can then be built around their strengths and weaknesses.

Organization and Staffing

Most of the elementary schools visited do not have organizational or staffing plans markedly different from those of conventional schools. A few programs have attempted different plans, however, and the following organizational and staffing practices were observed in one or more projects and seem to have promising qualities.

Ungraded Programs. The concept of an ungraded program was well established in last century's one-room schoolhouse. It has been recently rejuvenated and is now one of the "newest" curriculum ideas. In the ungraded program, pupils move from level to level when they are ready as opposed to when a graded curriculum dictates. Such programs claim to put the child "where he is and where he can grow at his own rate," a particular help to disadvantaged children. Following is a description of one ungraded elementary program that was observed.

> . . . After leaving an already established preschool program, the children in this school district begin their elementary school work in an ungraded program until they learn to read at a level determined by standardized tests. It may be as long as two years for some students, no longer than a year for others. After the child reaches a level of achievement equivalent to that of the normal second grade, he enters a second nongraded block which encompasses normal achievement through the fourth grade. After the fourth grade, children proceed into the usual graded elementary program. The rationale for this program is that under such a system every child entering fifth grade enters at the proper reading level. The school district hopes that such a system will eliminate the failure-built-on failure situation of disadvantaged children who have been passed from grade to grade without having achieved the proper knowledge and skills. The hope is that once students are "on the right track," they can progress at regular rates.

Although relatively few ungraded programs were seen, their potential seems worthy of further investigation by teachers and administrators.

The ungraded school organization is predicated on the belief that children do not learn in lock-step fashion. Research provides substantial evidence that pace and pattern of learning are individual and unique. Cannot then interage groupings provide opportunities for disadvantaged children in the elementary school to establish themselves in school without repeating grades and experiencing early school failure?

Another program observed handled differently the problem of promotion of children not ready for the work in the next grade. This program created a Junior First Grade which acted as a buffer zone between kindergarten and regular first grade. The class was made up of children who were judged by their kindergarten teachers to be unprepared for the work in regular first grade classes. Junior First Grade classes are small; individual attention is possible; and some students leave Junior First Grade for second grade while the others move into regular first grade classes.

Divided Day. One commonly used method of organizing the school day to increase the amount of individual attention given to students is the divided day. The class is divided roughly into two parts, often on the basis of reading ability, one group coming early and the other staying late. In one program observed, half the students in the first and second grades attend school from 9:00 a.m. to 2:00 p.m. The other half attend from 10:00 a.m. to 3:00 p.m. In a class of thirty students, the teacher spends one hour a day with each segment as a class of only fifteen, rather than thirty, students.

Such provisions to assure closer relationships and individual attention for each child seem particularly vital in work with the disadvantaged.

Class Size. Although some observers noted elementary classes with thirty or more students, Task Force members observed a definite trend in programs for the disadvantaged to have considerably smaller classes. In many programs classes of fifteen to seventeen students were not uncommon. Task Force observers were requested to note the number of students *in attendance* in the classes visited. The average was 23.1, excluding one class of 200 children watching a film. There is, of course, the possibility that classes were larger but that students were absent or had dropped out by the April-June visits. One fact that disturbed observers was the dropout rate among elementary students in certain states. In some areas of the country, little attention was paid to the lack of school attendance by young children of certain minority groups. Mississippi school officials, for example, pointed out that there is no compulsory attendance law in their state.

One important point should be made regarding class size. Small class size, in itself, does not automatically assure better learning experiences. If an elementary teacher uses the same techniques and the same assignments with a class of fifteen as opposed to a class of thirty, little or no increase in learning will result. However, the opportunities that a small class provides to work in individual instruction justifies lowering class size.

Children in a Migrant Workers' Camp in Pennsylvania Learn about Colors

Reading Clinics. District organization of elementary reading clinics generally took one of two forms: (1) Early intervention when first grade children, by their performance during prognosis, indicate probable difficulty in learning to read. In one program such students received clinical help in the form of compensatory experiences three times a week, in groups of four, for one-half hour periods. (2) Later intervention when students in grades 3 to 6 are obviously behind in their reading skills. Under such intervention retarded readers in grades 4 to 6 were given clinical instruction in groups of four, twice a week, for one hour.

Separation by Sex. One interesting organizational pattern observed in two schools was the division of elementary classes into separate classes for boys and girls at both upper elementary levels and the junior high levels. One elementary school principal in a highly disadvantaged area where classroom discipline is a severe problem felt that separation by sex was one very helpful way of handling discipline. Since observation of this kind was limited to two schools, it can only be said that such organization appeared to be working for the schools involved.

Specialized Personnel. Providing specialized personnel to assist teachers and children was a fairly common practice in the programs visited. The practice serves a number of purposes: inservice education, individualized teaching, release of teachers for intensive teaching, attention of individual needs in speech, and the involvement of parents in the education of children. Sometimes the service of specialized personnel is provided in lieu of reduced class size; more often it is in recognition of the need for specialized assistance of children and teachers. The following descriptions will indicate the range and diversity of specialized personnel that work directly with the teacher or the students.

1) A Remedial Reading Teacher is assigned to each of the elementary schools in the district. This teacher teaches three classes of ten children during the morning and works with homeroom teachers during the afternoon. Teachers are chosen not only for their professional competence in reading but also for their ability to work with people. This arrangement is designed to improve the teaching of reading to all students, not only to help thirty or fifty of the lowest.

2) A Reading Improvement Teacher is assigned to give teachers assistance in preparing reading lessons. She visits classes during the week and teaches nine student classes twice a week. The remainder of her time is spent in preparation and work with teachers. Students who score extremely low in reading tests are referred to a Correctional Reading Teacher. Class size is kept to a maximum of ten students so that intensive remedial instruction is possible.

Specialized help can also serve as a morale booster for teachers. The practices described not only assist in improving children's reading competence, but provide assistance to enable teachers to become more effective.

3) A Supernumerary Primary Teacher works within one school. This teacher is used to supplement the regular elementary program by visiting each primary classroom on a schedule to read to the class and to stimulate the children to speak clearly and listen attentively. Because this person is highly qualified and experienced, her example may constitute a form of informal inservice education for regular teachers.

A program of inservice training for all classroom teachers in the various aspects of teaching described above may be stimulating and challenging. But would not assigning special functions to a supernumerary teacher at the primary level be taking some of the more pleasurable aspects of teaching away from the regular teacher? Would there be merit in making the necessary materials and experiences available to the regular teacher?

4) A Cultural Improvement Teacher is hired in one large school to devote half time to music and half time to providing a program of cultural experiences for children, including field trips to art centers, museums, zoos, and the theater.

The classroom teacher should play an important part in the plans, participate in the excursions, and utilize the experiences provided by the trips. The use of a second teacher who has time to make the many arrangements for field trips could be extremely helpful. Could such work, however, be done by competent nonacademic personnel in consultation with teachers?

5) An Academic Improvement Teacher is available to take half a class while the regular teacher keeps the remainder. Both teachers can then work with only fifteen children rather than thirty.

6) Supportive Teachers are hired by one school to release the teacher for remedial instruction. These teachers are available to take a teacher's class so that the teacher can work with a small group of students requiring help. The theory is that the teacher of the class knows students and their problems best.

7) A Consultant, specially trained and with much experience in disadvantaged areas, moves from school to school and spends from a week to a month in each of the compensatory schools. This teacher gives demonstration lessons and helps teachers with whatever problems they might have.

The trend toward using a consultant teacher indicates that the service is of value. For districts in the early stages of programs, such an outside consultant can provide suggested materials and techniques to improve a program in a very short time.

Children in New York City Listen to a Story in the Library

8) Speech Therapists under the direction of the speech department of a local college are used in one school system. These speech teachers are assigned to one school one day a week for eleven weeks. Each teacher is able to work with an entire class for one half hour a week.

9) Another school system uses a Speech Improvement Teacher who visits selected classes and attempts to improve children's diction, usage, and speech. The classroom teacher audits the class from the rear of the room and makes notes of those children who need special attention from her during the course of regular classwork. Follow-up suggestions and additional materials provided by this type of speech teacher can be helpful to the classroom teacher.

Some work by speech teachers seemed to be limiting and unrealistic. In one case an entire fifty minute period was spent in drill work with second grade children on the *s* sound and the *th* sound.

10) Parent Aides are used in many projects. It is felt that hiring local people serves to free the teacher from many of the routine, non-instructional tasks of the classroom, and to help parents and those with whom they associate in the community to understand what the school is doing.

Practices and Methods

This section contains only a selection of the many practices and methods observed on the elementary school level. Classroom practices in programs for the disadvantaged reflect sharply conflicting attitudes to rigidity and permissiveness, to structure and nonstructure. They reflect, too, wide use of practices and methods based on commercial materials of instruction. In general, they imply markedly different philosophies, and varying degrees of knowledge and understanding of the needs, both social and academic, of the disadvantaged.

One extremely encouraging sign to Task Force observers was the considerable freedom given to most teachers, school administrators, and curriculum planners to evolve practices and methods that might be helpful to the disadvantaged child. In numerous interviews such educators stated that the only really severe handicap toward experimentation and change was the lack of funds. Nevertheless, the freedom to try something different did exist in most school districts. Using different teaching materials or methods does not necessarily result in better instruction, but meaningful experimentation helps to avoid complacency and stagnation. Since most disadvantaged students completing their elementary school education are not performing at a normal level of academic expectation, it is obvious that much of the elementary program needs revision. And it will be only through such revision that progress will be made.

Some teachers working in schools with a preponderance of disadvantaged children report that the approved district course of study or curriculum guide is unrealistic for the abilities and interests of their students. Such guides are normally written with the advantaged child in mind. Strong effort is needed to convince school authorities of the need to design specific programs for the disadvantaged.

One vital educational question that has not been answered is how research evidence can be brought to bear on the practices to effect academic achievement and student motivation. Research developments indicate that many common practices and methods do not produce the desired results, but that there are answers to many current educational problems. Certainly planners of any new program for the disadvantaged should be aware of the research pertinent to their area of work.

Reading. It is not within the scope or intent of this report to discuss the numerous controversies about methods of teaching reading. Such controversies are adequately covered in professional journals. Most schools visited used some form of a basal reader; others were using such approaches as Words in Color, i.t.a., Phonovisual, Language Experience, and individualized reading programs. Each approach will be discussed briefly, but its success or lack of success for use with disadvantaged children cannot be finally assessed in a one to three day visit. They are not the only approaches to teaching reading, but they are those observed by Task Force members.

Even a brief visit to research programs in reading revealed that more attention, materials, consultant help, and overall expectations were given to experimental groups as opposed to control groups. It would be interesting to reverse the procedure.

i.t.a. The Initial Teaching Alphabet or Augmented Roman Alphabet consists of a phonemic alphabet containing forty-four symbols. Each symbol represents one of the sounds in the English language. The Bethlehem, Pennsylvania, i.t.a. program was of particular interest to the Task Force since most of the students in the program were disadvantaged. The program has been in operation for two years, and the district's assessment of its value is indicated by the recent announcement that i.t.a. would be used in an increased number of the primary classes in the school district. Fifteen teachers were initially recruited to teach this new method of reading.

The test results of the Bethlehem project appear impressive. According to the latest published results of i.t.a.[1] and t.o. (traditional orthography) in the second year of school, some 25 percent of the i.t.a.-taught population are reading materials at 3-2 or above levels while none of the t.o.-trained population are in material of this difficulty level. Whether this is because of the success of i.t.a. or because students under t.o. instruction were not taught reading skills beyond their grade level is not known.

Some observers believe that impressive results from i.t.a. and other new approaches to reading result less from the new approach than from the emphasis placed on reading through the school day. They agree that reading should be emphasized but not by sacrificing other important experiences.

---

[1] *i.t.a. bulletin* (Initial Teaching Alphabet Publications, Inc.), 2, 4 (Summer 1965).

The Phonovisual Method. This method offers a structured approach to phonics instruction. It was observed in city schools in the East, where it is widely used.

The Phonovisual Method features the sequential introduction of sounds and the use of reading charts and games centered on this prescribed sequence. Ordinarily, it is taught separately from the basal reader. Since the basal reader is used for silent and oral reading, the basal teacher's manual is not used for phonics instruction.

On Phonovisual Consonant and Vowel Charts, consonants and vowels are arranged in order of sounds and voiced equivalents. The Charts, unlike i.t.a., do not attempt to present all sounds, but merely include the sounds and letters most often used.

Words in Color. This program is an attempt to show phonetic patterns through color patterns. Children are expected to work out words for themselves after a very limited amount of instruction. The materials consist of a series of charts on which vowels, consonants, vowel sounds, and consonant blends are depicted in many colors.

The Language-Experience Method. This method is based on the idea that reading should not be taught in isolation but should be based on the language experience of the child. Individual and class experiences are recorded, and children learn to read about what they have done in the classroom.

Second Grade Taos Indian Children Arranging the Bulletin Board (Donald J. Morrow, Photographer)

Class Activities in Reading. The following descriptions will give some indication of specific classroom activities in reading that were observed by Task Force members.

1) Grade 1 . . . The class activity was a demonstration of *Dialog I*— a programed phonics series. Children follow directions of a taped voice—this particular lesson on "s" and "t." Demonstration involved written and oral participation. After the demonstration, the children used their skill in phonics to "unlock" several words that the teacher wrote on the board. Using the word *splash,* children spelled for us *mash, lash, flash.* The teacher, when asked her opinion of *Dialog,* seemed to think the voice on the recorder did not pronounce beginning sounds properly. She seemed to think a local voice should be used.

2) Grade 3 . . . A discussion was in progress about a story which had been previously read, "Mr. Myrtle." The class had to recall the sequence of events in the story. The teacher then led the discussion to value judgments such as the virtues of the characters in the story.

3) Grades 4-5 . . . The emphasis was on phonics—sounding out the words—giving the meaning and using the word in a sentence. Children seemed interested and obviously knew basic phonic rules.

4) A Book Club was observed in the upper grade levels of an all-girl elementary school. Children seemed highly motivated, and all had brought at least one book with them that they were currently reading. The group had just finished *Little Women,* and three girls had started a project making a mosaic depicting several characters from the book. Each week girls submit a poster concerning reading, and the best poster wins a prize—a book. The winning girl received a copy of *Heidi,* the next book to be read. The teacher spent a large part of the period talking about the Swiss items she had brought with her. These were passed around. The girls seemed very anxious to read the book by the time she had finished.

5) One school developed what is termed a home library, a collection of children's books from which the children may borrow books to take home and keep as long as they like. The object is to make children and parents aware of the importance of books and to help foster a positive attitude toward reading. According to classroom teachers, this is the most popular feature of the program. Though return and control of books is relatively free, few books are lost or stolen. Since lower class homes typically have few books, such lending libraries are widely used by children.

6) In another school visited the librarian meets with a group of parents, discusses books the children may bring with them. Since many parents want to help their children, these practices should benefit all concerned.

Most programs in reading for the disadvantaged seem not to differ appreciably from those that would be seen in a school for advantaged children. This is particularly unfortunate because so much of the reading taught in regular programs is oriented toward a completely different social experience. Too few reading books, particularly basal readers, center on the interests of the urban child. Despite the increasing numbers of Americans who now live in urban centers, most reading material for primary children is based on suburban or farm life. Another common complaint is that in the past no basal reader and few other elementary readers showed Negroes and whites together. Some attempts to change this have been made. In at least one major reading series, the newly-appearing Negro children act and talk like the golden-haired, suburban members of the middle class. One gets the feeling that the illustrators were merely asked to "color their faces black."

Certain cautions should be observed in preparing urban-centered material for disadvantaged children. Showing a picture of a white policeman with the caption "The policeman is my friend" may draw a reaction from the Negro children in Harlem or in Philadelphia, Mississippi, quite different from that naturally expected by a middle class white teacher. Observers frequently noticed such unrealistic, middle class based material.

Oral Language. When oral work in language was observed, it was in activities such as class discussion, dramatics, puppetry, and story-telling. Most of the elementary programs were doing work in oral language, but much of it was unstructured. Little work, for example, was done in analyzing the oral language difficulties and deficiencies of students and developing specific programs to correct these problems. One of the most discouraging aspects of Task Force visits was, on the one hand, the acknowledgment by administrators and teachers of the severe language development problems of their students, and on the other hand the lack of any consistent effort to determine and solve these problems. Even the talking and discussing often were done more by the teacher than by the student.

The following items show some specific examples of the work that was observed in oral language:

> . . . In a first grade class, emphasis was on oral speaking and discussion. A large chart showed a park with several children in it doing many things. The chart

elicited much discussion. The teacher then demonstrated how one supplementary series of books was used. A small group read aloud or said the same words as were in the book. The book is designed in such a way that children easily see and readily adopt a pattern. (Example. I saw 1 white duck. He followed me home. I saw 2 pink ponies. They followed me home, etc).

. . . Hand puppets, flannel board figures, and other objects are used to reinforce dramatic activities and to allow the children to project themselves into characters of fantasy. The puppets are simple, made of brown paper sacks with faces painted and yarn glued on for hair. Teachers report that this kind of activity is most successful if the children have the opportunity to rehearse several times by themselves to experiment with the puppets and their characters.

. . . Another very successful language experience was a ''movie'' made of a roll of paper on a frame that is about 24″ wide. The paper is turned or rolled from the top to go in one direction and from the bottom to go in the opposite direction. The children paint, sketch, or draw pictures of a sequence of events of a trip they have taken or of any experience that is common to the group. Each child may narrate the illustration he has created. At times one child may be asked to narrate a series of pictures to strengthen his ability to recall and discuss a sequence.

. . . The administrator of this program stated that he thought improvement in speech and speaking habits was very important to the educational success of the students. Because such students are nonverbal, they need special assistance with their English speech habits. He recommends intensive work by each teacher on speech. He wants each teacher to stimulate the imagination of the students and try to make them aware of the world about them. He tries to communicate to all teachers the necessity of motivating the students in this manner.

. . . The use of speech teachers to come into elementary classrooms and help with the speech problems of the class was observed in three programs. Such a teacher operates in the manner of the art or music teacher who visits a class on specific occasions to work with the pupils. In one large city program, speech therapists are assigned to a school one day a week for eleven weeks. In 1964 the program was limited to the second grade. Interestingly, the program is now being moved down into the kindergarten and first grade in the belief that many problems are better prevented than corrected later.

Dialect. Teachers generally conducted class work on nonstandard dialect informally. If any conscious approach to problems of dialect was taken, it was usually either a teach-by-example approach, emphasizing the importance of teachers' speaking standard English, or a correction of student errors. Observers noted a tendency for teachers to ask students using a nonstandard dialect for the ''proper'' way of saying a word or phrase.

Some teachers were concerned about the possible conflict between the school language and the home language. They pointed out the problems of teaching an additional dialect in a manner that will not produce a home-school conflict. In teaching a second dialect, it is important to help the pupil understand that he may speak freely one way at home and to his friends but that there is another language he uses in the school. Frank discussion of the problem of dialects and the usefulness of learning the local prestige dialect, or in the words of the Negro student, "the Man's" language is essential. Further discussion of this point is made in Walter Loban's comments in Part III.

Although some teachers believe that the student's dialect should be fully accepted in school, the general feeling is that some work in standard English is necessary for greater social and job mobility by disadvantaged students with a strong regional or racial dialect. Methods used in teaching a second dialect cannot succeed without strong rapport between teacher and student. Otherwise, natural resistance can be expected when teachers attempt to teach a student a dialect he is unlikely to use at home or with his friends. The following description is of a class that appears to have achieved this necessary rapport in work with language and dialect.

> . . . The teacher had obviously done work with the class regarding dialect problems. When students were reading and one made a particularly apparent error in enunciation, she would ask the class for the proper way to say the word. One boy who was struggling to read also had to practice saying his "w" sound. He tried and tried and only with great difficulty produced an acceptable sound. Interestingly enough, the students did not resent this type of correction and indicated that they were aware of their speech problems, to the extent that the teacher had pointed them out. The attitude of the students regarding their school work, and in this case their dialect problems, was extremely wholesome. Also, this class had a mixture of Negro and non-Negro students, including one gypsy.

Composition. Composition was subordinated to reading instruction in virtually all of the programs visited. Several programs visited have adopted a noncritical approach to composition evaluation. Because academic work is, in many ways, a foreign experience to disadvantaged children, any form of criticism (especially of the red pencil type) was felt to be detrimental to motivation because it might inhibit more than it would help. As a result, such programs feature noncriticism; anything the student produces is acceptable. Ways of criticizing in a positive manner can be developed so that teachers need not accept just "anything."

In one program using a noncritical approach, the teacher returns the papers to the children only after he has compiled lists of spelling words and grammatical points for the following week's work. Another teacher uses essentially the same approach, but goes further; he has individualized spelling instruction and compiles each student's spelling lesson entirely from the misspelled words in his writing.

Some teachers stress "gentle" evaluation of composition; teachers quietly point out strengths and weaknesses. They feel there is merit in helping pupils through a constructive approach to criticism. In addition to stressing the strengths of a pupil, the teacher tries to suggest ways in which other aspects of composition can be strengthened. These need not involve the red pencil approach.

The Treanor Composition Program was observed in one school. The Treanor program is carefully structured, using a vocabulary building approach to various facets of teaching writing. Much drill is required, and it is not unusual to have each child repeat a phrase, a sentence, or a series of sentences in order to fix one idea. The overlearning seems to be a very helpful method to use with children who come to school with limited oral patterns of family speech.

The written phase of the program as it is practiced in the school observed seemed weaker than the oral portion. There was little evidence of written composition. One teacher reported that one pupil had made several copies of a letter before he produced a perfect one.

Visits indicated that stress is often placed upon the relationship of written expression to experiences. As a result, teachers take a careful look at all possible facets of student experience as motivation for written

Playground Activity in San Diego, California

90

expression. Work in such areas as poetry, ballads, and tall tales stimulated some interesting and exciting contributions from pupils. Teachers must select appropriate examples for motivating pupils.

One common practice includes the use of photographs of local landmarks, paintings, sculpture, and personal experience as writing stimulants. In general the stress in composition programs for elementary schools seems to be on the written expression of experience, because it is felt that this approach aids in developing greater self-awareness as well as facility with words.

Listening Skills. The English teaching profession has become increasingly aware of the need for and the importance of listening skills. Several school districts are attempting to identify certain necessary skills and to provide activities which will foster growth in these areas. A common reason cited for such activities is the high noise level in many of the children's homes and the resulting shutting out of sounds by children. The art of questioning certainly plays an important role in these activities, although there is a great need to review the kinds of questions that are asked of pupils.

One school district has designed a series of lessons presenting a variety of activities for listening to be used in the study centers in the primary classrooms. They use many approaches to motivation for listening as well as a variation in the method for child responses. These materials were considered only a beginning in this type of activity.

A number of teachers reported that "listening centers" provide a good means of furthering skill in listening. A listening center normally consists of a tape recorder or phonograph fitted with six to ten earphones. The material used may be either commercial recordings of music or stories or tape recordings made by the teacher. Older elementary children can, of course, operate the machines without help, but a teacher aide often has this responsibility in the primary grades. Another advantage of listening centers is the teacher's being freed to work with fewer children while the center is being used.

Dramatic Activities. Dramatic activities can be valuable aspects of the elementary school program. They have an important byproduct in that they are not only excellent expressive activities but also an effective means of developing listening skills in children. A child will usually pay close attention to his classmate who is playing the role of "mommy," of "teacher," or of another child. When he performs for his classmates, he usually is performing fairly close to the level of his peers, whereas the teacher may perform (as when reading a story) far above their level.

Task Force observers saw the following dramatic activities:

. . . The classes divide into groups, produce short plays (e.g., ''The Grasshopper and the Ant''), and perform them for the class and a tape recorder. The class goes over the tapes and evaluates the performance, voice inflections, pronunciations, etc.

This project was designed to encourage speaking—especially emphasizing phrases (due to emphasis on phonics in other programs) through the use of dramatic activity. The tape recorder is the principal factor here. The teacher reads sections of the playlet on tape; then children read each one aloud. After this, children rehearse the playlet in small groups, before classroom performance and tape recording. Children, under teacher guidance, then evaluate points such as pronunciation, diction, inflection, etc.

As the observers entered the classroom, the children and three teachers were getting ready to practice their play based on the story, ''Bremen Town Musicians.'' There were two basic groups of students: (1) the players on the stage and (2) the chorus sitting by the piano.

The stage had simple props that served the basic purpose of helping the audience and players imagine they were with the Bremen Town Musicians. Props on the stage consisted of a living room scene with table and chairs and, next to this, the yard with a tree around which the ''animals'' danced.

Perhaps the most impressive feature of this dramatic presentation was the relative freedom which the students obviously felt. They knew there were limitations to behavior, but they also knew that they had freedom that would not be evident in a regular classroom. The students could talk out loud and choose to participate or not to participate, as did the boy with the rooster mask.

Field Trips. Field trips and cultural experiences play a large role in most primary school programs visited. Such activities serve as writing and speaking stimuli, as an excellent exercise in acculturation, and are among priority items in most plans for program expansion.

Many elementary programs visited stressed firsthand experiences. Pupils can be expected to have difficulty in thinking and speaking if they must bare their thoughts and speech on an extremely limited range of experiences. Teachers interviewed by one Task Force member agreed that much growth in oral and written language resulted from the extension of experiences on field trips. Particularly noted was a growth of vocabulary. These teachers also felt that some pupils exhibited new interest in school and as a result there were fewer discipline problems. Pupils not only discussed the trips in class but also dictated or wrote stories about their experiences. Discussion was not limited to the classroom but continued on the playground and at home.

After such trips pupils not only discussed what they had seen and done in class, but also dictated or wrote stories, discussed them with their peers on the playground, and related them to their families. They appeared to have a better feeling about themselves when they could make an oral or written response to their experience.

In one program the teacher took pictures of the activities on the trip, so that only faces showed. Then a guessing game was conducted with the children attempting to guess the activity in the picture solely from the faces.

Field trips in the classroom are also being widely employed. Chicken incubators, class pets, and collections of rocks, insects, and other new objects can add much to the overall classroom environment. Whenever possible, many teachers coordinate such activities with the reading material or teaching units being used. Observations revealed many other classroom experiences which enriched the language background of the pupils. At primary levels some children were cooking pudding, making chocolate milk, making butter, and preparing jello. Their remarks and conversation showed an awareness of taste, color, texture, touch, and odor. They used such words as *bubbly, thick, hot,* and *cold.*

Trips to airports, fire stations, farms, etc., are regarded by teachers as stimulants for discussion, reading, and writing. One wonders, however, if a child living in Lower East Side in New York City with its variety of racial and religious people, stores, houses, and home situations has fewer experiences than an ''advantaged'' child living in a suburban community.

Martin Deutsch in one study notes that 65 percent of the Negro children had not been over twenty-five blocks away from their home. Surely, this is a disturbing statistic. Nevertheless, one wonders if such a child's range of life's experiences is *less* than that of an ''advantaged'' child living in a small midwestern farm community or a middle class suburban family. What an urban disadvantaged child does have are experiences *different from those which are expected in school.* Some schools are trying to make use of the urban child's experiences. Still, too many primary teachers were more concerned that their children could not distinguish farm animals or their size relationship than they were with what the children *did* know about their environment.

Parent Involvement. School administrators often stressed the need to involve the parents of the disadvantaged child in the school program. Without parental cooperation, the work of the school can be difficult. Despite wide agreement on the necessity of parental involvement in school activities, there was a split among administrators on the advisability of such programs. Some administrators claim high success in parent participation in school programs; others state that the parents in their area are reluctant to come to the school and that many students do not live with their parents. Not surprisingly, schools with high parent involvement attempt to fit programs to parental schedules, constantly keeping the parents informed of school activities, and in some cases even providing baby sitting services at the school.

Certainly parents visiting school need a genuine feeling of welcome by teachers and administrators. Parent group meetings should provide specific, helpful ways that parents can aid their children. In one parent participation program, parents are invited to school every Friday to learn what is happening in school and to help teachers prepare materials. Several projects hire parent aides, to help them understand what the school is doing as well as to assist the classroom teacher.

Materials

Books. Disadvantaged children own few books. Since students from disadvantaged families have limited chances to own books, book distribution usually takes the form of library loans. One school allows for half of each upper elementary class to be taken to the library once a week (by community volunteers) to check out a book. Books are read and then briefly reported on orally. Most classroom paperback libraries, where available, are available to students for home use. Most teachers think that it is important to get books in the children's homes.

Good books in adequate quantity are important in developing an academic orientation conducive to success in school. Some schools have initiated book clubs, in which paperbacks are ordered by the club and then bought by children for personal copies. Pride in book ownership is an important aim of the club. Another school has approached the problem with a key club in which students are given keys when they become members, the key symbolizing the importance of reading as a "key" to success. Reading parties are held at which parents and children celebrate the children's finishing a book, and the children read to their parents.

Visits revealed that several elementary schools are providing a library checkout service for children from disadvantaged families. In one instance the librarian was conducting meetings to explain to parents the purposes of the library, the use of the books, and to introduce to them books appropriate for children.

Visits also reveal many classes without classroom libraries or completely inadequate collections. Even more disturbing is the lack of school libraries. Classroom and school libraries should have the highest priority in the school budget. If students are expected to increase their reading skills, books must be made readily available to them.

Audiovisual. Audiovisual equipment and materials seem to be both widely used and highly recommended by teachers of the disadvantaged. They stress the abilities to listen and look among the least developed by young disadvantaged children. Audiovisual aids, because of their novelty and their central focus on a single thing (a screen, a piece of sound equipment, the shutting out of other stimuli by darkening a room, closing a door), interest students. Photographs in the primary grades aid children to relate themselves to the classroom group and the community. The use of tape recordings and filmstrips can bring literary experiences closer to the child.

The study center is becoming increasingly more valuable at the elementary level. A study center usually consists of a tape recorder, a record player, a filmstrip projector, a small table screen, and a group of six to ten sets of earphones. The study center does not require the darkening of the room because of the nature of the small screen. A combination of these audiovisual machines makes possible a valuable lesson with a small group of six to ten children while the teacher works elsewhere in the classroom with another group of children.

The opaque projector is used by a number of teachers who use it for one of the following reasons: (1) Illustrations in a book can be seen by an entire class. (2) Materials such as magazines, flat pictures, and student writings can be used in class discussions. (3) Attention is highly focused because many distracting stimuli are eliminated as rooms are darkened. (4) Teachers note that slower readers seem less likely to feel defeated and less concerned about being singled out for mistakes.

Children in Oakland, California, Visit the Zoo (Martin J. Cooney, Photographer)

English as a Second Language. One totally bilingual school was visited in an area with an equal proportion of native English- and Spanish-speaking children. At each grade level, there are two classes of native English speakers and two of native Spanish speakers.

A team teaching approach is used. Each English-speaking teacher teaches English vernacular to English-speaking children in the morning and English as a second language to Spanish-speaking children in the afternoon. Her teammate, in a similar manner, teaches Spanish vernacular to Spanish speakers in the morning and Spanish as a second language to English speakers in the afternoon. In this way, every student receives half his elementary school instruction in Spanish and half in English.

All the normal elementary school subjects are included in the curriculum; the only difference is that they are taught in two languages. The basic skills and concepts are introduced in the native language and incorporated later into the second language teaching. The idea of the school is to develop in the children mastery of two languages, both by means of direct teaching and by using them as a medium of instruction for all subjects.

Conclusions

Few of the elementary school programs for disadvantaged children observed by Task Force members differed radically from programs for the advantaged student. This is surprising since most teachers and administrators when questioned pointed out some very definite differences between the children in their school and advantaged children.

The NCTE Task Force recommends that, where such differences exist, elementary school programs reflect the particular educational needs of the disadvantaged student.

Despite the encouraging work of preschool and kindergarten programs, many disadvantaged children entering the first grade are not ready to begin a formal reading program. This fact should be recognized by school authorities so that they can establish special programs for these children. Such programs should broaden the children's backgrounds, particularly in language, and lead to greater opportunity for success when reading skills are formally taught. Especially, the programs need to relate the reading program to the spoken language of the children.

The NCTE Task Force recommends that first grade disadvantaged children not ready to enter a formal reading program should be enrolled in an intensive, language-oriented program.

Some children above the first grade, even some who have completed the special language-oriented program recommended above, will have serious difficulties in reading. These problems in reading are unlikely to be solved if the child is placed in a regular classroom situation and receives little individual attention.

The NCTE Task Force recommends that disadvantaged elementary children with serious deficiencies in reading should be placed in a special reading-and-language-centered curriculum taught by teachers specially prepared to teach reading in relation to language development.

Ungraded primary programs, such as discussed earlier in this report, may suggest one way of grouping children with special problems in reading and language development. Ungraded programs seem to possess advantages for other disadvantaged children as well. Too often graded organization operates as a ''mechanism'' to keep children from making academic progress. Failure is built in since students cannot succeed in the work they are required to do in their assigned grade level. Elementary schools in disadvantaged areas should consider the use of some type of nongraded program to overcome this common problem.

Therefore, the Task Force recommends that teachers and administrators consider the questionable effects of the traditional graded organization.

Undoubtedly the socioeconomic environment of the disadvantaged child is principally responsible for his educational problems. Regardless of how good a school program may be, the child still spends a substantial portion of his day in that environment. Any measures than can be taken to extend the schools' influence into that environment will help to make the schools' programs more effective.

The NCTE Task Force recommends that elementary schools involve the parents of disadvantaged children in assisting the school with its academic program.

Task Force members realize that the family structure of many disadvantaged groups makes implementation of such a recommendation difficult. However this should not deter schools from involving those parents who are able to participate.

Specialists commonly point out that the disadvantaged child ordinarily will find little reading material at home. Unfortunately, this lack of books at home is too often not compensated by an abundance of books in the school. Many classes visited had either no classroom library or one with an inadequate number of books. Two thirds of the nation's elementary schools are reported to have no school libraries. Although no formal attempt was made by the Task Force to describe school library facilities, observations substantiate this lack of classroom book collections and libraries in elementary schools serving disadvantaged children. Yet such facilities are imperative for successful programs in reading.

The Task Force recommends that every possible effort be made to provide good classroom and school libraries for elementary schools in disadvantaged areas.

Combined with the need for more book facilities is a further need for imaginative literature. Children's books of appropriate literary quality were seldom found in the schools. Such books should be emphasized on all levels of the elementary school program.

The importance of work in oral language in elementary education cannot be overemphasized. Students lacking oral language facility will be severely handicapped in their work in reading and writing.

The Task Force recommends that all elementary schools, but particularly those teaching disadvantaged children, reevaluate their programs in oral language development.

Appendix B lists major publications and current research in oral language. This work will be of considerable value to those organizing and to those teaching in language programs.

Secondary[*]

Introduction

Task Force observers visiting secondary programs saw a wide range of efforts—ex-Peace Corps workers serving as teacher interns, youth projects for potential dropouts, tutorial projects, work oriented curricula, a boys' school training program, and several school study programs. Many special projects organized outside the regular secondary school framework were novel, and much of their work appeared promising. Few of these imaginative experiences appeared in public schools, however. Much of the work in programs undertaken within schools seemed repetitive, questionably relevant, and insubstantial. Literature, when taught, was often found in commonly used anthologies of selections inappropriate to the interests and reading abilities of the students. Attempts to teach the intricacies of traditional grammar to students several years behind in reading skills occurred frequently. Few secondary schools observed had developed a program that recognized the needs of their students. Few had any well-defined objectives. Many secondary schools were providing experience in oral language, but little of it appeared helpful or professionally sound.

Although students within many classes varied widely in abilities to read, write, and speak, observers saw little in the way of individualized instruction. One exception was an emphasis on reading laboratories. In the best of such programs, students could work at their own level and see personal progress. Unfortunately, observers noted that much of the material used was of inferior or inappropriate quality. This comment was also made of the tapes used in oral language laboratories.

This pessimistic picture of secondary programs observed was by no means true of all schools. Observers were impressed about the work done in several secondary schools; some of these schools and their program will be discussed in this section.

Although observers are critical of the secondary school projects in English, they realize that establishing workable programs for these students is undoubtedly more difficult than for earlier grade levels. Large numbers of students find themselves further and further behind in their knowledge and application of the basic skills required in school.

---

[*] The observations in this chapter are based largely on 90 reports from observers on 54 separate programs.

Whereas most students start elementary school enthusiastically (or at the very least neutrally), many a disadvantaged student will enter junior high school or high school with several years of failure and frustration behind him. He has met with little school success; he is embittered by racial and social problems; he sees few realistic job opportunities ahead. These problems compound the difficulties for secondary schools in disadvantaged areas. Nevertheless, the Task Force believes strongly that a more realistic English curriculum, one that specifically attacks the problems of failure, bitterness, and bleakness, will do much to alleviate the problems of secondary school instruction. Several schools in the most difficult areas of the inner city showed observers that secondary English programs can be made exciting, challenging, and most important, can help to solve the language handicaps of the students.

Selecting Books for Outside Reading in a Cleveland, Ohio, Junior High School

Organization and Staffing

Administrative patterns, school curriculum, and staffing of secondary schools in disadvantaged areas did not basically differ from such practices in advantaged schools except perhaps in the size of classes. Nearly all of the schools visited had developed some form of homogeneous grouping or track system common to advantaged schools. Grouping practices were particularly noticeable in remedial reading programs. Although schools with homogeneous grouping had provisions for students to move from one group to another, it appeared in interviewing teachers and administrators that movement to upper tracks seldom happened. This may be the result of careful initial screening and proper placement of students, or the result of acceptance by teacher and student of the grouping classification assigned.

As in elementary schools, there was a strong attempt at the secondary level to reduce class size for disadvantaged students. In interviews both administrators and teachers felt that a smaller class size was important for successful programs. With smaller classes greater attention can be paid to the individual student, for it is then possible for a teacher to know all of his students better; and necessary remedial work can be done on the basis of individual need.

Most of the unique organization and staffing practices observed occurred outside the classroom. The following programs fall into this category and hold particular promise.

Orientation Program for Incoming Secondary Students

The transition between elementary and junior high school is frequently difficult even for the advantaged child. The problems that many disadvantaged children are likely to have in reading and in lack of overall school success undoubtedly cause even greater tensions as they enter the strange new world of junior high. Add to that the increasingly common situation where the junior high is also the first truly racially integrated school the child has attended, and problems increase. The following project shows one technique for handling such a situation.

During the last week in August and the first week in September, one school district set up an orientation program for students who would be going from an all Negro elementary school to the integrated junior high. A note was sent to every Negro family of a sixth grade child notifying them of the orientation project and inviting their children to participate. Thirty parents accepted, and their children came to each of the ten mornings of the project. The purpose of the orientation program was to introduce the children to the junior high program, to meet some of the administrators and teachers they would be working with, and to see the school itself. A Negro teacher whom the sixth graders knew and a white staff member met the children when they arrived on the first day. The principal welcomed them and spoke about junior high life in general, the student body officers answered their questions, and some of the teachers with whom they would be working when school started talked with the children and gave them an idea of the work they would be doing. The guidance counselor met the children informally at breaks so that he could get to know them better and told them that they should feel free to come to him in the new school if they had any problems. The nurse spoke to the girls and the gym teacher to the boys on personal hygiene. During the last session, the pupils toured the junior high building, met other teachers, and ate a picnic lunch. One teacher reported on the outcome:

> It was great! Tensions left, friendliness won over—the shy became relaxed and talkative and really participated. A follow-up toward the end of the year proved the value of this "special attention." Those thirty who had participated had come so much farther than the seventh graders who hadn't come to the early session.[1]

This type of orientation program is an excellent practice. However, it would be expected that those students whose parents encouraged them to participate would be the students most likely to adjust and to do well in a new school situation.

Pre-High School Educational Centers

The hypothesis that schools must concentrate solely upon those skills and subjects most requiring direct attention in order to achieve impressive results receives dramatic illustration in five nongraded educational centers established for adolescents in one large midwestern city. Concentrating on the twelve-to-sixteen-year-olds who seem too mature for elementary classrooms but too lacking in language skills to succeed in senior high schools, these educational centers provide programs which concentrate on language skills, reading, and arithmetic. Virtually all other subjects except physical education are eliminated. Boys and girls are enrolled for two-hour classes in the three subjects stressed. In language, for example, the students engage in planned oral practice, in listening activities, and in spelling and writing. Some students remain in the special centers for a single year; others may be there for three or four. As soon as the young people develop sufficient ability to indicate the likelihood that they can succeed in the regular high school, they are

---

[1] In letter from Rora Rashkis, Chapel Hill, North Carolina.

encouraged to leave the center. By focusing on two or three critical areas so as to produce a rapid acceleration in learning in particular areas, these educational centers in time should be reporting impressive results. Most have been in operation for only two years.

Tutoring Programs

Several tutorial programs using secondary students were observed by Task Force members. One of those that received high praise was the Homework Helper Program operated by Mobilization for Youth in the Lower East Side of New York in cooperation with the city schools. This program was designed for children at the elementary grade level who need help in their classwork. Tutors are high school upperclassmen normally hired to work on a one-to-one basis after school. They are also expected to escort the children home after each tutorial session. Work is done in several elementary schools, and each school's program is operated by an elementary teacher, designated as Master Teacher. This teacher is in charge of supervision and the inservice training of the tutors one afternoon a week.

Task Force members observing the work of the tutors were highly impressed with the dedication, rapport, and motivation of both the tutors and tutored. Several of the tutors displayed an intense drive and awareness of problems the tutored would face if they did not learn what was being taught. As a result, the children reacted seriously to the efforts of the tutors to advise and teach them.

Perhaps the following two examples of written work taken from a dittoed newspaper from this program will indicate the close ties between tutor and tutored in the Homework Helper Program.

My New Year's Resolutions

By Belisario Lago

At the beginning of each year, boys and girls and even grown-ups make New Year's Resolutions. My New Year's resolutions are:
1. I will obey my mother and father.
2. I will listen to everything my tutor John tells me.

My Pupil

By Ivan Kushner, Tutor

Since coming into this program, I have had one pupil who has attended the homework helper class consistently. This boy is John Delgado, from class 6-1. John is a very intelligent, ambitious, and, what is more important, serious boy. John has the desire and capacity to learn a great deal and tries very hard. We have covered much ground in math and he has learned some very important concepts. In keeping with the Christmas spirit, John and I exchanged gifts at Christmas time. He gave me a beautiful cuff links and tie clip set.

I enjoy working with John and only hope I can help him to learn more than he has already learned.

Another tutorial program established cooperatively by Mobilization for Youth and the New York City Schools is the Drop-Out Program. Unemployed school dropouts are carefully screened, given some training, and used as teacher aides at the kindergarten and first grade level. Part of the training for the dropouts includes a visit to Brooklyn College where some classes are held. In a sense, these potential teacher aides are going to college, for they eat with college students, attend classes there, and probably for the first time see what college life is generally like. This training and their work with students in class have brought about several interesting side effects. The coordinator of the program noted that several dropouts are now leaving the program to return to school— which is one indication that the job has given new direction to their lives.

At the North Carolina Advancement Schools, eighth grade under-achievers, in addition to having their own adult tutor, are given an opportunity to tutor fourth and fifth grade students in neighborhood schools. The director of the program reports that the experience of helping younger children contributes considerably to the adolescent's personal sense of importance.

Another tutoring program visited was the Volunteer Tutorial Service in Cincinnati, Ohio. This program attempts to match a tutor with educationally disadvantaged children who are behind in their classwork. The following information, used in recruiting volunteer aides, serves as a summary of the organization and objectives of the program.

VOLUNTEER TUTORS NEEDED BY CINCINNATI PUBLIC SCHOOLS

Enjoy the Satisfaction of Tutoring Children Who Need Your Help!

WHEN ARE YOU NEEDED?	Now until the end of May and again during the next school year.
HOW OFTEN?	Once or twice a week.
HOW LONG?	One hour or longer.
WHERE ARE YOU NEEDED?	At any one of 26 elementary schools, or at any one of 5 junior high schools.
WHAT TIME OF THE DAY?	Between 3:30 & 5:00 in the elementary schools, Monday through Thursday. Between 6:30 & 8:30 in the junior high schools, Monday through Thursday.

WHOM WILL YOU TUTOR?	"Educationally disadvantaged" children, who are lacking certain advantages other children have: encouragement; helpful experiences outside the school (travel, quiet place to study, success example to emulate, etc.). These children are often behind in their school achievement and may not succeed in their classroom work without the help of an interested adult who wants to help and can help.
WHAT SUBJECTS WILL YOU TUTOR?	Reading or arithmetic in the elementary schools. English, mathematics, science, social studies, foreign language, and other subjects in the junior high schools.
WHAT CAN YOU DO FOR THESE PUPILS?	Give them the extra help they need to succeed in school so they will have a chance to become successful citizens later in life. Raise their level of self-esteem, aspiration, and motivation by setting a good example, offering encouragement, and helping them become more efficient and self-reliant.
WHAT SPECIAL SKILLS MUST YOU HAVE?	Nothing special, just an interest in the subject you will tutor. You must have a warm and sincere interest in school age children. The average high school graduate can help these youngsters.
WHO WILL HELP YOU IN THIS PROGRAM?	Each school has a tutoring supervisor who will arrange your tutoring schedule. He will provide assistance on what and how to teach. Coordinators will help you to improve your skills in tutoring when needed. You will be informed of your pupil's difficulties and needs.
HOW MANY PUPILS WILL YOU TUTOR?	A pupil will be assigned to not more than one tutor in a subject. You may tutor one or more pupils depending on how much time you have.
WHERE DO YOU REGISTER?	Fill out a registration card from your place of employment, church, social club, or organization, or call Jim Jacobs, Division of Program Development, Cincinnati Board of Education.
HOW CAN YOU BENEFIT?	By getting the satisfaction that comes from helping a youngster who needs help and watching him benefit from your help. By participating in a community project which can be of significant influence upon the lives of hundreds of our future citizens.

A TEACHER AFFECTS ETERNITY:
HE CAN NEVER TELL WHERE HIS INFLUENCE STOPS!

Using Peace Corps Veterans as Interns

Two of the most obvious basic needs in schools with many disadvantaged students are a curriculum responsive to the interests and abilities of these students, and an increasing number of well-trained, informed, dedicated, and sympathetic teachers. One project visited that is attempting to combine these two needs is the Cardozo Project in Washington, D. C. The stated goals of the project are to develop and use curriculum materials and teaching methods with disadvantaged high school and junior high school students, and to develop a teacher training experience which will equip teachers for more effective service in the inner city schools.

The project employs sixteen Peace Corps returnees as intern teachers in Banneker Junior High School and at Cardozo High School in Washington, D.C., a practice now being used in several school districts. All of these ex-Peace Corps members have a B.A. degree and have taught abroad for two years. They bring to their classes the experience of teaching in such diverse places as Sierra Leone, Ethiopia, West Cameroon, and Ecuador. These interns attend seminars at Cardozo High School. Participation in the seminars and the credit given them by Howard University for their internship fulfills the requirements for eighteen credits in education for the Master of Arts in Teaching Degree.

Students at the North Carolina Advancement School Use a Teaching Machine to Supplement Their Regular Reading Instruction

Using ex-Peace Corps workers as teachers in disadvantaged areas should prove to be an excellent way of recruiting teachers interested in working with disadvantaged youth. Colleges and school districts should consider giving these workers credit for the work they have done. Such credit could be in the form of either course units or advancement on a salary schedule for experience and service.

Practices and Methods

Reading. One of the most obvious deficiencies in secondary reading programs is the lack of professionally trained teachers of reading. Some schools have attempted to solve this problem by hiring elementary school teachers to teach a remedial reading program; other schools use reading specialists, often as consultants.

A common complaint by both teachers and administrators is the lack of reading material suitable for mature students with a low reading ability. Certain textbook publishers have attempted to provide such students with books of simple vocabulary and supposed teenage appeal. On the whole, members of the Task Force found such material less than stimulating to students, even though recognizing that some teachers use it extensively.

The following practices and methods in reading were reported by Task Force observers.

. . . In the beginning each student participated in a session of oral reading in order to give the teacher an idea of his reading efficiency. As the students progressed, they were required to write out or discuss answers to exercises on vocabulary, phonics, and comprehension in reading.

. . . Students realize that they must be able to read so they can achieve some success elsewhere. Reading is the essential subject.

. . . In the core curriculum classes, there seemed to be no literature taught because of the ''emphasis on reading skills.'' There seemed to be equally little writing. The teaching of reading for one hour each day has become a requirement of the program, with teachers emphasizing word attack skills and reading for meaning. Reading specialists from the central office have conducted workshops and continue to work with the core teachers to help them learn the necessary techniques and skills.

Is there a definite danger that literature will be left out of programs that dwell almost exclusively on reading skills? Are disadvantaged students so retarded they need work only on word attack skills? Are such students able to read critically—even at their level?

. . . The reading teachers helped the children to develop an understanding that often a word may have several meanings. In some instances teachers clarified word meanings for the class by having someone describe or recall words with similar meanings, as cape, cloak; jolting, rough; border, boundary.

. . . Individualized work in reading as seen in elementary schools could be of considerable use on the secondary level in providing differentiated assignments. The following example observed in one high school is a good illustration. One group of students in the reading class worked with the teacher, a second group read books which they had selected; a third group used the tape recorder, reading a story along with the recorded voice and then completing reading themselves.

Educators constantly speak of the need for individualized instruction. Yet few programs observed provided such instruction. It is likely that such individualized work with a disadvantaged student is far more important than with an advantaged student because of the typical academic gap between the two groups. S. Alan Cohen shows the need for individualized instruction in his case description of two "homogenized" fifth grade boys,[2] who were ". . . part of a homogeneously grouped reading class matched on I.Q., reading grade level, and socioeconomic level." Despite this, according to Cohen, they are, educationally speaking, "homogeneous" in only two respects:

1) Their oral reading scores are two grade levels above placement.
2) They are both retarded readers.

In every other sense, they are different. Cohen's basic premise is that if schools are truly to educate such students, they must learn specifically what each child knows and doesn't know about what is to be taught, find out why he isn't learning, and by taking advantage of his strengths, teach to his specific weaknesses. It is one thing to label a child a slow reader; it is quite another to describe the specific reasons for his reading difficulty. For a tester merely to tell a teacher that a child is two grade levels below his group in reading is next to useless information. A teacher can, however, build lessons around this student's weaknesses if he knows, for example, that the student is unable to orally discriminate *en* from *ing*, has great difficulty in visually discriminating *ed* at the end of the words, etc. Or, as Cohen says, "The first requirement of effective individualized instruction is to think and operate as a learning specialist by isolating

---

[2] S. Alan Cohen, "A Psychology of Teaching Reading to Individuals," *Reading in the Elementary School,* ed. M. J. Weiss. New York: Odyssey Press, 1965.

specific operations to be taught. The more specific, the more likely the instruction will be successful."

Observers were able to see such a program in individualized instruction developed by Mr. Cohen at Woodrow Wilson Junior High School in Passaic, New Jersey. Students in the program were individually tested. Every Monday each student received his week's program that listed his specific weakness in reading, composition, and language. On the student's schedule was a list of study stations where he could work on his deficiencies. Although the program sounds mechanical, it was apparent to the observers that such personal attention to each student's needs resulted in some highly beneficial instruction.

Literature. Observers noted two rather distinct patterns in the teaching of literature on the secondary level. One was an emphasis on readings that were basically nonliterary, i.e., workbook texts and reading exercises; the other was literature for the disadvantaged taken from a district-adopted text of material either too difficult for the students or well outside their interest levels. As an example, one observer noted a teacher reading *Silas Marner* to a group of eleventh graders with severe reading problems. The entire book was being read to the class because, as the teacher later explained, the students were unable to read it themselves, yet the district required that the book be taught.

Balance is needed in chosing reading materials for the disadvantaged. Expository prose dealing with scientific, technological, or social events may provide appropriate reading for many instructional activities, but surely imaginative writing must not be neglected. Variety and change of pace in reading materials may be even more important in programs for the disadvantaged than in conventional classrooms.

Teaching and discussing literature with disadvantaged students on any level need not be done with diluted materials or adapted classics. Literature can and should be taught to all students at all levels. But the teacher of the disadvantaged needs the imagination and background to choose material that is not only stimulating to his students but also practical and effective.

Schools appear to be experimenting with several kinds of new literary materials in classes for the disadvantaged. Some large city schools are developing programs stressing American Negro literature. Selected literature from the traditional English programs is being reorganized elsewhere in new units on such topics as "The Hero in Jail."

To what extent is a "different" literature for disadvantaged students educationally defensible? Some minority group leaders argue that unless their children are taught the same literature as used in advantaged areas, schools will further perpetuate the disadvantaged child's academic problems. Should schools be influenced by this argument?

What should be the critical indices of literature specifically chosen for the disadvantaged student: vocabulary, setting, authors, minority group characters, literary theme (e.g., social protest, authority, problems of the underdog, etc.)?

One project achieving notable results in literature developed for New York City junior high students is the Hunter College Gateway English Program. These materials were developed at a curriculum study center supported by the United States Office of Education. The examples below will give the reader an idea of a successful literature and reading program for disadvantaged students. The spiral bound anthologies include songs, poems, short stories, and excerpts from novels.

One of the most successfully used stories is the excerpt "Valedictorian" from Richard Wright's biography *Black Boy*, included in *Coping*.[3] "Valedictorian" tells of Wright's dilemma when, after being selected valedictorian of his class, the school principal hands Wright a prepared speech to read. The conflict in the story centers on Richard, who wants to give his own speech, and the principal, who wants him to give the speech which has been prepared. The following material is an excerpt from the teacher's manual of *Coping*. Detailed, explicit guides of this kind offer one way of helping teachers to improve their instructional efforts.

AIM: To increase students' understanding of a complex situation. To reinforce the skill of basing opinions on evidence in the story.

APPROACH: ". . . The story we are about to read is called 'Valedictorian.' Do you know what the word means?"

(Have several students look it up in the dictionary.
Have students add it to their vocabulary lists.)

"In this story Richard Wright, who was attending an all-Negro school in the South, was chosen to be valedictorian at his graduation from ninth grade. If you were chosen to be valedictorian at *your* school, what would you do? This is what Richard Wright did.

"I shall begin to read the story aloud while you follow in your books. As soon

---

[3] *Coping*. Project English Curriculum Development Center, Marjorie B. Smiley, Director, Hunter College, New York, New York. Used by permission.

as I come to what you think may be the problem in the story, raise your hand and keep it up (but do not call out).''

Teacher reads until class recognizes the problem. (This will probably be when Wright says, ''But, professor, I've written my speech already.'')

Ask students what the problem is Richard must solve.

What alternatives does Richard have? Teacher writes on the board and fills in as students recite:

Alternatives

Richard:

1. To give principal's speech
2. To give his own speech
3. To quit school

Principal:

1. To insist upon his speech
2. To let Richard do as he wants

''I shall read on. Raise your hands when you find out which alternative Richard is going to choose. Let us see what you think will happen on the basis of what we have read so far. How many think Richard will give in? How many think the principal will give in?

''What do you think will happen? Read the rest of the story to find out.''

Following a reading of the entire story and a homework assignment based on some suggested questions is a continuation of the discussion of ''Valedictorian.''

AIMS: To help students recognize that people act from a mixture of motivations.

To help students understand that people are not all good or all bad.

To help students understand that one may attain his wishes and still not be happy.

APPROACH: ''Take up questions assigned for homework. These will bring out most of the events of the story. We have seen *what* the people in the story said and did. Now let us see *why*.

''Imagine that you are the principal in the story telling one of the teachers what happened when you offered Richard your speech.'' (Have a student take the part of the principal and another the part of a teacher. Have class discuss what the principal and the teacher would say, and then have two students act it out. Try to make the principal's motives come out in the dialogue: his fear that the school will be criticized, his fear that the whites in the audience will not think much of the Negro school, etc.)

''In the face of all this opposition, why does Richard persist in his decision to give his own speech? Does he think his speech is better than his principal's?''

Further discussion of the story is based on dialogue as a key to understanding character development and to discovering how an author signals

111

the manner in which his characters speak and act. Part of the class discussion is based on a transparency of a section of dialogue from "Valedictorian."

Included in Gateway English books are a considerable number of folk songs, one of which is Malvina Reynolds' "Sing Along":

O when I need a raise in pay and have to ask my boss,
If I go see him by myself I'm just a total loss,
But if we go together I'll do my part right pretty,
Cause I'm awf'ly nervous lonesome but I make a fine committee.

My congressman's important, he hobnob's with big biz,
He soon forgets the guys and gals who put him where he is,
I'll just write him a letter to tell him what I need,
With a hundred thousand signatures why even he can read.[4]

Some school districts or regional areas of the country would not choose these particular selections. Nevertheless, such work could elicit excellent response from even "slow" seventh grade children of minority groups.

Despite the use of many contemporary works, no literature program for any student should be devoid of works that are part of our literary heritage. In the Gateway English series, such works as excerpts from the *Odyssey*, Aesop's fables, Hebrew legends, and selections from the Old Testament are interspersed with more modern writings.

A glimpse at the overall orientation of the Gateway English program can be gained from a few excerpts from the teachers' manuals. Gateway English is an attempt to organize or develop materials. . .

. . . based on the asumption that the school must play an increasingly important role in helping junior high pupils to meet the unresolved problems of childhood. *(Who Am I?)*

. . . to cast each of the students in a positive "image" (e.g., good sportsman, loyal friend, dependable monitor, etc.) as he prefers. *(Identification and Image Stories)*

. . . to help these children identify the problems and to encourage them to find solutions. . . to help them to understand how their feelings developed and what now must be done to change them. *(Who Am I?)*

. . . to enable these discouraged youth to identify with individuals,

---

[4] Malvina Reynolds, "Sing Along," from *Little Boxes and Other Handemade Songs*. Words and music by Malvina Reynolds. © Copyright by Shroder Music Co. Used by permission. Quoted in *Coping*, Gateway English (New York, Hunter College Project English Curriculum Development Center, 1965), p. 77.

both real and fictional, who *have* coped with problems not unlike theirs with varying degrees of success. *(Coping)*

. . . to recognize that in some cases the conflict is not with extraneous people or forces but within the individual: between loyalty and responsibility, or between the comfort of status quo and the challenge of change. *(Coping)*

. . . of literary selections carefully chosen in terms of theme and quality . . . one of the principal outcomes should be the student's increased ability to read with insight and appreciation and a heightened desire to read many other books. *(Coping)*

. . . to create in them a consciousness of the power and usefulness of language. Not until we have stirred up in them a desire to know about and use language well can we hope to improve their skills in speech, in reading, and in writing—largely in that order. *(Stories in Verse)*

Literature selected for its relationship to the problems of students is the basis for the Gateway English Program. Therefore, the basic organization pattern is the unit, and each unit is assigned a theme to which all literature selected for study is related. The project staff considers that the themes are relevant for adolescents generally but that most of the materials are especially interesting to the disadvantaged because characters are from minority groups. These are the first literary materials developed for the culturally disadvantaged.

Themes such as "Who Am I?" and "Coping" are chosen for the units. One basic objective is to help the students to be introspective and to teach them to ask the right questions about problems by which they are directly affected. These titles suggest that the project is trying to develop in the student a "logical" approach to problem solving.

Language skills are woven into the general framework of the units. Composition and speaking are dealt with intensively. The material, relevant as it is to the lives of the students, can spark extensive language activity, both oral and written. Teachers are thus able to teach English for one of its most important uses—to communicate ideas and feelings.

Composition skills, according to the teachers, have improved remarkably since the program started last September. Students react favorably and write longer compositions without the teacher having to use authoritarian measures to get student cooperation.

Teachers report that reading is also improving because the materials the students read are interesting to them. The general reading scores have improved, and more important, the students now have more desire

113

to read. As in composition and speaking, once reading has begun, the teacher can make corrective suggestions.

Speech usually takes the form of a dialogue between teacher and students. Observers watched one speech class, but the other class was just beginning the unit. Dialogues are part of the structured English program.

Although the literary material chosen for the students served by the Gateway English Program appears to be well chosen, such material may be less useful elsewhere. One Task Force member in another city used some of the selections from the Gateway English series with disadvantaged seventh graders in her district's school. These students, however, could not read the material nor could tenth grade students in slow groups. Clearly no series of literary material offers a panacea for disadvantaged students. What is needed are teachers who attempt to find the best possible literature that the students in *their* classes can read. Since many disadvantaged students read from two to five years below grade level, teachers introduce high interest reading materials often not

Houston, Texas, Students Examine a Newspaper during Library Period

considered worthwhile literature, to stimulate them to read. Then, as soon as possible, teachers encourage their students to read more mature literary material.

Language Development. A vital need for programs involving oral work in English was noted in the preschool and elementary school sections. This need for work in oral language is no less important in secondary school programs, yet it seems to be receiving even less attention. Task Force observers noted that teachers and administrators seem to have less knowledge about oral language development and dialectology than about most other areas of English instruction.

The following excerpts from Task Force reports note some of the major problems observed in the study of language.

. . . Oral discussion in most instances consisted of a report of one kind or another. There was little interaction among the students; it was pupil-to-teacher and teacher-to-pupil kind of action; not a kind of group interaction.

. . . The major weakness in this program for disadvantaged junior high students is the lack of attention to oral language. Teachers admit this weakness but say they do not know how to handle the problem.

. . . Considerable work needs to be done in oral English. Observers indicated a great need for opportunities for individual students to stand before a group or in a committee where they can learn to express themselves with ease and self-assurance.

. . . The following dialogue will indicate the artificiality of the work seen in oral language. These eighth grade students had previously read a story about Paul Revere. The questioning proceeded as follows:

TEACHER: What was the name of the story?
STUDENT: "A Tooth for Paul Revere."
TEACHER: No, that's incorrect, answer the question completely.
STUDENT: The name of the story is "A Tooth for Paul Revere."
TEACHER: Who wrote the story? . . .
and so on.

. . . Oral work in English was being done in the recognition of single sounds and in the blending of sounds.

In work on recognizing single sounds, the students repeated after the teacher: "*K* has the sound of the *k* sound in *kiss*." Both *k*'s, however, were pronounced as *ka*, the letter name, rather than /k/, the value.

In the lesson on blending of sounds (bl + ess = bless, bl + ink = blink, etc.), the teacher did not pronounce the entire word for students to imitate or assimilate it by ear. Instead each student was asked to figure out the blending. When a student had difficulty, the teacher would supply hints by pronouncing repeatedly the component parts such as *bl* and *ess*.

115

Teachers often seem unaware of the distinctions between the production of the sound and the symbol of sound—of phonics, phonetics, and phonemics. Does not their confusion indicate an important emphasis for preservice and inservice programs of teacher education?

The following observations about language learning made by one Task Force observer summarize the problem.

> . . . It is rather easy to say that I observed a vast desert of knowledge about language learning and language teaching. But I suppose this is to be expected when people have had little or no education in this area. Practically no English teacher had studied the structure of English. Few secondary reading specialists had studied the English language or the teaching of reading.

> . . . I observed illiterate adults copying words from a blackboard (the teacher explained to me that these older people think this is education and won't have it any other way). I had a teacher tell me, ''There is no dialect problem here.'' I heard the students' English described as ugly and deplorable. I heard a teacher pronouncing lists such as *cob, cot, bog,* and *pod* with two difficult vowels while telling the children that they all had the same vowel. I heard English for Foreigners classes being taught to mispronounce *five* as *five-uh* (to stress the final consonant). I saw a teacher instruct Negroes to pronounce the g in *sing* / sIng / and *singer* / sIngɨr /. I saw English syntax mutilated by reading machines.

Some encouraging work in oral language was seen, however.

> . . . One class was working on the techniques of conversation. The students were not permitted to raise their hands but were expected to interrupt tactfully or to wait their turn following the conversation of their classmates. The teacher believes that the students need this kind of experience since they do not have it in a class situation or in their homes.

> . . . Enunciation and pronunciation are two aspects of oral English that were heavily stressed in one class, although the teacher's own dialect prevents the best example from coming through.

> . . . ''Nonstandard'' English is accepted at first in grade seven, but constant work on the part of the teacher helps the students realize that by the time they are seniors they should be able to use ''standard'' English. This was described as having subject and verb agree, etc. Pride in being able to speak correctly is stressed, and correct usage appears to be a status symbol.

> . . . The school places great emphasis on ''acceptable English.'' Idioms of the students' speech are being compiled by the English Department of the school. Common characteristics of their speech include the dropping of ''s'' from the third person singular and the pronunciation of ''th'' as ''Da.''

In most cases language work consisted of polite corrections of nonstandard answers or comments by students: ''Yes, John, the character in this play *did* accomplish it, didn't he?" Similarly when a boy commented, "They don't get nothin' out of it," the teacher replied, "Yes, they don't get anything out of it."

In this report and in various professional publications on dialects, teachers are asked to begin by accepting the dialect of their students for what it is, one form of oral communication, neither "good" nor "bad." It is one thing for teachers to say that they will accept the dialect and the language of their students; it is quite another for teachers to understand it. It was quite apparent in a number of visits that many teachers, particularly on the preschool and elementary levels, had difficulty communicating with their students. Patience, a good ear, and a willingness to understand different dialects can be highly profitable to teachers of the disadvantaged. Unobtrusive tape recordings of the speech of children with a particularly difficult dialect or speech pattern might be made and listened to later in the company of an "interpreter." Certainly a teacher could be far more successful in teaching the language patterns of standard American English to disadvantaged youngsters with nonstandard dialects if he better understood their language. In this way he would be able to aim language work at the basic differences between students' speech and standard informal English.

A teacher of English in disadvantaged schools not only should have a knowledge of the dialect spoken by his students, but he should also attempt to understand other aspects of the students' language. A well-intentioned white middle class elementary teacher in a disadvantaged school in such areas as Washington, D.C., and New York can unknowingly create a problem by using one of the most common and sacrosant of middle class words—*mother.* This word may denote in an abbreviated form (again depending on how and by whom it is used) one of the most vicious epithets in lower class language. Or, in a different context, it may more frequently denote the corner dope pusher than carry its usual middle class matriarchal meaning.

Although a degree of provinciality is apparent in analyzing the slang of disadvantaged groups, there is a national understanding among lower class of many terms. Such expressions as "cop out," "cool it," "gig," and "junk" are as familiar to youth in Brooklyn's Bedford-Stuyvesant area as those in Oakland, California, but no one suggests that this language of the streets be used by the classroom teachers.

While an English teacher in the Lower East Side may need to understand the difference between *farther* and *further,* he may also profit from learning that in his students' language *boss* means fine or stylish, and that *bad* can mean nice. A teacher who overhears a student saying that he has some *grass* or some *pluck* or a *shiv* in his locker may wish to know that these terms mean, respectively, marijuana, wine, and a knife. A teacher in a multiracial school may learn that *boots, member,* and *moulenjam* refer to his Negro students; *paddy, gray boy,* and *ofay* refer to his Caucasian students; and *hick, Marine tiger,* and *parakeet* to his Puerto Rican students. Knowing which of these terms can be used with impunity by students talking with one another in a mixed racial situation, and which terms could cause a riot, may be useful. A discussion of the grammatical function and varying inflective patterns of the word *tough* may prove to be far more meaningful and instructive than a discussion of the distinction of *shall* and *will.*

The following example shows how poetry and the language of lower class students can be used in language instruction.

MADISON AREA PROJECT

STUDENTS DIG JIVE WHEN IT'S PLAYED COOL[5]

> I play it cool and dig all jive.
> That's the reason I stay alive.
> My motto, as I live and learn,
> Is: Dig and Be Dug in Return.

This fine poem by Negro author Langston Hughes opened a new world of learning to a class of ninth graders at Madison Junior High.

The poem was presented to the class by Gerald Weinstein, curriculum coordinator of the Madison Area Project.

A teacher had complained to Weinstein that her students "practically fell asleep" when she read a poem called "The Magic Carpet" from a standard school anthology.

Weinstein came to the rescue with Hughes' "Motto" and distributed copies to the class. This is his account of what happened.

After the students read the poem, there was a long moment of silence. Then came the exclamations.

"Hey, this is tough."

"Hey, Mr. Weinstein, this cat is pretty cool."

"It's written in our talk."

But when asked the meaning of "playing it cool," the students had difficulty verbalizing the idea.

A boy volunteered to act it out.

Weinstein took the part of a teacher and the boy pretended he was walking down the hallway.

"Hey you," said the teacher, "you're on the wrong side of the hall. Get over where you belong."

---

[5] Robert Kanasola, "Students Dig Jive When It's Played Cool," *Syracuse Herald-Journal,* November 11, 1963. (A complete explication of this lesson appears in the January, 1965, issue of *Practical English.*)

Without looking up, the boy very calmly and slowly walked to the other side and continued without any indication of what was going on his his mind.

That was "playing it cool."

When Weinstein asked a boy to show what he would do when not playing it cool, a verbal battle ensued.

The class began offering definitions for "playing it cool": calm and collected, no strain.

Weinstein suggested another: nonchalant. A new word.

Next came a discussion of the phrase "dig all jive."

One student told how he once got into trouble because he didn't "dig the jive" of a group of streetcorner toughs.

So the message of Hughes' poem, the class discovered, was that he "stayed alive" because he "dug all jive"—understood all kinds of talk.

Hughes' motto was to "dig and be dug in return"—understand and be understood.

The students were amazed at their own analysis.

Weinstein asked the students how many kinds of jive they understood.

Why all kinds, of course.

The Madison Area Project official launched into an abstract essay on the nature of truth, using all the big words he could find.

The students looked blank.

He then asked them to test his understanding of their jive. They threw the colloquialisms at him and he got five out of six.

The class was impressed.

"According to Hughes, who has the better chance of staying alive," Weinstein asked, "You or I?"

You, they said, because you dig more than one kind of jive.

"The jive you have mastered is a beautiful one," Weinstein said. "But you have to dig the school jive, too, the jive that will occur in other situations."

"That's what school is for, to help you dig all jive and stay alive."

The enthusiasm of that class session led the students into more of Hughes' poetry. Later they moved into other kinds of literature in more conventional language.

But the students were not the only ones to learn from that exciting class. Weinstein learned, too.

He learned the advantage of being familiar with the language of the children you are teaching and establishing a rapport with them.

For if a teacher doesn't "start where the child is," Weinstein says, he only reinforces the failure and frustration that has become the normal pattern for disadvantaged students.

Exposure to the best cultural works produced no magical result and even less effective is the "phony" literature that often characterizes school readers, especially in the lower grades.

Exposure must begin "where the child is" and proceed to other varieties of art forms.

The method applies to all kinds of students, Weinstein says. For the student who has read Shakespeare but has not read Langston Hughes, for example, is also "disadvantaged."

Teachers new to a disadvantaged area should have a compilation of terms used by the students there. Since such a list will incorporate many words that are highly taboo by middle class standards, it is doubtful that a school district preparing such work will produce anything but a highly expurgated list. Nevertheless, at least one organization visited, Mobilization for Youth, did have an excellent compilation entitled "The Language of Gangs," from which many of the terms used to describe the language of Lower East Side students were taken.[6]

Composition. One teacher observed was visibly upset when, at the culmination of a writing assignment, few students had written anything to show to the observer. The assignment was "Think of something and write several sentences about it."

Fortunately, such assignments were rare; the following composition work observed intact suggests the considerable imagination teachers showed in setting composition assignments.

. . . Students were to pretend that they were reporters on board the *Titanic.* They were to write, on the basis of *A Night to Remember,* a newspaper article on the sinking. Each student was provided with a newspaper to use as a model for journalistic style.

. . . In one classroom the construction of the ballad was being studied. The students had written ballads after having some experience with reading them and studying the verse involved. As each student read his ballad, the class considered it. (This was the best example of pupil-to-pupil interaction. It also indicated some of the best thinking.) One ballad was put on the board with the class attempting to rewrite to bring in the appropriate verse meter.

. . . The question posed: twelve people in a bomb shelter with enough food and water for seven. Students were asked to discuss and decide which persons were to be eliminated and which to be kept in the shelter. There was much discussion. The following day oral presentations to the class were to be made on the subject, each person to talk *against* keeping one particular person in the shelter and each to talk *in favor* of keeping one particular person.

. . . Students in this program do writing every week. The emphasis is on the ability to organize an essay around a controlling idea. (Grades 11 and 12)

---

[6] "The Language of Gangs," *The Annotated Bibliography,* Mobilization for Youth Training Department, 1, 3 (January 1963), 1.

Creative writing in this class is stimulated by paintings and other visual means. The students exchange papers, discuss each others' papers in groups of two, and then rewrite them. Papers are then corrected by students in the class, rather than the teacher.

In classrooms where there are students with severe psychological and social problems, a different approach to composition may be needed. One interesting technique was seen in a corrective school for boys. In this school, composition began by the teacher's urging his students to write anything they wished. They could write about their reasons for not wanting to write; they could write simply the sentence, "I don't feel like writing," and sit in their seat for the remainder of the writing period; they could discuss their teacher's "hell uv a sens of humer"; they could write as much or as little as they wished. The teacher reports that in the beginning most of the papers came to him with the single sentence, "I don't want to write anything." After a while, the teacher began to precede the writing period by a discussion of an important topic, such as the merits of the system of parole used in the state for delinquent boys, or the importance of a father. Soon the boys were writing, some of them swearing about their drunken fathers, their "whore mothers," and so forth; some were telling the teacher about how terrible he was, and others were wanting him to adopt them. The teacher feels that this writing exercise motivates the students' writing. The teacher respects the students' wish that these papers be confidential and never shows them to anyone else except by the boys' permission. This practice requires a teacher who doesn't mind being offended, who doesn't mind reading violently antisocial, anti-anything writing. The practice would be killed at the first move by the teacher chastising a boy for swearing, or for criticizing "sacred cows."

Although the above observations note some interesting techniques, few schools had any sequential plan for the teaching of writing. Most school programs appeared to rely on individual assignments that were usually corrected in some way, but they had no definite plan that attacked the specific writing problems of the students.

Traditional Grammar. Members of the Task Force saw in many classes extensive work in traditional schoolroom grammar and traditional formal English usage. They commonly found students with poor reading skills being taught the difference between *shall* and *will* or pupils with serious difficulties in speech diagraming sentences. Interestingly, observations by the Task Force reveal far more extensive teaching of traditional grammar in this study of language programs for the disadvantaged than observers saw in the National Study of High School English Programs, a survey on comprehensive high schools known to be achieving important results in English with college-bound students. In effect, those students least able to understand or to use traditional grammar seem to be given more work in this subject than those students able to comprehend the abstractions of such a grammar.

Teachers who were stressing the traditional schoolroom grammar approach admitted that students seemed unable to remember the most basic grammatical rules and definitions; none suggested that their students applied the work in traditional grammar to their writing or speech. The practice of teaching traditional grammar to disadvantaged students points out the disparity between what is known and what is being taught. For years empirical research has shown little significant relationship between the knowledge of traditional grammar and mental discipline, understanding and appreciation of literature, composition, the learning of a foreign language, and oral speech. The authors of *Research in Written Composition* state:

> In view of the widespread agreement of research studies of many types of students and teachers, the conclusion can be stated in strong and unqualified terms: the teaching of formal grammar has a negligible or, because it usually displaces some instruction and practice in actual composition, even a harmful effect on the improvement of writing. [7]

Surely such a displacement of students' time is indefensible when he has such imperative needs in other academic work as the typical disadvantaged child. If a student is able to comprehend the intricacies of traditional grammar, it is highly unlikely that he is disadvantaged.

The nature and amount of teaching of formal grammar varied considerably among programs visited. The following excerpts from observers' reports indicate this range. Several excerpts will also show some typical instances of class work in grammar.

> . . . In all cases traditional grammar was taught in a traditional manner, and deviation from this approach was made only when the students were severely educationally retarded.

> . . . Most teachers simply attack grammar as it comes up in composition. Formal training in grammar is left to the discretion of the teacher.

> . . . There is no direct teaching of grammar in this project.

> . . . The entire session was spent on a few students working at the board and all working at their desk chairs with the conjugation of verbs. It was noted that those who had a knowledge of English seemed to have only a little difficulty

---

[7] Richard Braddock, Richard Lloyd-Jones, and Lowell Schoer, *Research in Written Composition* (Champaign, Ill.: National Council of Teachers of English, 1963).

with this activity, whereas those with a bilingual background were making errors in sentence construction in addition to the conjugation of the verbs. The teacher circulated among the students and helped them correct errors.

. . . In one junior high school class the teacher told the observer that she knew that the grammar work just taught would not help her students' reading, speech, or composition work. She felt, however, that despite the students' serious deficiencies in English, it was necessary to teach formal grammar, for such knowledge was required in the district's high school. She knew that her students would do poorly in high school English without this type of training.

The following excerpt from a Task Force report summarizes the type of instruction too frequently seen.

. . . We spent some time in a ninth grade English class for above-average children. As we entered the room, the students were diagraming sentences from an exercise in a well-known grammar book. They did not seem very interested. They seemed to be reviewing a previously done lesson. The teacher called this "tearing sentences apart." The he said they would now "put sentences together." He listed words at random on the board and asked students to build sentences from them. Then began an extraordinarily confused mixing of traditional and structural grammar presentations. Form, function, and everything else were combined:

"Who did what?"   ANSWER: direct object
"Pick out *the* noun."   (actually there were *three* in the sentence)
"Pick out the verb."   ANSWER: *was going*

Few students replied to the teacher's questions, and most of them seemed to answer automatically and usually incorrectly.

This young teacher seemed very uncertain about his objectives for this group. He said he planned to spend "four more weeks on grammar, and then about six weeks on work in the anthology." The materials being used with these students were the state adopted texts—the same as those being used with most of the children in other schools.

When the observer got there, the class was already under way. Written all over the blackboard, in large handwriting, were definitions of a sentence and the parts of speech, together with some diagraming of sentences and a list of spelling words. The subject of discussion was the usage "It was me, not him." The teacher explained in detail why such expression was bad English and should be avoided.

The teacher was as enthusiastic about his students as he was about English grammar. He challenged the observer to point out the two students who made the greatest progress. When the observer admitted that she could not, he singled out two boys with obvious pride and urged them to tell the visitor how much they had learned in his class, adding that these boys had progressed four grades in twelve weeks.

Despite the multitude of research, publications, and current professional interest in modern language study, Task Force observers noted little impact in secondary schools for the disadvantaged. Perhaps modern grammars should not be taught to the disadvantaged student any more than traditional grammars. But perhaps some understanding about language and its operation should consciously affect curricular practice. All that the Task Force learned about modern grammar instruction in disadvantaged schools is that it was seldom seen in the classes observed and that it exerted little influence in the programs visited.

Although many Task Force members insist that grammar should be taught as a humanistic study, important in its own right for able students in college preparatory programs, most believe that for the disadvantaged student direct instruction in grammar cannot be justified on the basis of improving that student's ability to write, speak, or read. Of course the total program in language instruction for all pupils must be based on sound linguistic principles.

Observations and Impressions of Total School Programs

The observations and impressions of secondary school programs presented below are only a brief summary of what Task Force visitors encountered. They considered the following descriptions of three programs to be outstanding examples of secondary programs for disadvantaged students. Descriptions are included not only because these were among the best programs observed, but also because they offer some especially unique qualities and approaches to organizing school programs.

North Carolina Advancement School (Winston-Salem)

Although this school was dedicated in November 1964, it has already received national recognition for the work it is doing. The North Carolina Advancement School is a residential school for underachieving eighth grade students. Because the school seeks to remedy educational deficiencies and to equip its students with skills and attitudes they need for success in school and adult life, it works with many students normally classed as disadvantaged.

The following are unique aspects of this school:

a. Only eighth grade students who are residents of North Carolina can be admitted to the schools. They must be of average or above-average potential, but operating at below grade level in reading, writing, and arithmetic. Nominations are made by principals and/or superintendents on the basis of test scores, school records, and teacher evaluation.

b. The school has four eleven-week sessions each year. A maximum of 350 students and 50 teachers can be brought to the school each quarter.

c. Tuition, board and room, books and instructional materials are provided free for those selected, and a round-the-clock program is maintained to provide for both instruction and recreation.

d. The school has an inservice education program for North Carolina teachers. Fifty teachers come each quarter, many from the same district as the pupils, to work with the faculty and students, and they make new ideas and methods conceived in the Advancement School available to public schools. The work of these teachers supplements that of the regular staff and makes possible much small group activity.

e. New and different instructional materials and methods, from film projectors and TV to specialized "Auto-tutors," are being used extensively in the school. Testing and evaluation of such aids should result in the most promising and successful use of materials and methods, and subsequent use in public schools of North Carolina.

f. One unique feature is the emphasis upon tutorial work. Many students attending the schools have adult tutors (volunteers from neighboring Salem State College and Wake Forest College) who meet regularly with them to supplement class instruction. Since the students, staff, and incoming teachers are integrated (75 percent of the students are white, 25 percent are Negro—about equal to the percentage of these groups in the state), the school is being seen in part as a demonstration that integrated student bodies and facilities can work in the South. A summer Civil Rights Institute was even established for North Carolina teachers to better prepare them for teaching newly desegregated districts.

g. The program in English stresses reading. After careful diagnosis of specific deficiencies in a school operated clinic, most children are assigned to special teachers for reading instruction in small groups of five or six students each. A library maintained by the boarding schools is open evenings as well as during the day. In addition, the regular English classes stress wide reading and the communication of ideas in topical units.

Task Force observers were impressed with the empathy and understanding towards the school's students by both faculty and administrations. The variety of the staff impressed one observer to note, "The conglomeration of teachers, missionaries, college-near-dropouts, volunteer tutors, visiting teachers, and a retired admiral make for an interesting, differentiated, and inventive staff." Observers were impressed with the high degree of discipline; boys moved around the school in orderly groups. Although student attitudes seemed positive, there was some question as to whether eleven weeks give students enough time for such attitudes to take hold permanently. However, returning teachers are encouraged to oversee some continuing attitudes, and administrators of the school who have studied students' progress after returning to public schools stated that the attitude of many generally continues to improve. This "re-entry problem" causes primary concern, since improvement in attitude depends to a great extent on sympathetic teaching. Without sympathy from teachers, the chances for a student to improve in attitude are slight.

Administrators seem unquestionably sure that they are getting results. Contrary to same beliefs that possibly a three-month quarter is too short, students have gained an average of two months in tested achievement for every one month spent at school. In specific subjects or areas, the gains are sometimes dramatic. For example, one boy surged four years in reading ability tested by a standardized examination after only three months in the school; many others gained from one to three years in the same period. The most noticeable gains, however, were reported in areas of motivation.

A Comprehensive High School

The following lengthy description of one comprehensive high school's English program is included for several reasons. This school shows what *can* be done without major foundation or government funds, but with intelligent and dedicated planning. It also shows the importance of an enthusiastic staff, and a school curriculum tailored to the needs and abilities of the student body. The school's program is new; teachers and administrators readily admit that it is far from perfect. Nevertheless, this is a good example of what one school can accomplish.

The school is a four-year comprehensive high school with a student body of about 1,200. Twenty-five percent of the students are Mexican, 60 percent are Negro, and the remainder are white (who are referred to as Anglo). If 15 percent are white, many of them must have been absent, as observers saw few white children in the classes they visited.

The principal is a dedicated man who believes that the curriculum for a school like this must be developed by the teachers in the building, using the strengths of the individual members as an important factor in determining class offerings.

The school's present principal volunteered for the job, asking that his faculty be given permission to experiment with a special curriculum and not be held to the districtwide guides. Teacher turnover had been very high; some of the experienced teachers with long tenure in the building were asking to be transferred.

The school's English program is just a few months old, but it showed considerable initiative and creativity on the part of the teachers. Teachers have worked out what they call a four phase program in English. Phases indicate to a large extent the ability and skill of the students in English fundamentals. The phase one sections are for the top groups, and the phase two sections are for the average students. The major difference between phase three and phase four is that phase four students are those whose attitudes and motivation are so poor that they can hardly be taught anything. The teachers readily admit that they don't know what to do with this last group but feel that it is best for the other students to keep them separated for the time being. Ninth grade students are not included in the nongraded phases because the teachers do not at this time know them well enough to place them.

Oral drill receives much emphasis in the reading laboratory. On the first day of the visit, the teacher was playing oral language tapes for a lesson on the parts of speech. The teacher later told the observer that these tapes were not very appropriate material for these children. The teachers plan to make their own tapes when they have time. These tapes sounded stilted, and the vocabulary seemed to be over the children's heads. Although they didn't appear to understand what the words they were repeating meant, they were pronouncing them well and seemed to like what they were doing.

In the room were a few Language Master machines. The student sends the carded tape through the machine, then repeats the sentence on the card and listens to his voice on the machine. The teachers were very enthusiastic about this activity and hope to have about fifteen of these machines by next year—money forthcoming. But they feel that much of the material on tape is inappropriate for this situation and plan to devise their own materials.

These laboratories are unique in appearance. An attempt has been made to make them attractive and as little like a standard classroom as possible. The floors are covered with carpets, a folding door separates the two rooms and, in the reading lab, tables and chairs are used in place of desks.

Nearly every day the students begin the period in the writing laboratory by writing for about five minutes in a notebook called a journal. They write anything they want to write, even if it is only "I don't feel like writing today." They understand that no one except their lab teacher will read their journal. Students write about their job problems, their love lives, their illnesses, and their animosities toward other students. The teacher reads the journals from time to time but makes few

127

corrections on the papers. The teachers say that this activity seems to have a therapeutic effect on many students.

Actually, not much of the time in the reading lab is spent on reading; most is spent on oral drill and vocabulary work.

The composition laboratory is much like the reading laboratory and is located in the adjoining room. Sometimes the folding doors are opened, and the two groups work together with the two teachers helping on an individual basis.

During one class the composition teacher returned a short composition which the students had written the day before on the topic *Spring*. They were asked to correct the errors and recopy the paragraphs. The teacher often uses one word topics for the essays. *Death, Love,* and *Hate* are some that she used with success. The students write anything they wish about the topic.

The lab teachers were very enthusiastic about their plan, although they readily admitted that they really didn't know where they were headed most of the time. They found it far less frustrating when they were able to separate students by ability, cut down the class load, and work on fundamental skills with special emphasis on oral drill. They felt that a two-hour lab period some days would be a good time block.

By far the most popular class in the school is one called American Negro Literature, taught by a second year teacher of Portuguese-Irish descent. A visit to her class showed why every seat in the room was occupied. She is an extraordinary teacher.

The class was reading "A Member of the Wedding" by Carson Mc-Cullers. The teacher was reading the major role, and the students were taking the other parts. She read excellently with great force and many gestures—a real extrovert. The class loved it. Often she would stop and ask the students what they thought of certain lines: "Do you see why Frankie felt this way?" "Did you ever feel left out like this?" And the class members read with real gusto, too. The teacher would stop one of them once in a while and say, "Come on. You can say that line with more feeling that that, can't you?" And he would.

When the period was nearly over, the teacher made an assignment for the next day. She told the class to read on in the play—just a few pages—and be ready to write a short character sketch on one of the characters, although she would not tell them which one. She clearly set the limits for the students, giving some examples of the kinds of things they might want to write about. They knew exactly what was expected of them.

After class, seven students flocked to her desk to talk to her about books they were reading. There was an obvious mutual respect between her and the students. To one she said, "Remember what you promised. You wouldn't stop reading that book until you had read at least two chapters."

In class the teacher read aloud "taboo" words if they appeared in literature. Once she highly recommended an article in *True* magazine: a condensation of *nigger*, an autobiography of Dick Gregory. The teacher reported that there have been no repercussions from the students or parents about the use of these terms.

All in all, this is a very exciting school. The teacher morale seems high, and the principal is letting teachers and students experiment.

Task Force observers noted generally that administrators need an enlightened attitude toward discipline and toward freedom to experiment. Some of the poorest teaching observed occurred in classes where the teacher thought he was doing the students a great service by being altogether permissive. But the other extreme, where a teacher went to class with only a preconceived lesson in mind and taught it strictly according to plan, could also produce poor teaching. Task Force members believe that administrators should insist that the teacher be so well prepared for every class and every day's lesson that he knows when to digress from the plan for the sake of spontaneous learning: to capitalize

Miami, Florida, Students Use a Listening Center

on an unexpected moment of interest and readiness, to probe a problem in depth, to build a clearer understanding. An administrator then would know that a digression from the planned curriculum is not a distraction but an enrichment.

A Comprehensive Junior High School

The junior high school described here has a flexible program based upon students' abilities as revealed by test results and by elementary teachers' recommendations. The program has been set up on a ten-track concept. Students may be in one track for English—called Language Arts here—and in different tracks for math and social studies. Physical education and vocational training courses use heterogeneous grouping in classes. Some double periods of fifty minutes each are scheduled with one or two teachers being responsible for subject matter in two fields. Classes for low tracks are limited to twenty students each, with several having only fifteen or sixteen. To compensate, high track students are put in larger classes; none is larger than thirty-seven.

The attitude of teachers and administrators in this school is one of both sympathy and concern for the students. They admit frankly that the problems of teaching the disadvantaged student seemed overwhelming at first. However, all school personnel have pooled ideas and efforts in an attempt to solve their difficulties. Rapport among staff and administration is very good. The atmosphere is one of mutual respect and a deep dedication for helping youngsters. The staff seems anxious to try any technique or method considered educationally sound. All observed have liking for youngsters, exhibiting a good sense of humor in the classroom and in their corridor contact with students.

The ethnic composition of the school is 75 percent Negro, 12 percent Japanese, $5\frac{1}{2}$ percent Caucasian, with smaller percentages of Chinese, Filipino, and American Indian students. Teachers consider Oriental students to be generally superior students, with much family encouragement for academic achievement. Negro and Indian children are said to have difficulty in getting to school or classes on time, and they suffer from dialects which seem strange to this geographical area.

Students are clean, well groomed, and generally well behaved. Discipline is good, although it is obvious that teachers have worked very hard to develop it. Since there is much individual instruction, as well as many conferences with students, the school faculty seem well aware of their students' strengths and weaknesses.

The English program chiefly emphasizes the development of reading skills. Since students read several levels below grade, teachers believe the

130

emphasis necessary. Teachers have experienced difficulty in attempting to use traditional English materials for lower tracks. Challenging materials, however, are used for higher tracks.

Teachers pay much attention to spelling and vocabulary development. In fact, every teacher in the school is responsible for vocabulary in each of his classes. Students in higher tracks handle traditional types of English. Although they come from culturally disadvantaged areas, these students perform at a high level.

Administrators and teachers are generally pleased with the reading program, although they express concern about the lack of reading materials with simple vocabulary and high teenage appeal. They use a reading skills approach, with word attack an integral part of most lessons. Classes use overhead projectors for vocabulary, spelling, and testing. Teachers require definitions for randomly selected words and expect students to give synonyms, antonyms, and homonyms of any word on the vocabulary or spelling list.

Classes are democratically organized, with class president and secretary who handle some of the routine tasks, thus relieving teachers for more work with groups and/or individuals. Students' work is displayed prominently. Bulletin boards are covered with challenging materials brought in both by teachers and students.

As noted above, the major weakness in this program is a lack of attention to oral language. Teachers admit this weakness, but they say they do not know how to handle the problem.

In general this is an excellent junior high English program carefully planned for special needs of youngsters and for curriculum materials to implement goals set forth by competent, eager, dedicated teachers and administrators. The value of small classes with a variety of approaches being used in each class is inestimable. Certainly, other schools in similar districts may find it worth emulating.

Three Unsuccessful Programs. As noted elsewhere in this report, observers of classroom practices in secondary schools found many programs falling far short of their written and oral descriptions. Although Task Force observations necessarily lasted only one to three days, it was quite obvious in classroom visits and discussions with students, teachers, and local administrators, that often highly publicized programs, exciting in concept and description, simply did not coincide with what was happening in the individual classrooms.

Although this report is meant to present positive aspects of English programs for the disadvantaged student, a description of some of the less successful programs seems necessary to balance the description of the secondary schools visited. The following three programs are not named, and slight revisions have been made to preserve their anonymity. Comments have been taken directly from the observer's reports.

School A

OBSERVER 1: Classes at A High School are conducted in the usual secondary school pattern. Students are tracked according to achievement test scores, intelligence test scores, and teacher adjustment. Classes are not, however, homogeneous. One teacher reported that some pupils in grades 11 and 12 in all tracks have reading scores as low as the second grade level.

The school does not have department heads with any observable responsibilities or power. The English chairman acts only as the conveyor of information from the central office and as a securer of materials. He is given no time for other activities.

Although the administrators all declare their interest in the disadvantaged student, they are too pressed with other work to know exactly what the instructional program is or to evaluate its effectiveness. Teachers do what they can to improve the oral and written English of their students, but each teacher must find his own materials and work out his own methods.

Paperback editions of literature are used, but no other materials are apparently available for student use. All rooms were bare, and no supplementary reading materials were on hand.

That part of the program concerned with the teaching of literature to the college-bound seems effective, but the same materials and methods are used with students of lower achievement.

OBSERVER 2: All students in this school are theoretically grouped in three tracks: Basic, Regular, and Honors. Several teachers expressed the opinion, however, that the track system is very loosely organized, reporting that most classes contain pupils with a wide range of ability. While some of the classes actually observed appeared to be fairly homogeneous, others bore out the teachers' assessments.

In one Basic class, registration had shrunk from forty-one in September to seventeen in May.

Administrators are cordial and cooperative. They appear to understand the classroom teacher's problems and are sympathetic to the students. They are alert, guardedly optimistic, and at times highly enthusiastic about the programs in progress. Administrators unanimously complained of the lack of financial support for their school

132

programs, a complaint borne out by observations of materials, equipment, and staffing.

The English content in the classes visited is uniformly poor. Suitable books and reading material are notably missing (according to the teachers, because of "lack of funds"). There is, however, no shortage of reading workbooks and even reading "kits" which to several of the teachers seem to be the answer. The most obvious weaknesses in the teaching are lack of imagination and insecurity with subject matter. However, the weaknesses are no more pronounced in the classes visited than in the classes of some more advantaged schools observers have known.

District B

OBSERVER 1: This program was set up because students from the district had been doing so poorly on most yearly tests. Parents in each school district were called together, an appeal was made to their desires for their children to get ahead in the world, and they were asked to cooperate in an organized, closely supervised program. This program's chief purpose was to inspire and help their children pass the track tests and to raise the children's self-image.

In instituting the program, administrators cut class size, employed extra teachers, and inaugurated after school and evening programs.

Teachers here are generally understanding, although often frustrated, about the complicated factors involved in child growth and development. They seem to understand language problems, and many show they are trying to overcome those problems. They do, however, lack professional training in this field. Observation showed that teachers are more concerned in practice about teaching for tests than about oral language.

One teacher had worked out an original approach for book reports, but in most cases students work at their desks while teachers circulate, answering questions as needed. Although the school pays lip service to democratic classroom organization, there is little evidence of it. In the classes observed, emphasis in English content is upon meeting requirements of annual track tests. Teachers show great concern for preparing students to pass these track tests. Those who fail are put into a terminal program where they may stay for two years before being dropped from the schools. Pressures are great; teachers told stories of tears, illnesses, and more serious trouble resulting when students fail. There has been some discussion about discontinuing these tests, and some concern about the necessity for teaching towards them.

133

Program C

This program is an experimental course in a large urban school district for disadvantaged high school students who have acquired only a limited skill in English. The administrators and teachers are conscious of the needs of the students and sympathetic toward them. One teacher feels that his own experience and preferences in teaching make him less effective with the students assigned to this program than he is with other classes. However, the observer thought he was the most effective teacher in the program.

The classes visited were all composed of Negro pupils, some with white teachers. While no disciplinary problems were apparent, the students showed no enthusiasm for the program. The program is quite impressive on paper, but in practice the problems of motivation, materials, and adequately training teachers remain unsolved.

The program is designed to give pupils an opportunity to read, write, and speak daily. While variety and change of pace are necessary for students of the type assigned to Program C, trying to do all three of these activities within a forty to fifty minute period does not allow enough time to do any one thing well. Many things are attempted and few completed. Jotting for ten or fifteen minutes does not give these pupils time to plan what they wish to say, or to get more than one sentence on paper. The ''jotting sessions'' in the students' composition work might be worthwhile if the pupils had something pertinent to write about, but the composition subject on the day of the visit was ''Behavior in Auditorium Programs.''

Program C has been expanded since its beginning several years ago and, according to administrative personnel, is the most promising secondary school English program for the culturally disadvantaged. Teachers report some satisfaction with it but mention they are hindered by a lack of suitable materials. The problem cited is that of finding master teachers who are willing to teach these classes. Too many teachers feel that unless they are teaching advanced courses for the very able college-bound student, they are not fulfilling their duty. Present plans are to continue and expand the program.

Materials

Task Force observers noted an overwhelming use of two kinds of materials, (1) pre-packaged reading kits and (2) mechanical reading equipment. Most textbooks used were either standard anthology or grammar texts supplemented by easy reading high interest books. Many classes used workbooks in grammar and usage, and several junior high schools were using elementary basal readers. With the exception of the materials in the Gateway English Program, few books were specifically chosen for use by disadvantaged students. Very few observers saw adequate classroom libraries that might be used to supplement the texts given to the student.

Several schools observed made extensive use of magazines and newspapers in their reading programs. Such magazines as *Scope,* a magazine published specifically for the disadvantaged slow reader, and *Ebony,* used in predominantly Negro classes, were available in several classrooms. *Reader's Digest,* particularly its graded reading series, was used by many schools. Certainly magazines can be helpful in supplementing the inadequate and unappealing texts presented to most disadvantaged secondary students.

Audiovisual. Educational television was observed in many schools. One impressive program observed, however, was the Educational Television Project in Detroit. A Task Force observer reported on the television broadcast of a reading lesson.

> . . . The series is broadcast twice each week in the morning and repeated in the afternoon. The TV teacher makes the reading lesson and story come to life. The great feature about this television reading series is the very close relationship that has developed between the TV teacher and the classroom teachers. The teachers look to her for guidance, ask questions, write to her, make suggestions for improving the program, and have a one-day workshop every semester. In the TV lesson a story is introduced and a background of experience is built. This can be done very well on television because they have the facilities and time to develop extensive audiovisual aids, build models, etc. The teacher then takes over in the classroom to read the story and develop reading skills.
>
> This program seems especially valuable because of the large number of students—approximately 15,000—it reaches. Television seems to be excellent as a background builder. So many things can be shown on television that the typical classroom teacher would not be able to provide. For example, a few weeks ago they came to a story about a rodeo. They decided to produce a real rodeo, televising it from the parking lot outside the studio. This program appears very successful, especially among disadvantaged children who really need that type of direct visual experience.
>
> Every month the program is evaluated by approximately 4,000 teachers. Probably the greatest effect that this program has results from the teacher training that the demonstration teacher can do during the television series. The series is growing rapidly. The tapes for this year's series have been sold to many suburbs.

Another interesting audiovisual practice in the Banneker District of St. Louis is the use of a radio program featuring stories of Negroes who have made significant accomplishments in their field of interest. The program apparently is well received by both teachers and students. One teacher was assigned as an administrative assistant to assume many duties involved in writing and producing the program. She has help from a committee of teachers and principals.

Many reading programs observed emphasized extensive use of such audiovisual equipment as reading pacers, controlled readers, tachistoscopes, and machines to photograph eye movement. Although Task Force members felt that such hardware could produce limited gains in reading skills, they saw some programs in English being based almost entirely on this mechanistic approach. As a result of emphasis on the reading laboratory and its machines, some English programs did little work in language, dialect, literature, or composition. Such overemphasis on one phase of English must be seriously questioned.

The Task Force visited several language programs using tape recordings as used in a language laboratory. Though this technique could be a valuable aid to oral language instruction, programs visited were reported disappointing. An observer noted that the format of the tapes in one program said in effect, "Don't say it this way. That is wrong. Say it this way instead," and that students when responding were doing so in a mechanical and embarrassed manner. Another observer reported that the tapes heard were on the uses of the conjunction with students being asked to repeat a list of conjunctions named. Another lesson was on adjectives and adverbs. Observers felt that such an emphasis on tradi-

Small Group Discussion in a Miami, Florida, Secondary School

tional grammar was of little help in modifying the language patterns of the students.

Task Force members still believe that the use of tapes in teaching language, particularly standard informal English, can be a useful way of supplementing language instruction. To do this, however, requires better material than Task Force members observed.

Conclusions

The need for increased work in language instruction has been stressed continually in this report. Unfortunately, few teachers or administrators have had any training in it.

The Task Force recommends that teachers and administrators inform themselves about recent developments in language instruction.

College courses and inservice training are sound means of improving language instruction; familiarity with the content of language books in Appendix B is another means. Whatever methods employed, Task Force observers agree that knowledge about language instruction is necessary before useful, overall programs of English instruction for the disadvantaged can be established.

Many disadvantaged students speak dialects that are considered socially unacceptable in middle and upper class society.

The Task Force recommends that secondary English programs include oral work in standard informal English for students with nonstandard dialects. Instead of downgrading or attempting to eliminate students' dialects, teachers should teach standard informal English as a second dialect.

In developing an effective language program, schools can learn much from the considerable work already done in the area of teaching English as a second language. Many methods and techniques can be incorporated with caution. For example, the Social Dialects Conference of 1964 brought forth this comment:

> . . . It is fair to say, I believe, that we reached a general concurrence on three points. The first is a matter of terminology. Recently there has been a tendency on the part of some of us to equate the teaching of standard English to the culturally deprived—or whatever the euphemism happens to be this month—with the teaching of English as a foreign language. It is undoubtedly true that some of the approaches and methods of teaching English as a foreign language can be advantageously employed in teaching the standard language to speakers of substandard English, but . . . it is unwise and even foolhardy to speak of it

137

in those terms. On the one hand, we may be treading on the feelings of those who are sensitive about their recent immigrant status, and on the other we may be relegating to the role of the recently arrived certain groups who have been in this country for generations. If we must have a term or label for what we are doing, let it be accurate and at the same time nonpejorative.[8]

In a recent survey of changes in language instruction in schools, Vera Louise Higgins reported [9] that over the previous two decades, those schools with the ablest and most advantaged students have jettisoned formal grammar, while schools with slower and disadvantaged students have clung tenaciously to it. Both kinds of schools have retained in varying degrees the teaching of usage; but formal grammar concerned with abstractions and terminology has been taught mostly to students who are least likely to succeed with it. A comparison of the forthcoming *High School Departments of English: Their Organization, Administration, and Supervision* with this Task Force report corroborates the findings of this study.

The time devoted to teaching formal grammar to disadvantaged students can be better spent in other areas of English instruction. Grammar instruction, as observed by Task Force members, was considered unlikely to help students to write, speak, or read with greater proficiency.

The Task Force, therefore, recommends that traditional grammar instruction be deemphasized in programs for the disadvantaged.

As previously noted, many Task Force members believe that grammar should be taught as a humanistic study to able students, including college-bound students in disadvantaged schools.

Literature of little significance or inherent appeal to disadvantaged students was observed in many classroom visits. In general, literature was being neglected for work on the development of reading skills, usually through some kind of mechanical equipment or grammar instruction drills. Much of the reading done by the disadvantaged secondary students is vapid, nonliterary, and is unlikely to initiate worthwhile class discussion.

The Task Force recommends that literature appropriate to the interests and abilities of the students be studied at all secondary levels of English instruction.

Encouraging and teaching students to read is of primary importance.

---

[8] Albert H. Marckwardt, ''Review of the Conference,'' *Social Dialects and Language Learning*, ed. Roger W. Shuy (Champaign, Ill.: National Council of Teachers of English, 1965).

[9] Vera Louise Higgins, in a speech made at the 1965 NEA National Convention, New York, New York, July, 1965.

Initially, material of little literary significance but of high reader interest may provide the teacher with a way of arresting the attention of pupils and directing them to books.

Literature does not have to be presented in written form. Records, tape recordings, and films of literary quality or on literary subjects can be used successfully. Teachers with wide reading backgrounds do not have to rely on literature anthologies but can make use of materials resembling those suggested by Gateway English. Paperbacks can be useful in such work. Even literature in standard anthologies can be taught successfully by inspired teachers, and again, excellent teaching in any program for the disadvantaged must be paramount. One Task Force member saw Keats' "The Eve of St. Agnes" taught successfully to a class of Negro students, which the following observation points out:

> . . . The interesting aspect of this visit was that the students were actively participating. Upon leaving, I was more dubious than ever about the worth of "programs" as contrasted to the "gifted teacher." I had just observed a very artistic teacher work with Keats and do so with a high degree of success. Judging from my experience, it would appear that the teacher who has philosophical insight enough to extract the human elements from life and from literature is the most effective teacher of the culturally disadvantaged. Perhaps what I am trying to say is that the average teachers are superficial in their approach, and consequently what they personally and professionally perceive in life is commonplace and meaningless to the culturally disadvantaged student.

Adult Basic Education

In 1964 under a grant from the Cooperative Research Branch of the U. S. Office of Education and the Ohio State University Research Foundation, Robert F. Barnes and Andrew Hendrickson directed a study of thirty-five major adult basic education programs in various sections of America.[1] Barnes was assisted in making the site visits by Robert D. Boyd, Edward G. Summers, and Harold L. Wise.

Since a repetition of this study seemed unnecessary, the Task Force concentrated on visiting representative programs so that it could provide information to supplement the Barnes study. This section of the Task Force report, therefore, consists of a portion of the report of the Ohio State study, "A Review and Appraisal of Adult Literacy Materials and Programs," followed by additional comments and observations based on the NCTE visits.

[1] Robert F. Barnes, "A Review and Appraisal of Adult Literacy Materials and Programs," Report on Research Project G-029 (Unpublished report to United States Office of Education, October, 1965).

Problems in Adult Basic Education

ROBERT F. BARNES

Today one constantly reads of or hears about the many different and perplexing problems facing administrators and teachers in adult basic education. As everyone interprets these problems in the light of his own special interests, I discuss them in light of the findings of a research project that I am now completing. In this project we attempted to identify the problems existing in this field by (1) visiting thirty-five programs in fifteen states with a team of four persons who observed classes and interviewed administrators, teachers, and students, and (2) collecting some 1,300 pieces of instructional material from commercial publishers and public agencies. These materials were reviewed and appraised by a panel of three consultants—one university reading authority and two teachers who had taught adult basic courses for several years.

An Adult Basic Education Class in New York City

One of the major problems facing the majority of the adult literacy programs observed was a marked lack of written operational objectives designed around the students' goals and needs. Factors that the team identified which probably contributed to the absence of such objectives were (1) the newness of the programs, (2) the rapid expansion of programs, (3) teacher load, and (4) teacher time. In almost all programs, when the question was raised concerning objectives, the answer was the same—"to teach the illiterate adult to read and write." This is a very commendable objective, but it must be classified as an ultimate objective which in no way indicates what the teacher does or should do to encourage and help the student to develop such skills.

For the most part, the few objectives that the programs purported to have were established by the administration or staff and were based more on theory than on the objectives, goals, and needs of the individual students within the program. From their observations and interviews, the team came to feel that only in the more successful classes did the teachers of adult illiterates take the students' objectives into consideration in their formulation of operational objectives. In these cases, the teachers were cognizant of the significant difference that exists between literate and illiterate adults, and of its effects upon the students.

In general, we noted that the classes were structured into three rather broad classes which we designated as levels 1, 2, and 3. Classes were so organized and divided primarily because of the rather small enrollments. Level 1 was roughly equivalent to grades 1, 2, and 3; level 2 to grades 4, 5, and 6; and level 3 to grades 7 and 8.

For the most part we noted a marked heterogeneity of class structure; foreign born or foreign-speaking students were consistently placed in the same classrooms with the native born, English-speaking students, thereby compounding teachers' problems.

Another characteristic of the adult basic education programs observed was their teacher recruitment policies. In general, depending of course upon the type of program—public school, voluntary, or private foundation—the teachers were recruited from four groups—elementary teachers, secondary teachers, retired teachers, and married women with excess leisure.

A fifth factor typical of the programs observed was an air of complacency toward the program displayed by administrators and some of the teachers. This complacency was generally displayed in the form of comments such as: "We're doing a good job right now. We are filling our classrooms, etc." In such programs, never did the team hear any mention or concern that, even though the classrooms available were full, only a small percent of the illiterates in the community were being reached.

While this complacency was not nearly so prevalent among the teachers as it was among administrators, it was found most often in programs where persons who were teaching a full load in elementary or secondary schools were also teaching adult basic education classes at night. In many cases, this attitude appeared in direct correlation to "overwork and underpay." The team feels quite strongly that if administrators are to have successful adult basic education programs using day school teachers for staff, they must make some provision to provide relief time for these people. Teachers of adult illiterates must be extremely enthusiastic and at the peak of their efficiency if they are to do the best possible job in teaching these people. For adult basic education programs to be effective, they absolutely cannot be considered as a "sideline" by anyone in the system—the administration, teaching staff, or board of education.

Another area which is often identified as a problem is the marked lack of suitable instructional materials. As a result of our research project, however, we have identified between 400 and 500 pieces of instructional material that are satisfactory for use in adult basic education programs. I grant that there is not a great deal of this material that could be called outstanding, but nonetheless there is satisfactory material available. *There is a crying need for sound, well-designed field testing of available instructional material before a lot of time and money are ploughed into the development of new material. By this I do not mean field testing done by several agencies, each using his own design, but field testing using a common design that is sound and of adequate depth and scope to produce meaningful, valid results.*

As the situation now stands, the single greatest problem in adult basic education is providing adequate education for existing teachers and for the multitude that will be recruited for the Title 11-B programs. The education needs that have been identified will be discussed in the following sections of this report, though it must be emphasized here that such education cannot be accomplished by a few one-day meetings or by a one- or two-week conference. To adequately educate these teachers we must provide an institute of at least six weeks' (preferably ten or twelve weeks') duration, followed by a series of organized inservice experiences.

What of the students we saw; what of those that you have faced or will face? What did we learn that teachers of illiterate adults should know about these students. Who are they? What are they? And why are they?

First, who are they? Of course, they are the low-income, un- or undereducated. I would wager that this is the definition many of you might give. Generally this is true, but let me caution you that not all can be classified as low-income, nor can they always be physically recognizable—perhaps a bit on the unclean side or poorly or shabbily dressed. By the same token, a great many of our low-income population are not un- or undereducated.

Why is it so important that teachers and administrators know, or be aware of, these factors? One of the primary reasons is that teachers and administrators cannot enter into such a program with the attitude that the illiterate population must be made to master the basic literacy skills so that they will no longer be an albatross about the neck of our middle class society. These same teachers and administrators must understand the pressures, barriers, and problems facing the illiterates and be brought to accept them as human beings who generally are capable of being taught. I feel that only when we can accomplish this, and then are able to sell adult basic education to community leaders as a thing of value, will such a program be totally effective at the level and magnitude envisioned by the proponents of the Economic Opportunity Act.

Another major factor to consider is that adult illiterates are aware that the middle class mass has stigmatized their inability and has stereotyped them. Illiterates have suffered a lifetime of rejections, rebuffs, and unpleasant school experiences. Even if they never went to school, they have friends who went.

As a result of all these factors, they have many fears and barriers discouraging their participation in education of any form, and they have literally been forced to develop an almost fanatic system of defenses. Among those we can list are a mastery of oral expression, always carrying a book or paper, a battery of multicolored ball point pens in a conspicuous place, and such comments as, "I forgot my glasses," "My hand is injured and I can't write."

I have a great respect for anyone who enrolls in any adult literacy class. When he does this, he is in effect, saying to the world "Look at me, I can't read or write," and I ask, how many of you would have the courage to do this?

Even in order to grasp the door knob of the school where the class is offered, the illiterate must overcome a great many barriers. Those identified by the observers were classified as (1) economic, (2) family, (3) social, and (4) psychological.

1) The barrier caused by *economic pressures* was noted in all programs observed, whether or not fees were charged. It must be granted

that, where fees were charged, they were quite modest—in most instances about $2.00 per year. An additional expense in most programs was transportation and, in some, pencils, paper, and similar materials. Another instance of this barrier was pointed out by some of the students when they noted that "At first I wouldn't come to this class because I didn't have any decent clothes to wear." For a person with a very low family income, where the primary needs are physiological, this could be a difficult barrier to overcome. Although this particular barrier was not noted as often as some of the others, there is a strong possibility that it is preventing those who would list it from entering this type of class at all.

2) Closely related to economic pressures is the problem of *family pressure*. Questions like "What was the most difficult thing you had to face when you decided to enroll in this class?" elicited such responses as, "I didn't have enough money for a babysitter and had no one to leave the children with." Other typical responses were "There was an invalid member in the family and no one to leave him with"; "After I took care of the family all day, I didn't feel like coming"; or "After working all day, I was too tired."

3) Of the four types of barriers indicated, the social and psychological were listed often. Among *social pressures* affecting the decision to enroll, reluctance to admit to friends and neighbors the inability to read and write was listed most often, even though many of these people were in the same situation. Another attitude held by some social groups was the belief that school was only for children and that older people can't learn in school. A typical observation was made by one student in North Carolina: "The toughest part about startin' in this class was listenin' to my friends telling me that 'You're too old to learn anything in books, and besides school is for kids.' Now that I'm in school, they don't say anything; they just look at me and grin."

Another belief harbored by some segments of society in the areas visited is that if a person once fails in school, drops out for any reason, or has never attended school at all, he is too "dumb" to learn anything. Along this line the observers heard such statements as, "I almost didn't come because I was afraid that I was too dumb to learn anything," or "If it hadn't been for _____, I would never have started in this class because all my people and my friends told me I was just too stupid to learn anything in school. Now I know better, but I still can't tell them a thing." The great majority of the people in adult literacy classes certainly are far from being stupid. To the contrary, because of their inability to read or write, they have been forced to "live by their wits" in a highly literate society.

4) The most difficult barriers to identify were the *psychological barriers*. Although there are probably more of these affecting the student's decision to enroll in an adult literacy class than are identified here, the observers chose to categorize those that are listed by students into three general divisions. They are (a) fear of failure; (b) fear of school; and (c) fear of change.

a) *Fear of failure* was the one psychological barrier that appeared most often. This barrier was usually apparent in statements such as, "I didn't start in this class for a long time after I heard about it, because I wasn't really sure that I could learn anything. Maybe I *was* too dumb to learn." Although this was stated in many ways, they all basically expressed the fear that the person involved would fail in this new endeavor as he had in others throughout his life.

b) The *fear of school experience* was a barrier that was noted almost exclusively by those students who had had some past school experience. When this fear was reported, it was connected almost always with an unpleasant experience such as placement by physical size rather than ability; ridicule by either teacher or pupils because they were slower than other students; not being accepted by pupils because they were unable to attend regularly; and other similar experiences. This fear was adequately summed up by one statement heard by one of the observers: "If I'd have had people who understand me like these people do and had a teacher like the one I have now when I was a child, I don't think they'd have ever got me out of school."

c) The third psychological barrier listed, *fear of change,* was mentioned least often by the students interviewed; the observers, however, felt that this barrier probably confronted the majority of these students at one time or another. This fear of change or, in essence, "Fear of the unknown" was most often reported to the observers in a form dealing with the student's concern over the effect that this new experience might have on his relationship with his family, friends, and society in general.

Although it may have been presumptuous of the observers to categorize the psychological barriers in this fashion, it was felt that these categories most aptly described those reported by those students interviewed during the site visits. It is important to remember that, while the barriers were listed separately, they are interrelated, and the absolute effect of one upon the other is unknown. In spite of this, it is believed that the economic and family barriers are closely related and tend to reinforce each other and that the social and psychological barriers are similarly interwoven. It is further believed that teachers and admini-strators must be aware of these barriers facing the adult illiterate and must be ready and willing to help him overcome them if the programs are to be effective.

Although the existence of these barriers can be documented, the observers feel that it would be wise to explore such questions as:

1. What effect does each barrier have upon the other?

2. Are some of the various types of barriers really more closely related than are others?

3. Are there really four distinct types of barriers affecting the participation of the adult illiterate, or in reality can it be said that all are the result of a factor such as economic deficiencies, racial problems, etc.?

Why do these people attend adult basic education classes? The answer to this is not as simple as might be imagined. Certainly, they wish to develop needed skills in reading, writing, and arithmetic, but *why* do they feel a need to master these skills? There is no question in the minds of the team members that many of these people have gotten along reasonably well without such skills. After visiting with many of these students, the observers were able to identify several forces that were compelling these people to admit that they lacked these basic skills and to enroll in the adult literacy classes. These factors can be grouped into two general categories—vocational and self-improvement (self-actualization). The observers were aware of these two general forces before they started their site visits; however, they had been led to believe that the majority of the people in the classes would be there because of the vocational motivation.

The observers found that the students who listed a vocationally oriented motivation, fell into two classifications: (1) job seeking and (2) job improvement. Those persons who fell into the job-seeking category could be further subdivided into one group which had never been em-ployed and a second group which had been employed but were currently out of work and were interested in developing a new vocational skill.

Those persons classified as job-seeking who had never been employed were primarily women who felt that it was necessary for them to go to work. Reasons listed by these women for going to work were as follows: (1) change in marital status through death of husband, divorce, or separation; (2) husband out of work; (3) need to supplement husband's income because of increased expenses; and (4) desire to "get off the welfare rolls."

The majority of the individuals who were identified as job-seeking unemployed were males; however, in the highly industrialized areas many women fell into this category. Most of these were unskilled or semiskilled workers who had been displaced by automation. In some instances, the observers were told that the former employers had recommended that these persons, some of whom were long-time employees, attend the local adult literacy classes in order to retrain for a skilled job.

Persons attending the literacy classes to retrain or to improve their present employment status were predominantly male. These people for the most part reported that they were attending the literacy classes to increase their reading, writing, and arithmetic skills to a level that would allow them to enter specific vocational training programs. However, some of them indicated that it would be necessary to master these literacy skills in order to either retain their present job or be in line for a promotion to a job at a supervisory level.

Some of the specific reasons given by students wishing to enroll in literacy classes for the purpose of job improvement indicated, rather emphatically, that a great many of them are quite intelligent. One man had been employed as a rural mail carrier for over fifteen years even though he could neither read nor write. He had simply had his son ride with him to read the names and addresses. Now that the son was entering the military service, this person found it necessary to learn to read in order to hold his job.[1]

Another individual had been employed as a shipping clerk for a number of years, and only when his employer wanted to promote him to supervisor of the shipping department did it become known that he could only write his name and had no reading ability. This man had memorized the labels on the packaged material, and, when the typed orders came to him, could identify the material needed, assemble the order, and attach the order to the package. From there it went to another person who attached the shipping labels.

Many similar instances were cited, all emphasizing that much of the illiterate population do hold responsible positions by virtue of their native intelligence and ability. As would be expected, these persons are among those who make the most rapid progress in the adult literacy programs.

Analysis of the responses from persons whom the observers identified as ''self-improvement'' motivated showed that the responses could gen-

---

[1] When the observers asked how this person had gotten this rural mail carrier job, they were informed that he had been given the civil service examination orally as the result of a ''political debt.''

erally be divided into seven categories. These categories are: (1) parent image; (2) helping children; (3) social status; (4) "operation bootstrap"; (5) group interaction; (6) religion; and (7) social outlet. True, some of these overlap those motivational forces classified as vocational. The context in which they were given to the observers, however, led to the belief that the students listing them were thinking of these forces primarily in terms of self-improvement (self-actualization), and that any vocational motivation was secondary in their minds. A discussion of the seven categories follows:

1) Most often, those persons who were identified as motivated by the *parent image* force quite frankly admitted to the observers that they felt that, if their children found that they could not read or write, it would destroy or decrease the children's desire to finish school. One said that he was in the class because one of his children was threatening to drop out of school "because you can't read or write and get along all right, so why should I finish school?" This person believed that if he could get an eighth grade equivalency certificate, his youngster's argument would be ineffective. Surprisingly enough, some people in this category were grandparents concerned about their grandchildren.

2) Of the persons motivated by the desire to be able to *help their children*, the observers identified two different groups. One group was interested only in being able to help their children and, in some cases, grandchildren with their schoolwork; the other feared that if it were known that they could not read or write, their children's circle of friends (peer group) would be limited.

3) One of the more common motivational forces identified as "self-improvement" was that of improving or maintaining one's *social status* by becoming proficient in those literacy skills previously listed. Although one might expect this reason to be given most often by the Negro students, the observers noted that it was listed by white students just as frequently. Indeed it would appear that some of the low-income whites are realizing that, with civil rights legislation and the Negro drive for self-improvement they must improve themselves just to maintain the relative social status.

4) Closely related to the preceding motivational forces, yet different enough that the observers felt they should be identified separately, were the forces called "operation bootstrap" and "group interaction." The *"operation bootstrap"* motivation was listed exclusively by Negro students. Persons in this category made such statements as, "It looks like my people are beginning to get some breaks, and, if we are going to make anything of the breaks, it's up to us to get as much education as we can,"

or "If our people are ever going to amount to anything, it's up to me and people like me who ain't got no learnin' to get that learnin' just as fast as we can."

5) The students classified as *group interaction* motivated were those who seemed most concerned with their increasing inability to "talk to" or "visit with" their friends and neighbors, and with people in general. One lady stated, "I feel very uncomfortable and nervous when I try to talk to my friends. And, I can hardly bring myself to talk to people I don't know very well because I just know that they will know that I never went to school as soon as I open my mouth."

6) Some of the students interviewed by the observers stated quite bluntly that the only reason they were enrolled in the literacy classes was to learn to read the Bible. Most of the persons with *religious motivation* were older, and the majority were found in the southern states visited.

7) The last self-improvement motivational force identified was *social outlet*. This motivation was found most commonly among those persons who were either receiving welfare payments or whose family income was extremely low. In one instance an individual made the statement, "I come to this class because it is the only chance I have to get away from the kids and the old man."

It must be noted that some of the motivational forces identified in this section are not those which educators feel students should have for the most effective learning. However, regardless of the type of motivation, the observers believe that the teacher must recognize it for what it is, and if the motivation is weak, the teacher must use that force as a means of developing other, more powerful ones in the student.

Based on the preceding statement and on observations and interviews with teachers and administrators, the observation team believes strongly that the one key to the success of any adult basic education program is the *teacher*. Therefore, one of the more critical questions asked of administrators was, "What are the qualifications you look for in hiring your instructors?" Usually this was answered in terms of the kind of teacher employed and the attributes most commonly found. The six kinds in public school programs can be identified as: (1) the elementary school teacher, (2) the secondary school teacher, (3) the retired teacher, (4) the married woman with excess leisure, (5) the master teacher, and (6) the manager.

1) The elementary teacher

   a) is more firmly grounded in the basic developmental phases of reading, writing, and arithmetic than are other day school teachers;

b) is more accustomed to moving at a slow rate and, therefore, tends to be more patient with illiterate adults;

c) is better acquainted with developmental materials;

d) generally knows more about how to teach the basic literacy skills than do teachers at higher levels.

2) The secondary teacher

a) is used to working with older students. Therefore, he would be able to relate more readily to adults;

b) is accustomed to the psychology of working with adolescents in a learning situation, which more closely parallels working with adults than does the psychology involved in working with elementary students.

c) has more flexible and more varied teaching load.

3) The retired teacher

a) is available on a part-time basis and generally has more flexible schedule;

b) is more sympathetic toward the adult illiterate student;

c) has to spend time in preparation of lessons, and as a result is usually more conscientious in his efforts.

4) The married woman with excess leisure

a) is available on a part-time basis and generally has a more flexible schedule;

b) has to spend time in preparation of lessons, and as a result is usually more conscientious in her efforts;

c) is usually strongly motivated in either a service or religious aspect.

5) The fifth category identified was *the master teacher*. A considerably smaller number of directors took the position that it does not matter from which grade level the teacher comes so long as he is a "good teacher." It was extremely difficult to get an operational definition of a "good teacher" from these directors. From observations of and interviews with some of the most successful teachers in the programs visited, the observation team believes that this success was due primarily to the fact that the individual teacher:

a) had well in mind those objectives pertaining to teaching the basic literacy skills;

b) established rapport with the individual students as soon as possible in order to determine, or perhaps to develop, their individual objectives;

151

c) was familiar with or had a sensitivity for methods and techniques that are effective in teaching adults;

d) used all identifiable objectives in developing a ''main course'' to follow in teaching the class, and yet maintained sufficient flexibility so that, if necessary, the main course could be changed;

e) used the individual student's objectives to design individual ''subsidiary courses'' to either supplement the main course or to help the student master the content of the main course;

f) understood the students—who, what, and why they are what they are;

g) was able to accept the student for what he is—a person of value who is capable of learning;

h) began instruction of each student at his own level of achievement and taught in terms of the student's value system and culture;

i) was able to recognize the individual student's goals;

j) had a firm understanding of human relations;

k) had an understanding of group dynamics and their value in the classroom.

While a few of the systems did offer sound teacher training programs, most public school programs had only an orientation period at the beginning of the school year or semester. Generally, these orientation periods were five to ten hours in length, the major portion of the time being devoted to administrative matters. The sessions were conducted by means of a lecture-discussion format, covering such topics as the differences between teaching adults and teaching children, available instructional materials, and administrative details.

A summary of the responses made by administrators to an inquiry concerning the value and need of teacher training yielded several excuses for the deficiencies in their programs:

a. One director argued, ''If a teacher was a good teacher to begin with, what needs to be done?'' The implication was *nothing*. He dismissed the question, ''What is a good teacher?'' as an academician's ''ivory tower'' problem.

b. There is no money in the budget, nor is there any likelihood of getting any.

c. The changing and part-time teaching staff would make the expense of such workshops too great in terms of the direct returns.

d. It is questionable whether or not there is enough known about education to make such workshops profitable.

e. Part-time staff would not come.

f. The staff is too busy as it is, meeting the demands of adult students and the community.

Teachers interviewed throughout the thiry-five programs all seemed to feel that there was a great need for teacher training, regardless of whether their own administration offered such a program. A summary of remarks of teachers related to teacher training indicates that there are a great many training needs which should be met in order to develop effective teachers for adult basic education programs.

Teachers specifically needed training in:

1. Psychological and sociological peculiarities of adult illiterates
2. Adult learning principles as they pertain to adult illiterates
3. Psychology of the slow reader as applied to adult illiterates
4. Group dynamics in the adult basic education classroom
5. Human relations
6. Identifying needs and immediate goals of the individual student
7. Establishing attainable, measurable objectives
8. Formulation of objectives around the individual's needs and goals
9. Program evaluation
10. Selection and evaluation of instructional materials
11. Developing supplemental materials to meet individual needs
12. Testing and the place of testing in the program

While a great many of these needs could be presented through lectures and seminars to increase the effectiveness of the training experience, provision must be made for practical experience and application. A majority of the trainees will not have had experience in the adult basic education classroom.

In order to cover both the theoretical and practical aspects outlined above, it is proposed that an institute of a minimum duration of eight weeks be planned. The proposed institute format includes regularly scheduled formal lectures, seminars, laboratory sessions, and practicums, to be described in detail in the following discussion. Such an institute could do much in strengthening adult literacy programs.

Institute Program

1. Lectures
   a. General Survey of Teaching Adults—8:00 and 9:00 a.m., daily. To be taken by all participants. One half of the group would take it at 8:00 and the other half at 9:00. Planned to serve as a foundation for other institute activities, the course will develop an understanding of the basic principles and theories relative to:

—Psychological and sociological differences of the adult illiterate
—Adult learning
—Adult education methods and techniques
—Group dynamics as a tool
—Human relations
—Identifying adult illiterate needs

b. General Survey of Teaching Reading to Adult Illiterates—8:00 and 9:00 a.m., daily. To be taken by all participants with course "a" and should serve as a strong foundation for developing a good understanding of methods and materials to be employed in developing their own teaching materials. Will also serve as a foundation for the seminars, labs, and practicums. Designed to develop an understanding of the principles relative to:

—The process of reading

—Word attack skills

—Comprehension, rate, and study skills

—Problems of readability

—Motivation and reading interests

—Developing maturity in reading

—Causes of reading disability

2. Laboratory Sessions—10:00 to 11:50 a.m., Monday and Wednesday. The staff will carry joint responsibility for this phase. Lab sessions will be related to the lectures as follows:

a. Trainees will participate in demonstrations in the use of adult teaching methods and techniques.

b. Participants will be expected to review and evaluate available materials and develop some degree of competency in developing their own teaching materials.

c. During the latter stages of the institute the participants, with guidance from staff, will develop a tentative teaching plan.

3. Supervised Practicum—10:00 to 4:50 p.m., Tuesday and Thursday. Staff members will supervise this segment of the institute which will relate to both the lecture and laboratory sections. The practicum sessions will require a high level of student participation as follows:

a. On the basis of criteria to be developed in the lecture and labora-

154

tory sessions, the students will spend some time each day critically reviewing and evaluating instructional materials and available testing instruments.

    b. Students will observe adult basic education classes in operation and will evaluate practices observed.

    c. Students will plan and teach lessons under the supervision of both the staff and the classroom teacher.

    d. The students will administer and interpret achievement and diagnostic tests, after demonstrations and practice administration with other institute participants.

4. Seminar—1:00 to 4:50 p.m., Monday and Wednesday. Students will have the opportunity to explore in depth, topics related to

An Adult Student at the Blackboard in New York City Teacher Education

the programs that are of interest to them and report the results of their study in the seminar sessions. The primary purpose of the seminar will be to encourage thorough study and critical discussion and evaluation of significant problems in the field. Topics and/or problems will be identified by the staff and appropriate related references will be supplied for beginning exploration.

5. Staff Conferences with Participants—10:00 a.m. to 4:50 p.m., Friday. All staff available including classroom teachers. This consultation period is provided to allow ample time for individual consultation with those participants who need additional help.

Institute Weekly Schedule

	Monday	Tuesday	Wednesday	Thursday	Friday
8:00– 8:50 a.m.	Lecture	Lecture	Lecture	Lecture	Lecture
9:00– 9:50 a.m.	Lecture	Lecture	Lecture	Lecture	Lecture
10:00–11:50 a.m.	Lab.	Practicum	Lab.	Practicum	Staff-trainee consultation
11:50–12:50 p.m.	Lunch	Lunch	Lunch	Lunch	Lunch
1:00– 4:50 p.m.	Seminar	Practicum	Seminar	Practicum	Staff-trainee consultation

Observations of the Task Force[*]

A relatively small amount of professional energy has been spent to develop new curricula and materials for the education of adults. Nevertheless, a number of sound, effective programs have emerged despite very limited resources of money and personnel.

Recruitment of Students

Because they often encounter social problems when they return to school, many adults who realize their need for education are reluctant to try again. The adult literacy program that aims for maximum enrollment, therefore, does not simply wait for potential students to come knocking on the administrator's door; it reaches out into the community to sell itself and to attract students. Of course, nearly every program uses the usual forms of publicity—posters, newspaper stories, and pamphlets or brochures, but the nonliterate person has difficulty reading printed materials. *Program directors state that the most effective means of recruitment is personal contact with potential students.*

A number of projects that the Task Force visited recruit through the offices of various community services, employment agencies, and welfare agencies. The program representative (teacher, administrator, community relations worker) may even locate himself in these offices, thus making himself available to people interested in basic education. Sometimes program personnel make themselves available for speaking engagements at community meetings which potential students might attend. A less direct means of word-of-mouth publicity is to inform community agencies, clergymen, teachers, and employers about the program so that they in turn will recommend it to those who can benefit.

Another recruitment practice reported is that of advertising the program from a sound truck driven through neighborhoods of the disadvantaged. If non-English speaking students are sought, the broadcasting should be in their native language.

Some programs enlist volunteers to go door-to-door to inform people of the program. This practice requires considerable organization but can succeed if the volunteers are well informed and can communicate effectively with disadvantaged adults.

---

[*] The observations in this chapter are based on 19 separate reports from observers on programs providing for English instruction to adults. Six programs which deal exclusively with adults were visited.

Student Placement

Virtually all programs group students according to their mastery of reading. Useful in many classroom teaching situations, homogeneous grouping has a special justification in programs for adults. This motivation of an adult may be destroyed if he is placed in a class in which he is far below or above the average. A class which is too advanced for him can frustrate and discourage him, whereas a class which slowly covers material which he has already mastered may bore him. The adult wants to complete his education as quickly and effortlessly as possible. If the teaching, the level of the class, and the rate of progress are satisfactory, an adult is less likely to drop a program than is a younger student. This problem is a continuing one for even in the most successful programs as many as 50 percent do drop out.

In practice, there is disagreement about the soundest ways of determining the language proficiency of students. Some programs administer formal tests at enrollment time while others do not. Directors who do not administer tests told Task Force members that immediate confrontation with a battery of tests frightens many potential students. Those who use tests say that proper initial counseling to inform the student of the need for the examination and for proper placement can erase or mitigate the negative effect of a formal achievement examination.

Classroom Teaching

Teachers reported that the closer a program comes to providing individual instruction, the more effective it will be. Teachers who had taught in regular elementary schools stated that individualized instruction is especially important for adults, who typically want to spend as little time as possible on material which they know.

Some teachers divide their class period into two sections: the first for presentation of new material to the group, the second for individual work. During the first portion of the class period, they may present practical uses for the language skills which students are learning. For instance, they may show students how to fill out Social Security information forms, representative job application forms, etc. Teachers reported that including such materials in even a beginning class increases the incentive to learn and to continue to attend class.

During the second part of the class period, students work on individual assignments. Each student works at his own rate of speed while the teacher circulates from student to student. Teachers said that it is very important to devote approximately equal attention to all students during recitation and individual instruction periods. Even a high achiever may become discouraged if he receives less attention than he feels he deserves. Teachers also stated that an adult student is less likely to surrender to a temptation to stay away from class if he feels that the teacher will miss him personally.

Teachers use wide variety of approaches to evaluation of student work. Some teachers "red pencil" students' work liberally while others restrict evaluation to such marginal comments as "Well done," or "Not as well as you did last week," or to casual circling or underlining of errors. One teacher explained that she adjusts her rate of progress to the number of errors on her students' written work. If most of the work contains few errors, she moves on to new material; if, on the other hand, she sees many errors, she reviews material.

Teachers must consider the students as individuals. If one or two students retard the progress of the class, the teacher may do one of several things. If the principal causes are lack of ability or inadequate academic preparation, the teacher may suggest that the student transfer to a "slower" or less advanced class. If, however, a student's poor performance is due to failure to attend class or failure to work industriously, most teachers talk to the person privately to attempt to solve the difficulty. Nearly all teachers stated that one must not embarrass an adult student by reprimanding him before the entire class. Although a teacher must make casual or routine corrections during oral recitation or individual classroom work, the teacher who makes the student appear "stupid" before the class produces negative results, in both attitude and attendance.

Most teachers use a fairly traditional approach to instruction in reading and writing. Considerable emphasis on training in phonics, accompanied by drill-writing, spelling, weekly testing, review, and retesting, was observed in adult programs. Several reasons for a traditional approach were reported. Some teachers stated that adult students expect, and indeed even *want*, a traditional approach so they will feel that "they are really going to school." Other teachers said that adult students, if properly counseled and taught, are willing to work very hard to learn and that the traditional approaches are therefore most appropriate. Others contended that written workbook and dictation exercises, corrected and graded by the teacher, give the students concrete evidence of progress and that success is possible if the exercises challenge the students. Teachers reported that both real progress and successful experiences are needed to sustain students' motivation.

One basic education instructor uses the Initial Teaching Alphabet to teach beginning reading. He said that his students probably like the method because it is different from the ways which were used unsuccessfully with them in previous experiences in school. He reported that both the learning of the i.t.a. and the transition from it to traditional orthography are probably less difficult for adults than for children, for adults can understand sophisticated explanations. The same teacher pointed out that the adult student, therefore, can have the advantage of the augmented alphabet for encoding and decoding words without the danger of the "alphabet confusion" feared by some teachers of children. No evidence was reported about experiments with the use of i.t.a. for adults.

Spelling receives considerable attention in most programs visited. Many teachers have acquired or compiled lists of important or difficult words as a base from which to work. A "Words in Color" modification of the traditional approach to the teaching of spelling was observed. The teachers concerned felt that the appearance of letters and syllables in different colors is an aid to phonetic identification skill and thus ultimately to spelling.

One teacher working with illiterates stated that students who confuse letters and words sometimes learn to write faster when they drill with kinesthetic writing exercises. For example, when students have trouble differentiating the letters "b" and "d," she has them practice them by "writing" them on sandpaper with their fingers. She reports success with this approach on the spelling of words such as *receive*.

Materials

Virtually every teacher reported the great need for materials for adult literacy education. Many teachers use elementary school basal readers because they have not seen any more appropriate materials available. A significant number of teachers, however, told Task Force members that although there are pitifully few materials for adults who are beginning readers, the problem is not as severe as it may seem. They contended that many adults do not mind reading about "Dick and Jane" or "ponies and circuses"; adult illiterates who have decided to attend school simply want to learn to read and write. Some teachers said, in fact, that adults who dropped out when they were in elementary school may *expect* to use traditional elementary school materials and are neither surprised nor disturbed when confronted with them. Other teachers argued that although traditional materials do not motivate adults significantly, they do not block student motivation. Some indicated that new materials would be especially valuable if they treated social studies or other disciplines not usually taught in basic education programs. It should be pointed out that these same teachers were unaware of a great deal of instructional material that is available.

There are, of course, commercial materials available for adult literacy education, but none have the endorsement of all teachers. Books of readings for adult beginners seem to be in both the greatest need and the smallest supply.

Most of the available materials written specifically for adults are at the intermediate and upper reading levels (grades 3–8). At these levels, two types of commercial materials were in use in many basic education programs which had not developed their own materials. One is a series of graded readers containing simplified stories originally written for adults. Teachers use these primarily as supplementary reading materials; some divide the set into materials for class use and those for home reading. In other instances, these books are used as basic texts, since the content appeals to adults more than does that of the traditional elementary school readers.

A second type of commercial material was observed in a number of programs where funds are available for books. These are individualized reading "kits." The kits are used primarily to afford maximum opportunity for practice, as students are able to progress at their individual rates of speed, correcting their work as they go. Most teachers reported that, to insure satisfactory progress of those using kits, they must check individual work sheets regularly.

Although individualized reading kits are intended by their manufacturers to be *supplementary* materials, some Task Force members were surprised to note the number of teachers who seem to regard such kits as a total reading program.

Almost all programs encourge students to read newspapers and magazines as soon as they are able, and in some programs, such materials are read in the classrooms. Teachers reported that the vocabulary requisite for the vocational needs of the students is basically that of the newspaper and popular magazine, and that concentration on reading them is important, especially in terminal courses.

The dearth of commercially produced materials for adult literacy programs has forced a number of programs to develop their own. One program distributes to its teachers a mimeographed bulletin containing hints for teaching adults. Recognizing that most teachers have been trained for work in regular elementary or secondary schools, such programs have undertaken to acquaint their teachers with the special needs and characteristics of adult students. Such bulletins typically contain suggestions for presenting materials, for coping with attendance problems, for setting academic standards, and for effecting satisfactory relationships with students.

Though only a few programs have developed their own text materials, much can be gained from their efforts. One important example of such a program is the adult education department of a large city in which a significant percentage of the population is nonliterate. Each set of the mimeographed materials consists of a reading booklet and a workbook. The content of the materials is based on everyday experience. A sample lesson is included below.

LESSON I [1]

CLERK: Good morning.
MR. BLACK: Good morning. I want a hat.
CLERK: Here is a good hat.
MR. BLACK: How much is the hat?
CLERK: The hat is $15.
MR. BLACK: I want the hat. Here is $15.
CLERK: Thank you. Here is the hat.

* * * * * * *

I want a hat.
You want a hat.
Mrs. Black wants a hat.
Mr. Black wants a hat.
The clerk wants $15.

Accompanying the booklet of such lessons is a workbook of exercises which afford practice with sentence structure and vocabulary.

Another set of materials features a realistic account of two people who have migrated to the city in which the program is located. It contains, in sequential lessons, stories, letters, and dialogues. The workbook consists of writing exercises based on the lessons. These exercises require the student to answer questions about the content and to fill in blanks with appropriate words. The notable feature of the material is that it is based on the community from which the students come. The characters in the stories are typical residents with whom the students can readily identify.

---

[1] Oakland Public Schools, Department of Adult Education, *Lessons in English* A-100, September, 1963.

Another program, not a part of a local school system, has made a somewhat different and perhaps more sophisticated attempt to develop its own materials. Diagnostic tests of the adults in this program revealed that at least 80 percent who had inadequate literacy skills were severely handicapped in auditory or visual discrimination skills.[2] The administrators of the program, therefore, devised a "linguistic alphabetic-phonetic" system which makes use of auditory, visual, and kinesthetic senses. From the simplest operation, that of tracing individual letters with a pencil, to the most complex, new material is introduced according to a carefully regulated progression of difficulty. After the student has begun with *a* and *t*, he learns additional letters, *p, h, l,* and *c*. Next he learns to form, consecutively, the words, *pat, hat, cap, cat,* and so on. Because the procedure and the sequence are explained in detail in the teacher's manual, they will not be described further in this report. The important feature of the material is that it results from an attempt to build from the very beginning a literacy program intended specifically for adults, developed to meet the unique educational problems of adults, and aimed at their particular educational goals. The materials are used in a one-to-one tutorial situation, by a volunteer staff comprised of retired teachers and other interested members of the community. The program trains the volunteers to use the materials and to understand the theories on which the materials are based.

These materials are mentioned not because they are the only notable work that has been done in this area, nor because they represent the last word in materials development; they do, however, provide concrete examples of what can be done.

English as a Second Language

Students who speak a native language other than English present special problems to adult basic education programs. Programs for Latin-American students predominated among those visited by the Task Force. A few, however, have immigrants from Europe and Asia as well. Supplanting many of the problems of motivation that characterize native born semiliterates and illiterates are differences in culture which cause other problems. Teachers reported, for example, that Mexican immigrants typically have difficulty adjusting to such requisite matters as punctuality and regularity of attendance.

Approaches to the teaching of English as a second language to adults were highly varied from program to program. Some teachers reported

---

[2] Charles Drake (ed.), *Read, Write and Spell* (Boston: Massachusetts Council for Public Schools, Inc., 1964).

that they teach it in the same manner as they teach English to native speakers. In other programs, where there are not enough such students to justify a separate class, the non-English speakers are put into the lowest levels of the regular program.

Generally, however, where there is any significant number of non-English speakers, there are special classes, and sometimes special teachers. Task Force members seldom observed that teachers of English as a second language to adults had had special training in this area. These teachers seem especially to lack awareness of modern approaches to language learning. Even though many of these teachers use special text materials for English as a second language, their experience is in regular elementary or secondary teaching and they are feeling their way.

The programs that seemed to be the most successful were those that use a pattern drill approach comparable to that used for the teaching of foreign languages to speakers of English. These successful programs used texts designed for such application. Many of these approaches and materials are based on linguistics such as are described in the recent report, *On Teaching English to Speakers of Other Languages.*[3]

Conclusions

Visits to programs of adult basic education confirmed the need for much work to be done in the development of a body of theory, founded on research, for adult education. It is the exception rather than the rule to find a teacher who is well informed and confident that he knows where he is going. Teachers of adults who have special education for the teaching of adults are almost unheard of. Commercial materials prepared especially for adults are rare, and teachers consider only a few of them adequate.

Appropriate materials and curricula for adult education will be designed after research has provided additional professional knowledge about what is involved in the education of adults. Colleges and universities must bear their share of the needed research and development if this problem is to be solved soon. (The cooperation of adult education programs themselves is needed if efforts at social research are to succeed.)

Extensive work on the educational and social characteristics of undereducated and illiterate adults is necessary. Only after more is known about the sociology and psychology of these members of society can programs be designed which have the greatest possible attraction and

---

[3] Virginia French Allen (ed.), *On Teaching English to Speakers of Other Languages* (Champaign, Ill.: National Council of Teachers of English, 1965).

holding power for adult students. Social scientists and social welfare workers must serve as consultants when programs are designed.

At the upper levels of basic education, teachers must provide some work in composition. Often the concentration is almost entirely on reading, single sentence writing, and spelling. Of course all the problems faced by regular elementary teachers of composition are compounded in the adult basic education situation. Once again, student motivation is the primary consideration. Few adult students will attend classes regularly for which they are asked to "Describe your favorite. . . ," or to do most of the assignments which can be given to elementary students. In fact, in adult education, the possibilities for composition diminish considerably, for the adult student is typically interested only in practical material. Such an emphasis is important, but it should not be the only concern in such programs. More work in oral communication and in writing is needed. As one reviews composition lessons appropriate for use in elementary schools, very little is found that is transferable to the adult student situation.

Those programs which teach any composition at all normally stress letter writing more than any other activity. This has practical applications which are obvious to adult students.

Most of the staffs visited included guidance counselors whose counseling duties usually involved testing and placing students. It is common in adult literacy programs visited for more than half the students enrolled to drop out during the first six months of classes. Many program directors feel that, next to effective teachers, a good counselor is the most important person in an adult program. By regular counseling with all students, many problems of attitude and attendance can be met and solved before they result in dropouts from school. Like teachers, guidance counselors are usually trained in regular elementary or secondary work and have to "play by ear" the situations which are characteristic only of adult students. In a few programs, unfortunately, the counselors seemed more concerned with the tests than with the students.

A reorganization of adult education programs in relation to local school system administration is also necessary. Most programs operated by the local school systems are merely added to the routine work of local administrations. If the problem of adult undereducation is to be attacked effectively, it must receive full attention as a regular part of the public school system. So long as adult programs remain "special" programs for "special" people, problems of recruiting teachers, developing materials, and providing adequate funds are not likely to receive the permanent attention that they require. Furthermore, it may well be that the "specialness" of current programs is one of the greatest obstacles to attendance by undereducated adults. If the programs seemed to be part of the public continuing education and if regular attendance were more routine, the social pressures against trying school again could be lessened.

Teacher Education*

For many an English teacher a classroom of disadvantaged students is a crucible. In it, otherwise insignificant handicaps are starkly revealed. A gap in preparation, a narrow view of man, a limited tolerance for variety in human nature—any of which might pass unnoticed in another setting—not only come to the surface, but virtually guarantee failure. This failure is rooted partly in general education programs that fail to provide a broad view of man, in academic specialization divorced from the demands of the work, in professional training that provides

Institute Participants Examine School Facilities in the Teaching of Reading at Wayne State University, Detroit, Michigan.

---

* The observations in this chapter are based largely on visits to 28 programs which stressed the education of teachers of the disadvantaged. Ten reports from observers were obtained on institutes or programs devoted exclusively to teacher education.

neither the rationale nor the skill needed for teaching disadvantaged children.

What follows is not an indictment of English teachers. Indeed, it grows principally from their own evaluation of themselves and thus provides at least an indirect assessment of their preparation for working with disadvantaged children. It is based in part upon comments and reports of administrators, who, unaware of the demands or lacking other candidates, have enlisted or conscripted for service with disadvantaged youth teachers prepared for other programs. It grows, too, from the insights of those who see better now what is needed and who are directing special programs for teachers of the disadvantaged. But neither the administrators nor the directors have pointed to problems which the teachers, observed and interviewed by Task Force members, have not identified themselves. The weaknesses and the needs which the teachers themselves report provide the best clues for needed changes and additions to inservice programs.

The dominant impression from observations and interviews is a widespread lack of fit between the teacher's preparation—personal, academic, professional—and the demands of teaching disadvantaged children. Fully certified and experienced teachers find themselves frustrated, their expectations disappointed, traditional materials ineffective. Supplementary services in the form of classroom aides and additional equipment, though meant to help, provide little assistance. The teacher is frequently unsure how best to deploy the former or how to use the latter. Meanwhile, increasing concentration of minority poor in urban centers and earnest efforts at desegregation have produced rapid changes in student population that intensify the problem. Furthermore, vast appropriations for urban and rural projects catapult increasing numbers of teachers into programs for the disadvantaged. As the scope of the problem increases, so too does the need for a major effort in teacher education in behalf of teachers in service as well as candidates in training.

The teacher is a product of his own culture, his professional and academic background, his past experience, and the teaching materials he has become accustomed to using. In varying degrees these forces have produced a series of misconceptions which underlie many classroom practices and which seriously impair the effectiveness of any program for disadvantaged youth. There is, for example, a general confusion of "culturally deprived" with "uncultured." Neither general education nor professional education sufficiently changes ethnocentric notions which identify "Culture" with the culture of the dominant prestige group. Consequently, departure from the dominant norms is often taken to mean

168

an absence of culture or an imperfect or corrupted version of the dominant culture. Similarly, the fact that the disadvantaged frequently fail to succeed in the conventional academic program leads to a mistaken assumption of mental incapacity, or "dullness."

If attitudes are a key to solving the problem, if in fact attitudes themselves constitute part of the problem, how do we assess them? More important, how do we make it not only possible but virtually unavoidable for teachers to assess their own attitudes? How can they come to see not only the strengths, but the limits of their own culture?

Although it surely impairs their work, this false view of the nature of the disadvantaged is, of course, not restricted to English teachers. They share with colleagues in other fields a cluster of misconceptions about learning: the belief that "telling" is teaching, for example; that "induction" or "discovery" is a method of learning appropriate only for "normal" or "advantaged" children; that teaching reading is a responsibility for elementary schools; that instruction in mechanics of reading must precede reading for enjoyment, for pleasure, for esthetic growth. And though teachers at all levels recognize a reading problem, they continue to tax students at this most vulnerable point, while failing to take sufficient advantage of new educational media.

In course content and objectives and in classroom practice the misconceptions peculiar to English come into clearest light. For all that has been learned in recent years about the nature of language and how it is learned, teaching still continues to reflect such misconceptions as the belief that to teach language is to teach grammar alone; that there is one prevailing standard English dialect; that there is one dominant nonstandard English; that the difference between the standard and the nonstandard dialect is that the latter has no "grammar"; that one teaches standard English by identifying discrete nonstandard items one by one or anticipating their possible occurrence and by substituting their standard counterparts, rather than working with language patterns. (In some dialects, for example, *ain't* is not a single usage problem; it is the only negative linking verb and the only negative form of the auxiliary that occurs.)

In literature some teachers think it best to avoid or at least postpone indefinitely the introduction of fiction or poetry. They stress the expository or the factual to the exclusion of the imaginative and the esthetic. Few teachers claim any knowledge or training in the literature of minority groups. Virtually no teacher in secondary schools is confident of his ability to teach reading.

Underlying the whole program at its worst is a tendency to dichotomize English into two programs: one for the average and the gifted students, another for the underprivileged or "slow" students. The former is literature, literary appreciation, expository and sometimes creative writing. The second, and from the point of view of professional prestige, the *second class* English consists of the mechanics of reading and such writing mechanics as will enable the student to fill out forms and write letters of application.

Once more it should be stated that this is not an indictment of teachers. Next to the disadvantaged students, the teachers themselves are possibly the most obvious victims of the current educational plight. They charge, and often rightly, that their prior training did nothing to prepare them for their present assignments; that this training "lacked practical applications," "stressed theoretical abstractions and inappropriate subject matter too much," and "generally failed to face up to the problem adequately." When classroom practice of course content is inappropriate or even certain to fail, the comments of teachers in informal conversation or formal interview make clear why they are still carrying on. Some are convinced that what they are doing is right and *should* work, and nothing in their education or experience has made clear that it will not. Others, more pathetically, do what they do simply because they do not know what else to do.

Objectives of Programs

The objectives of the teacher education programs for teachers of the disadvantaged are without exception more emphatically pluralistic than those of programs for English teachers in more conventional curricula. It is currently fashionable to discount methodology, even to blur the important distinction between a methods course in a particular field taught by a specialist in that field and a general, all-purpose, all-subject methods course. Many collegiate institutes and some local inservice programs are a response to widespread reports of inadequate preparation in the subject field itself, rather than in professional courses. No project proposal in any of the programs visited discounted the importance of subject matter preparation. But in no program—whether an NDEA institute or a local inservice project—was this the major single concern. Rather, most project directors were willing generally to assume at least minimum acceptable background in English or elementary language arts. They stressed both the unique aspects of English relevant to disadvantaged programs and related concepts and insights from behavioral and social sciences that successful and unsuccessful programs, in their different ways, show to be essential.

The difference in objectives between conventional programs and those for teachers of disadvantaged children is underscored in *A Manual for the Preparation of Proposals for NDEA Institutes,* published in 1965 by the Office of Education of the U.S. Department of Health, Education, and Welfare for institutes authorized under the National Defense Education Act. Although the Congress clearly intended the institutes generally to concern themselves with "advanced study," this same pluralism is reflected in the guidelines for institutes on teaching disadvantaged youth. Here it is made clear that "Institutes should emphasize the basic understandings, develop the competencies, and study the materials needed for work with young people of diverse cultures. Institutes should include instruction in the psychological and sociological characteristics of disadvantaged and in ways of motivating them to seek further education."

Whether preschool or secondary school, whether preservice or inservice, the objectives of these teacher education programs reflected the same recurring theme:

1. To understand the lives and the learning styles of children in depressed areas.
2. To understand the psychological and sociological roots of prejudice and the problems within and between ethnic groups.
3. To develop a positive attitude toward serving in programs for disadvantaged students.
4. To develop, through study and supervised experience, teaching skills and patterns appropriate for working with disadvantaged children.
5. To develop new curriculum guides and, sometimes, original teaching materials that reflect not only an awareness of the needs and the special disabilities of disadvantaged children, but that also capitalize on their interests and their abilities.

Of the five categories or types of objectives listed above, No. 5 is fairly easy to evaluate. Either the materials were forthcoming, or they were not. Either they worked or they did not. No. 4 is harder, but skilled observation and supervision would do the job. But what of the others? If we are satisfied with No. 4 and No. 5, can we assume that the others have been achieved? If not, and if they are important enough to be objectives, how do we measure success?

However, teachers' attitudes received far more than passing lip service in many of the programs. Some project staffs attempted to assess attitudes as a condition for participation. Others attempted to measure attitudes at the beginning and the end of training programs to determine whether the program was successful in shaping attitudes. Further discussion of this measurement of attitudes appears below under ''Practices and Methods.''

Practices and Methods

School district and other project-related programs provide a variety of opportunities for inservice growth. One index to the range of these opportunities emerges from the following excerpts from but a few reports by Task Force members:

. . . Compulsory time is set aside on Mondays for teacher meetings and inservice training.

. . . Teachers are freed during the day from regular duties to attend the inservice education class . . . in the morning when teachers were fresh rather than exhausted from a hard day's work.

. . . Some inservice training classes are provided. They are recommended, but not compulsory. No credit or salary is given for attendance.

. . . Special summer workshop is organized. Teachers receive a stipend for attending.

. . . A two-week orientation period at the beginning of the year includes detailed treatment of the culture and habits of the Navajo.

. . . Regularly scheduled staff meetings, including all-day meetings early in the program; plus carefully planned workshops; plus interschool visitation; plus encouragement to attend local, state, and national meetings.

. . . Summer workshops involving a team of at least three representatives—e.g., a teacher, counselor, and principal—from each participating school.

In short, most of the projects surveyed and discussed elsewhere in this volume claimed some kind of inservice education. Sometimes they were short term orientation meetings to explain the aims of the project; brief institutes with guest speakers on the needs and characteristics of the population served; periodic meetings with consultants; workshops to discuss problems and prepare materials; training sessions, most frequently with a reading specialist, or sometimes with a demonstration of elementary school teaching methods for secondary teachers. Most involved a single person or small team directing the inservice project and anything from a single consultant to any number of consultants—sometimes as many as fifteen in succession—speaking on particular problems, topics, or issues.

Task Force members also observed a limited number of NDEA institutes for the disadvantaged. Most were distinct from any particular school or community project, although one was coupled with a summer project sponsored by the Office of Economic Opportunity. Here, the participants in the institute were also teachers or supervisors in the summer classes taught under the auspices of OEO. The NDEA program consisted of a two-week introductory program, thrice weekly seminars in conjunction with the summer teaching and a follow-up two-week workshop to prepare new materials.

But regardless of their connection with or disassociation from any of the school or community projects, each of these NDEA programs placed a premium on field work. In the program cited above, the teachers would teach half days for a six-week period. In another, they spent a total of twenty hours teaching or supervising the teaching of their peers in at least two or four cooperating schools. The minimum field work reported in any of these institutes was fifteen hours. That is, unlike the other NDEA programs principally concerned with subject matter fields, the institutes for the teachers of disadvantaged students—regardless of length or recency of the teachers' experience—still expected teachers to relate summer study to concurrent classroom practice.

Measuring attitudes is difficult and the results often questioned. Yet, changes in attitude are essential to improved programs for the disadvantaged. Some project directors have been ingenious and resourceful in finding or devising approaches which place minimum or negligible reliance on the most vulnerable of all approaches, the paper and pencil test. In one project the principal method of measuring attitudes is through a series of role playing situations. First, the candidate is given a passage from Warren Miller's *Cool World* to read, and then in role playing he is to take the role of the Negro adolescent and describe to a friend the school he attends and his teachers. Then he reads a short description of the system of checks and balances in the United States government and "explains" this system to another person playing the role of a Puerto Rican immigrant who finds it hard to understand. Finally, he takes the role of a teacher in a seventh grade classroom, where staff members of the project play the roles of a number of recalcitrant students.

In one of the NDEA institutes the applicants were not selected or rejected for attitudes, but a condition of final acceptance was their taping and submitting a twenty-minute recording of their teaching a morning class for the disadvantaged and similar recording of an afternoon class. These tapes will be analyzed in the light of a seven-point scale, devised by John Withal, to assess social and emotional climate in the classroom. (See

Journal of Experimental Education, 1949; *Journal of Teacher Education*, September 1963.) Without knowing the particular use or analysis made of these tapes, the teacher will again tape two twenty-minute sessions as part of a follow-up planned for fall. Through comparing the analyses, the project staff hopes to learn whether attitudes did change as a result of the institute experience. Another institute relied partly on written responses to certain projective questions, but principally on a taped interview, adapted from preliminary work on attitude measurement done by Melvin Tumin, Princeton University.

The assignment was, "Write a paragraph on *"Why Young People Rebel."* The seventh grader wrote:

> I get rebeled when teachers say you doing the wrong think and you are not that happened today (English) so when it happens to me I do nothing the rest of the periout to make up for things they say I didn't do.
>
> Most periot English
> and Social Studies
> Yours truly x x x

Is it a spelling lesson he needs most? Or instruction on sentence structure and punctuation? Or is it something else?

As one would expect, a principal difference between the summer programs sponsored under NDEA and ongoing inservice programs in schools is the added weight which the former place on the substantive content of English. Especially in institutes for secondary teachers, one comes to expect to find formal courses or course components devoted to the subject matter of English, to literature, to language, to oral and written expression. But as often as not, such courses are taught by persons with a dual competence in English and in education, and with experience in schools. Not uncommon is a separate course in urban sociology or cultural anthropology. Moreover, visiting consultants are typically chosen not so much for their specialized work in English, but for their strength in one of the behavioral or social sciences whose findings have special relevance for programs for disadvantaged students.

Observations and Impressions

Despite frustrations and setbacks in classrooms, in their pursuit of preservice or inservice education, teachers of disadvantaged students are almost universally characterized by the Task Force observers as "dedi-

Demonstration Teaching at Hofstra University, Hempstead, New York

cated, hard working, and very much concerned about the problems of the disadvantaged and the discovery of practical solutions. . . ." At times the mood is one of grim determination rather than high enthusiasm, but the point of view and the vision are the same: the goal is achieveable. Although the mood of participation was reported on more favorably in projects that provided released time and ideal conditions, at least as significant were the reports of consistently high attendance and participation in other programs: late afternoon programs, Saturday programs, programs without stipends or credit, but programs regularly attended by large numbers of teachers who were not required to take part.

The use of consultants drew particular comments. Whether intensive or spread out over long periods, programs which relied principally on a succession of consultants who rarely knew or met each other, and who worked for an hour or a day and then left with no chance for follow-up, were never as effective as those which engaged consultants for a longer period of time and provided for frequent contact between participants and consultants in a variety of settings. Clearly the rarest pattern, though possibly one of the most valuable, was the concurrent engagement of two

175

or more consultants from different disciplines who might, through their exchanges, make important connections that would otherwise be left to chance.

The teacher's praise for demonstration teaching and for interschool visitation suggests that such activities are far more valuable than relatively infrequent scheduling would suggest.

The concern for providing teachers with additional training in the uses of audiovisual equipment and the preparation of materials for use with this equipment was almost universal. That this concern is well placed is apparent in the limited uses of such equipment described in other sections of this volume. Of particular concern in some programs were the preparation of oral language drills and the use of recording equipment, including in at least two centers the use of language laboratories. Apart from recording equipment useful in teaching standard English dialects, the most frequent efforts were with using simpler—and perhaps less intimidating equipment—such as overhead projectors. Each of the NDEA institutes visited has as one of its general requirements the demonstration of ability to use a variety of equipment and the preparation of sample materials, including oral English pattern drills.

The most unsettling report came from one of the NDEA Institute directors reporting on a regional conference of those directing NDEA institutes for the teachers of the disadvantaged. The conference was held at about midcourse during the first summer institutes. It was no surprise that participants felt overworked. But what was crucial was their impatience for *the answer,* for a kit of whatever size and contents that would enable them with certainty to teach language, say, or reading to the disadvantaged children.

> Born partly of a desire to help the disadvantaged, partly of frustration, is a clear sense of urgent need for "the answer." How do we help teachers live for a time without the answer? And by what criteria should they judge curriculum kits and packaged programs which, over the next few years, will presume to provide "the answer"?

Conclusions

As the detailed descriptions of programs from preschool through adult make clear, the principal issue in teaching the disadvantaged is *language,* as it is broadly conceived in the opening sections of this volume. Successful programs are based on sound principles of language and of language teaching. Programs that fail are most often rooted in a microscopic or an obsolete view of language.

The NCTE Task Force recommends that the teacher of disadvantaged students be knowledgeable about the structure of language, particularly of the English language, and about language learning.

"Language" here refers not only its sounds, word formation, and syntax, but also its social, geographical, and historical manifestations. Of particular but not sole importance is the emerging work in social dialectology. Field workers in linguistics are at work preparing scientific, accurate descriptions of nonstandard dialects, descriptions which can provide considerable help to teachers of the disadvantaged. First and most dramatic is the problem of the teachers in one project who reported that initially it took them "six weeks or more before they could understand what the Negro children were saying." Of more enduring importance, however, are the implications that these studies will have for step-by-step instruction in standard informal English based not on the "internal logic of grammar," but on contrastive features between dialects. Teachers in projects for the disadvantaged need access both to published material in dialect study and to the field workers themselves who are advancing these studies.

The teacher should understand that there are many social and regional dialects of English and that children must develop a repertoire of dialects for appropriate situations. He needs, moreover, special instruction in the processes of language development in the psychology of language learning.

Related to linguistic differences among social and ethnic groups are important cultural differences and cultural drifts. The teacher of the disadvantaged has to understand and to appreciate the different backgrounds in customs, language, and attitudes which children from these backgrounds manifest. In particular, he must be informed about the particular subculture with which he deals, whether its salient and differentiating characteristics stem from special community or ethnic viewpoints or from differences in subcultural dialects.

The NCTE Task Force recommends that the teacher of the disadvantaged include in his preparation work in such fields as cultural anthropology and urban sociology.

In some NDEA institutes and other college-related programs, this problem has been attacked through formal course requirements, through collateral reading assignments, and through judicious scheduling of visiting speakers. In the best of the inservice programs, it is met by engaging one or more continuing consultants to work with the staff in designing the program and, importantly, in the continuing evaluation and revision of the program.

The issue here is not one of particular courses or departments. Rather, it is one of background understanding and of operational concepts. The background will forestall the "cultural shock" that often blocks communication between students and teacher and renders efforts at teaching futile. The operational concepts will not only help teachers to choose material and teaching styles appropriate to the students, but will enable teachers and project directors to study their students objectively before designing a program for them and to evaluate the program as it goes on.

In programs for the disadvantaged, reading and literature stand in a peculiar relationship. In middle or upper class settings, the ablest student soon becomes an independent reader and can explore literature without concurrent instruction in reading. By high school the average student from a middle class home normally has similar abilities. Although one never "masters" reading, these students are able to achieve a level of performance that gives them access to literature without additional instruction in reading. But one of the more common characteristics

Use of the Overhead Projector to Teach Lesson Planning at a Summer Institute at Wayne State University, Detroit, Michigan

of the disadvantaged student is his severe retardation in reading. To teach him reading without providing experiences in literature is to deny at least half the *raison d'être* for reading. To assign him literature without instruction in reading is to condemn him to frustration and failure.

The NCTE Task Force recommends that preparatory and inservice programs for teachers of the disadvantaged at ANY level include both work in the teaching of reading and in literature appropriate for the students.

This problem is not confined to teachers of the disadvantaged. One national survey reported in 1964 that fully 90 percent of secondary teachers of English felt inadequately trained to teach reading. Asked to rank their interest in a variety of courses, elementary teachers in the same survey ranked *reading* first and *children's literature* second. But if the problem is not confined to programs for disadvantaged, it is certainly heightened there. The argument about whether or not reading instruction is principally a responsibility of the elementary schools is a fruitless one here. The problem exists at all levels. And unless the professional is going to write off tens of thousands of adolescents and adults, it is going to attack this problem in secondary schools and adult programs as well as the elementary school.

The program in reading and literature for teachers of the disadvantaged will include a number of related components. To be sure, it will deal with such reading activities as "word attack skills" and "finding key ideas." But it will also direct attention to literary works and selections, rarely found in traditional anthologies, that promise most to capture the interests of the disadvantaged. Special provision must be made for uses of films and filmstrips, recordings, and still pictures which can provide intellectual or esthetic reinforcement necessary for the child from a background that has not encouraged his reading. Finally, it will pay particular attention to the literature of minority groups. Few programs will build their entire literature curriculum on literature from a particular minority group. Indeed few English teachers have read extensively enough in these areas to make intelligent selections for an entire program. Moreover, the diversity that America treasures is quite different from the cultural barriers and exaggerated differences which threaten to split it. But both out of respect for their students and for a literature program that reflects cultural diversity, teachers will be widely read in literature from many cultural groups and will reflect this reading in the literature programs they plan for their students.

Characteristics of disadvantaged homes—absence of books, of reading adults, of rewards and incentives for reading—make clear that motivation for reading and reinforcement of the written symbol are at least as important as "efficiency." Even though teachers may see the value in reducing the number of eye-fixations per line and in finding the key idea in a paragraph about Brazilian exports, the students often will not. Perhaps part of the clue is in this report from one teacher in the BRIDGE Project:

> . . . Since motivation is really the key to learning in our situation, I find biographical material highly useful. The way we treated John Brown and the raid at Harper's Ferry can be used as a case in point. We used a section of the poem by Stephen Vincent Benét, pictures, part of a filmstrip, a dramatization, and text material for homework, as well as the song sung by Paul Robeson to enrich the basic material. . .[1]

Regarding programs for teachers in service, whether conducted by schools or project centers or universities, the NCTE Task Force members make no single general recommendation. They recognize, rather, the complexity of the task and the variety of settings in which it is carried out.

The Task Force makes the following specific recommendations:

1. **That time for inservice activities not be added to a full teaching schedule.** The inservice program may be offered in either a separate summer program or during a released period in the school day.

2. **That the approach be interdisciplinary.** The problem is not just one of the content of English. If teachers regard themselves as surrogates of the dominant culture, or if the students so regard them, the problem is sociological and anthropological. To the extent that a second dialect needs to be taught, the problem lies partly in the psychology of verbal learning. If evaluation is going to mean anything, the problem lies partly in the behavioral sciences and in statistics. No approach that relies on less than a team of several instructors or consultants from these fields can hope for much.

3. **That contact with consultants extend over a period of time and in a variety of settings.** Projects which use consultants as after dinner speakers waste their great potential. Consultants should visit classes and discuss with teachers the application of principle to practice. The consultants who help initially to design the program should take part in the evaluation and in the analysis of the results.

---

[1] Helen Storen and Robert Edgar (compilers), *Learning to Teach in Difficult Schools* (Flushing, N. Y.: Queens College Department of Education, n.d.).

4. **That inservice programs provide for a variety of activities rather than relying on one approach.** Workshops alone sometimes have cathartic value and may even provide opportunities for disseminating information about devices, lessons, and the like. Lectures alone may instruct and entertain, but without opportunity for dialogue, practical applications are unlikely to follow. For certain matters, the teaching of reading, for example, nothing is as valuable as demonstrations by a skillful teacher working with a class of ''typical'' students.

So far this discussion has been concerned with teachers who are working with the disadvantaged or preparing to do so. Another issue still remains—the implications for the academic and professional education of other teachers of English. Not everyone will teach disadvantaged students. And to a considerable measure, teaching disadvantaged students requires special training over and above that education which all teachers should share. But if the approach is entirely that of preparing specialists for these programs, will the gulf between professional levels widen? The Task Force members did not unanimously recommend that all teachers of English take work in urban sociology, in teaching standard English as a second dialect, in the literature and the history of American minority groups. They do recommend, however, that preparatory and inservice programs educate those not teaching the disadvantaged to understand the problems *and* the satisfactions of those who do.

For all the unanswered questions and debated issues, one overriding trend is still clear. Uncertainty may leave people uncomfortable, but in one sense it reassures. Worse than living without the answer is selling out too soon to a wrong answer. There are new academic courses, new field activities in classrooms and after school centers. At least some of the experiments are subjected to close and thorough evaluation. Through it all comes the justifiable hope, if not the clear vision, of both theoretical frameworks and practical experiences to effect a profound change in the attitudes and the skill that teachers bring to the task of educating the disadvantaged.

Program Administration*

Strong, bold, and imaginative leadership is of prime importance in administering programs for the disadvantaged. Successful attack on the myriad of problems—social, cultural, and educational—in such programs requires a high degree of administrative skill. Nevertheless, certain practices were reported to Task Force observers which diminish the possibility of competent leadership. Too often weak and unsuccessful

Crowded Classroom in a Large City: School Districts Struggle to Avoid Such Situations

---

* The comments in this chapter on project administration are based on observations of 115 separate administrations. Observers reported concentrating on project administration in 14 separate reports.

administrators are "sent down" to schools in disadvantaged areas, and new school administrators and teachers "first serve their time" in such areas before they can transfer to advantaged schools. Several cities require all new administrators and teachers to work a two-year minimum term in inner city schools. Those administrators successful in this area are often promoted, leaving vacancies difficult to fill.

There is, however, a discernible and encouraging trend in the opposite direction, although the right answers often emerge for the wrong reasons. Just as the programs and overall attention for the exceptional child drew great attention in educational circles in the late 1950's and into the early 1960's, so now are the programs for the disadvantaged. As one administrator noted, the disadvantaged are presently an "In" group in education, a group for whom vast federal funds are becoming increasingly available. In 1965-66 an administrator in an urban area may be able to achieve a professional reputation faster by developing successful programs for the disadvantaged than he can for programs for the gifted. So the pendulum swings.

The pendulum of educational concern *can* move rapidly. Many large city school superintendents are under fire because of problems concerning the disadvantaged and, more specifically, the Negro student. In the past, public pressure for good school programs has come for schools serving the advantaged student. One result of such pressure was the assigning of weak school personnel to disadvantaged areas. Now, the struggle for equal rights for minority groups includes a call for equal educational opportunities. This call will increase in intensity where opportunities are still unequal. An urban superintendent will now seriously reconsider sending his weakest administrators into disadvantaged areas, for his own position may be in jeopardy if he is unable to solve the major problems of the disadvantaged student, especially those of certain minority groups. In this respect, at least, the administration of programs for the disadvantaged looks promising.

Implementation of Programs

Many observers noted the disparity between curriculum guides describing programs for the disadvantaged—often well publicized—and then enactment of these programs in the classroom. Such programs presented lofty objectives and goals, an elaborate administrative structure, and a well-designed program. The programs *were* outstanding— on paper. What was missing was an effective method of putting them into action.

As might be expected, the disparity between the program described and its enactment increased in proportion to the distance between the administrator and the teacher. Administrators who work regularly with teachers, frequently visit classes, and know the students could usually discuss their programs realistically with Task Force observers. Administrators unfamiliar with the teachers and students usually could not. This disparity was not common to all programs. But the administrators who impressed observers with their knowledge of the program, the teachers, and, most important, the students were in the minority. The disparity between the design of a program and its practice was one of the major administrative problems observed.

Importance of Evaluation

To keep administrative reports accurate and reliable, school boards and superintendents should require both external and internal evaluation of their programs. They should ask subject matter specialists and specialists in the education of the disadvantaged to interview district and local school administrators and teachers, visit classrooms, and test students. Too often only the administrators of the program test the progress of students; outside testing can support or interpret the conclusions. Because Task Force members found classroom observation indispensable in evaluation of programs, they recommend that both administrators and consultants always include classroom observation as one basis for evaluation.

Qualifications Needed by Program Administrators

Observers noted that outstanding directors of the programs observed had two predominant qualities: imagination and a willingness to try new approaches. Change and experimentation, however, must be based on professional knowledge about the disadvantaged and on the research that is becoming available in this field. When Task Force members found unsuccessful language programs, one reason for the inadequacy was usually the administrator's lack of awareness of the subject. Few administrators interviewed had even a rudimentary knowledge of such vital areas in language development, dialectology, and linguistics. It is one thing to study, test, and analyze, and, on the basis of one's knowledge in a specific school situation, reject the use of foreign language labs in teaching standard English usage; it is quite another thing never to have heard or thought about such a possibility.

184

Administrative Structure

The Task Force noticed no dominant pattern in the administrative structuring of programs for the disadvantaged. As would be expected, line and staff relationship varied from district to district. Typically, program directors operated at a level below that of an assistant superintendent. When funds for a program came from outside the school district, lines of staff relationships became more tenuous, and cooperation between program directors and district administrators was uneven.

A large eastern city has an interesting administrative structure; it has established a "Model School District" as a district within a district. Programs in this district are developed from within and are adopted without usual clearance by departmental and curriculum offices. The assistant superintendent in the Model School District is answerable only to the superintendent and the school board. Though such an arrangement may create ill feeling among department chairmen and curriculum coordinators who are bypassed, it has a potential for putting programs into operation quickly.

Administrative Staff Responsibilities

Superintendent. School superintendents and assistant superintendents are ultimately responsible for the initiation of school programs and curriculum development. But because the shortness of time forced Task Force observers to emphasize interviews with program directors and their staff, they interviewed only a few superintendents. This report will therefore discuss other administrators instead.

Program Director. When a project becomes part of the established school or district program, the project director generally becomes the program director. It was clear to observers that one person needs to coordinate and oversee the program activities, with the help of assistants in large districts. One observer made the suggestion that a continuing policy of training assistants to take over when necessary insures continuity in the program.

In several programs visited, the staff relationship between the program director or coordinator and higher level district administrators seemed confused, a situation particularly unfortunate when it interfered with staff members' obtaining materials and facilities needed for working with the disadvantaged.

Principals. Numerous comments by program directors indicated that a supportive principal was the key to whatever success they enjoyed. Without a strong, competent, cooperative principal, particularly at the elementary level, programs were doomed from the start. Task

Force observations reinforced these comments. The best programs revealed a strong commitment by both director and principal to the goals of the program.

Consultants and Specialists. A program that covers a wide geographical area or includes a number of different classrooms or schools generally has one or more consultants. The Task Force noticed that a consultant, usually a specialist in a subject area, has one or more of the following duties: (1) to be a liaison between the administration and the program teachers and assistants, (2) to consult with teachers both within and without his area of specialization (for example, in several programs visited, one of the duties of the reading consultant is to help the social studies teachers to understand reading instruction so that, although social studies material is being read, the teacher can work to improve reading as well), (3) to evaluate the program.

Task Force observers noted that effective consultants worked well with teachers and other school personnel, advised without offending, and helped without inhibiting; communicated accurately and effectively on both professional and personal matters; could distinguish between causes and symptoms of a problem; knew their areas of specialization and professional literature. Certainly language arts or English consultants should be well versed on research and programs in language learning. Unfortunately, such consultants seem to be in the minority, according to Task Force members.

Outside Consultants. Too frequently, outside consultants brought in to guide the initial stages of a project were not given the chance to visit classes and teachers after the project was underway. As a result, they were more often inspirational than effective. Having outside consultants follow up with continuing help to administrators and teachers can translate ideas for programs and techniques into actual practice without undue frustration.

Classroom Teacher. The classroom teacher is the most important person in the program; no program, no matter how well conceived, will succeed with weak or mediocre teachers. Yet the classroom teacher is too often considered the least important person—in salary, prestige, status, and influence. Programs are initiated and curricula established without including a large representation of teachers in all stages of development. A program so conceived can and will be impressive only in its "paper" form unless teachers are thoroughly involved in its planning.

Noncertified Classroom Personnel. For forty years the American elementary classroom has been self-contained: one teacher teaching one

186

class of students at a time. Now school districts are using lay readers, tutorial programs, and teacher aides to assist the teacher. Is such help an infringement upon the professional status of teachers, or does it free teachers from routine clerical duties? Should noncertified personnel be used in such nonteaching jobs as taking care of the milk money, classifying books in the library, and relieving teachers of playground duties at lunch time, or should they actually teach children? For example, some of the most impressive teaching seen by Task Force observers was done by high school students working with elementary pupils. Chapters on the grade level sections include further discussion of the use of noncredentialed personnel. The administrators and teachers of each district will have to decide how best to use these classroom assistants.

The Administration, the Program, and Public Relations

The best kind of public relations results from a successful program, but the community needs to hear about it. Community support can help to obtain funds and enlist student participation in the program. The local, as well as national, press has assisted teacher recruitment.

Project visits reveal numerous methods of maintaining public relations. The following list indicates the wide range of methods used:

1. Several projects coordinate their activities with those of other community agencies, such as the Urban League, NAACP, and social welfare agencies.

2. In one preschool education project, attendance by parents at a weekly meeting is mandatory. These meetings are held to (1) inform the parents about what the program is attempting to do for their children, (2) educate the parents in hygiene, child care, employment, community activities, (3) encourage parents to assist in certain phases of program planning and to take an active role in children's field trips, children's parties, and the building and making of teaching materials.

3. Projects frequently ask parents to approve participation in programs for their children. Although the real reason for many parent approval slips for field trips is a legal one, such requests also alert parents to what is being done in the school program. However, one observer noted in reading over comments by parents at the end of the school year that many parents felt trips to the zoo, airport, and fire station were merely for "fun" and did not serve any real educational purpose. Directors need to explain to parents why and how such trips are educational.

4. Teachers' visits to the children's homes can be used to gain support from parents. Some programs insist that teachers make at least one visit to the home, preferably at the beginning of the school year. Teachers, of course, especially if unfamiliar with the social patterns of the school's neighborhood, need some prior preparation for those visits.

5. Some project directors send informal progress bulletins to parents and other interested people.

6. School-community representatives and parent aides help to build good public relations.

7. Articles in newspapers and professional journals spread the word of promising programs.

8. One school district operates a Community and Parent Reception Room. A team of two teachers, a school community agent, a counselor, a child welfare agent, a corrective physical education teacher, and a doctor give attention to in-migrant parents and their children.

9. One large urban district has a weekly radio program featuring stories of Negroes who have become successful. One teacher was assigned as an administrative assistant to write and produce the program. A committee of teachers and principals helped the teacher.

10. In several programs visited, an informal speaker's bureau is established. Through this bureau, members of the program staff and faculty are available as speakers to community organizations. Often certain audiovisual materials are developed to promote the program and assist the speakers.

Communication within Program

Lack of communication between administrators on various levels and the classroom teacher often accounts for discrepancies between descriptions of programs and programs actually in practice. Task Force members did, however, observe the following solutions to the problems of communication within the organizational structures of programs.

1. The consultant regularly holds a meeting of all teachers for the dual purpose of inservice education and interfaculty and administration communication.

2. The administration issues a mimeographed pamphlet for regular classroom teachers. The pamphlets contain information and suggestions about teaching, materials, and receiving new students.

3. Faculty workshops are held to develop materials, to discuss new organizational procedures and developments, and to set up curricula.

4. Administrators collect and distribute materials developed within the project as well as those obtained from outside sources.

5. The administration distributes to all teachers a "Program Evaluation Form" on which teachers may record their suggestions and criticisms of the program. This information is used by the administration when they plan the following year's program.

6. Frequent inservice training programs are conducted.

7. The program provides for interdistrict teacher visits which allow one teacher in a program to see how the program is handled in other classrooms. Although many school districts provide for such visits, more teachers need to be encouraged to make them.

8. A local university holds inservice classes on Saturdays for interested teachers and administrators.

Night Classes in Oakland, California

Conclusions

The **NCTE Task Force** recommends that school districts evaluate their hiring procedures to insure that the least experienced or least effective administrators and teachers do not serve as the bulk of personnel assigned to schools serving disadvantaged students. Successful educational programs in disadvantaged areas cannot be established with well-meaning but ill-prepared personnel. Although some educators have suggested that the worst educational areas should secure the best teachers and administrators, such a policy would result in imbalance in another direction. All schools need a balance of personnel, with teachers assigned according to training, experience, and temperament.

The Task Force recommends that principals and program directors have extensive preservice and inservice training in teaching the basic skills to disadvantaged children. Such training should include some study in oral language, language development, reading, and composition. It is particularly important that school principals be carefully chosen and oriented to the problems of the area they serve. The success of educational programs depends significantly on their interest and leadership. Unless the principals and directors are knowledgeable in these specialized areas, they will be unable to lead the development of language programs. Obviously not all principals can have extensive training in English, but all need greater awareness of modern concepts than many presently possess. Where a subject supervisor in English is assigned to a special project, the principal can, of course, rely on expert advice in day-to-day decisions.

District administrators should do everything possible to cut administrative red tape that prevents teachers from receiving the books and materials they need. Too often teachers must wait a year or more for inexpensive materials that might help a specific classroom situation. School budgets should make provisions for the specialized needs of a project such as consultant help, outside evaluation, and special material. Perhaps a larger provision for a petty cash fund or other monies that are instantly available within the school building can help teachers and principals capitalize on immediate interest in new ideas and materials.

The Task Force recommends occasional evaluation of programs for the disadvantaged by qualified consultants chosen from outside the school district. Evaluations by these consultants should include classroom visits and interviews with teachers. The necessary enthusiasm that an administrator must have for his program makes it difficult for him to be objective about the program he directs.

Most of the Task Force observers are either working with or have worked with disadvantaged students. They have visited some of the most deprived areas in the country. As a result, they are much aware of the problems facing school and project administrators working in areas serving disadvantaged students. They realize that the problems are bigger than the school; schools are too often asked to solve the major weaknesses of society. Nevertheless, problems must be resolved. In order to find solutions, administrators of programs to educate disadvantaged students must be willing to experiment with new approaches to education, many of which may call for radically different patterns of operation than those characteristic of conventional schools.

Part III

COMMENTARY ON THE TASK FORCE FINDINGS

Academic Instruction and Preschool Children
CARL BEREITER

Group Identity and Educating the Disadvantaged
SOL TAX

Dialects, Education, and the Contribution of Linguistics
JANET SAWYER

A Sustained Program of Language Learning
WALTER LOBAN

The French Lick Conference participants found especially valuable the knowledge and insights of the consultants who observed and participated throughout the sessions. After considering the recommendations and observations of the Task Force with reference to specific programs and visits, each consultant was asked to summarize his impressions, his observations regarding the reports, and his specific concerns. The comments of the consultants were taped and are reproduced here in the order in which they were presented. Because their views reflect varying approaches to language learning for the disadvantaged, groups designing projects may find them particularly helpful. Also included are the reactions of participants to each of the statements.

Academic Instruction and Preschool Children

CARL BEREITER

It is a truism of academic life that a scholar will magnify the importance of whatever he devotes his life to studying. It is not surprising, then, that a person studying the feet comes to believe that the feet are the most important part of the body. I therefore find it somewhat incongruous to be telling a group of people whose primary interest is in language that they do not seem to appreciate its full importance, but this is the distinct impression I have received both from the reports delivered and from the conversation at this meeting. There seem to be two reasons for this unusual state of affairs. One is a basic lack of realization of the gravity of the whole problem of cultural disadvantage, and the other is a somewhat limited conception of the language problems of disadvantaged children.

We have heard it said at this conference that disadvantaged children are not culturally deprived, but only culturally different, and that there are intelligent and capable children in every disadvantaged group.

Volunteer Classroom Aide Reads to Children in a Baltimore Preschool

Charitable as these comments may be, they nevertheless serve to divert our attention from the fundamental problems. Let me summarize for you several facts which in my opinion no responsible educator, whatever his particular interest may be in disadvantaged children, can in good conscience ignore:

1) By the time they are five years old, disadvantaged children of almost every kind are typically one to two years retarded in language development. This is supported by virtually any index of language development one cares to look at.

2) Half a century of studies on the prediction of school success clearly establishes that verbal abilities are the best single predictors of achievement in a wide variety of school subjects. Thus the child who

196

enters school markedly behind in the development of verbal abilities enters with a severe handicap.

3) School failure is the expected rather than the occasional fate of disadvantaged children. From the evidence I have seen, half the children in the many low income area schools repeat one or more grades during elementary school, though this fact is sometimes hidden behind administrative labels for special classes. This proportion of failure does not include the children designated as mentally retarded and assigned to special classes. Lower class areas produce at least twice the average number of children labeled mentally retarded as middle and upper class areas. We are all familar with the high dropout rate among lower class children and with the fact that most of these children are hopelessly behind in school when they drop out. What is less commonly known is the miserable level of attainment that characterizes even those disadvantaged children who remain in school. I do not have solid data on this point, but the estimate given me by people who have studied the matter closely is that in the most disadvantaged segments of our society, such as the southern Negroes, the average terminal level of achievement reached by high school graduates is around seventh grade. The fact that an occasional disadvantaged child goes on to achieve high academic excellence should not blind us to the fact that all the odds are against it. Recent statistics on high school seniors reaching the final round of the National Merit Scholarship screening process indicate that a child from a prosperous family has from four to thirty times the chance that a child from a poor family does, depending on the state. This is one among many possible indexes of the extent to which disadvantaged children, if not deprived of the culture content necessary to the formal educational process, are at least deprived of the opportunities which educational attainment can provide in this country.

4) If a child who starts out behind is to catch up, he has to progress at a faster than normal rate. This is not an empirical fact but a logical one. It follows, therefore, that any educational program that claims to be helping children overcome their environmental handicaps must be able to show not just a normal rate of progress but a superior rate. I have the impression from the reports of Task Force members that little attention was given to rate of progress at all, and that in many cases a program that looked good in other respects may have been producing progress at a slower rate than is normal for children of the age involved.

5) It is too much to expect that programs can be accelerated above the normal level in all areas of development at once. If this is true, it follows that educational programs for disadvantaged children must be

selective in their goals, striving for maximum progress in those things that are judged to be most crucial for later success in school. It is therefore necessary, in evaluating an educational program, to look not only at the rate of progress but at its content and to ask whether five minutes devoted to one kind of learning might not better have been devoted to some other kind.

If these facts are taken to heart, they give the whole problem of education for disadvantaged children a tremendous urgency. One is forced to recognize that time is against the disadvantaged child, and one becomes impatient with any teacher who wastes that precious time. The disadvantaged four-year-old, happily shoveling sand at a sand table, gives the impression that he will be four years old forever. But for the teacher to act as if this were true is disastrous. She should be constantly aware that the first grade is hurtling toward that child like an express train, and that the child's fate may well depend on what she as a teacher is able to do and how quickly.

The Task Force members have reported observing enthusiasm, optimism, and dedication among the teachers of disadvantaged children, but none of this sense of urgency. I must report that I find it lacking in this group as well. One reason, in addition to a natural tendency to look on the bright side, may be that you have selected as your major concern the problem of teaching a standard English dialect to children whose native dialect is of some other sort. Though this is one of the problems of disadvantaged children that deserves attention, it is atypical in that no great urgency attends it. Some time during his schooling the child should master the standard English dialect, but it does not much matter when, and thus nothing is wrong with a gradual, drawn-out approach to teaching it. This is not true of the more fundamental language skills because these are instrumental to the whole process of education. Reading provides the clearest example of this point. If reading were only of value once the child gets out into the world, it would not matter if he did not learn to read until his last year of school. But because reading is instrumental to school learning, because progress in most other academic areas is held down to the rate at which children progress in reading, it is important that the child learn to read as early as possible in his school career. The child who falls behind in reading is held back in all other areas.

In the same way, oral language may be conceived of as an instrument of learning and thinking, and it is from this point of view that the problem of retarded language development in disadvantaged children becomes an urgent one, requiring the quickest and most powerful remedies.

The paper that I have been circulating by Siegfried Engelmann is an attempt to identify those specific weaknesses in the language of pre-school disadvantaged children that seem on logical grounds to be crucial from the point of view of academic learning.[1] On the basis of this kind of analysis we have constructed a preschool program that tries, through direct and intensive teaching, to remedy these lacks. We have not been very much concerned with many of those aspects of language which serve mainly social or expressive purposes—standard vocabulary, idiomatic expressions, intonation, niceties of agreement and the like. It has not bothered us so much that a child may not know the word *sheep* as that he does not know the word *not,* for while in the former case a child might encounter an occasional difficulty, in the latter case he is deprived of one of the most powerful logical tools our language provides—a tool, moreover, which it is assumed in school work that a child possesses from the very beginning. In our program, we have been less concerned with the child's lack of empirical knowledge than with his lack of ability to derive knowledge from statements. It seems to us far less serious that a child might not know that milk comes from cows than that he might not be able to tell you where milk came from after he had been told.

The children we have worked with have for the most part been four-year-old Negro children from the most disadvantaged stratum of the lowest income urban Negro group in the state of Illinois. I can perhaps accomplish two things at once by listing for you some of the specific performance goals of the language program we employed. This list will serve first of all to indicate the nature and severity of these children's language handicaps, for I can state that not one child of the fifteen we worked with was able initially to meet a single one of these criteria. The list will also serve as one indication of the effectiveness of the program, for after eight months of instruction, all but one of the children were able to meet all of the criteria, the one exception being a definitely retarded child who has not come close to any of the goals. The goals are as follows:

1) Ability to use both affirmative and ''not'' statements in reply to the question, ''What is this?'': ''This is a ball. This is not a book.''

2) Ability to handle polar opposites (''If it is not _____, it must be _____.'') for at least four concept pairs: e.g., big-little, up-down, long-short, fat-skinny.

---

[1] S. E. Engelmann, *Cultural Deprivation—Description and Remedy* (Urbana, Ill.: University of Illinois Institute for Research on Exceptional Children). Mimeographed.

3) Ability to use the following prepositions correctly in statements describing arrangements of objects: *on, in, under, over, between.* Example: "Where is the pencil?" "The pencil is under the book."

4) Ability to name positive and negative instances for at least four classes, such as tools, weapons, pieces of furniture, wild animals, farm animals, and vehicles. Example: "Tell me something that is a weapon." "A gun is a weapon." "Tell me something that is not a weapon." "A cow is not a weapon."

5) Ability to perform simple "if-then" deductions. Example: The child is presented a diagram containing big squares and little squares. All the big squares are red, but the little squares are of various other colors. "If the square is big, what do you know about it?" "It's red." (This use of *if* should not be confused with the antecedent-consequent use that appears in such expressions as, "If you do that again, I'm going to hit you," and which the child may already be able to understand.)

6) Ability to use "not" in deductions: "If the square is little, what else can you say about it?" "It is not red."

7) Ability to use *or* in simple deductions: "If the square is little, then it is not red. What else can you say about it?" "It's blue or yellow."

Using Oral Language in a Los Angeles Preschool

This list, of course, is not exhaustive. Many of the childen have gone far beyond these goals. But they have proved to be focal points of difficulty and progress in many different kinds of learning of these basic tools. Although I cannot elaborate on the matter here, it should not be difficult to see how important these language operations are for understanding concepts of all kinds and for logical thinking and problem solving. If it seems premature to worry about logic at the preschool level, one has only to consider that middle class children are typically able to handle all of these operations at this age and that a great deal of what they learn from their parents and teachers and even from each other is made possible because of this. Disadvantaged children would learn them in time also, but the longer it is delayed the more retarded would be their whole conceptual development.

In teaching these logical statement patterns we have placed strong emphasis on learning to produce them and not merely respond to them. We have made continual use of pattern drills not unlike those used in the teaching of foreign languages to college students. Initially the children could not even repeat statements of the kind illustrated, let alone produce ones appropriate to the situation. But the drills have been used to teach new language operations rather than to replace old patterns, and thus we have avoided the conflicts that arise when children have already learned to express the same thoughts in nonstandard ways. This has also made motivation easier, because the children are not merely learning a way of expressing themselves that is more acceptable to the teacher but are acquiring tools that enable them to do things intel- lectually that they had not been able to do before.

In keeping with the principle enunciated previously, we have been highly selective as to what went into the program in order to produce maximum learning in the areas chosen as most important. A great many of what we would acknowledge to be desirable preschool experiences have been minimized or left out altogether—such things as arts and crafts, group play, dramatic play, block play, and so on. Singing has been included, but with songs specially composed to supplement the instructional program. What has knowingly been left out has been left out for one or both of two reasons: because it seemed less important than what took its place or because it seemed that out-of-class experience adequately made up for the lack. (Unlike some of our more relativistic colleagues we do not regard the disadvantaged child's home environment as a void.) We cannot claim infallibility, however, and so we always welcome observations on the important things that have been left out of our program. What we do insist, however, is that some things must be left out if an above-average rate of progress is to be maintained. Thus, any suggested addition must be justified as worthy of replacing something already in the program—unless, as is sometimes possible, additions can be made without additional use of time.

It may seem to you that the approach we are taking to language places it within the realm of logic or psychology and outside the range of interests of English and language arts teachers. To this I can only say that if English and language arts teachers do not assume the responsibility for teaching disadvantaged children the cognitive uses of language, I don't know who will. Except for a few experimental projects such as ours, there are no logicians or cognitive psychologists in the schools, but there are plenty of teachers who are supposed to be concerned with teaching language. It seems to me inexcusable that they should decline an interest in one of language's most important functions. If it is language as an instrument of social communication that separates man from apes, it is language as a tool of thought that separates civilized men from barbarians. It is this latter use of language which, if I read my history correctly, was the legacy of ancient Greece. If the term "cultural deprivation" has any legitimate meaning, then it means to me that two thousand years later millions of people in our society have yet to receive their full share of this legacy.

Discussion

Conference participants discussed the extent to which generalizations for other situations could be derived exclusively from the preschool experiment which Mr. Bereiter is directing at the University of Illinois. Although the apparent increases in intelligence as indicated on tests were admittedly impressive, Task Force members thought them predictable because of the heavy emphasis placed in such tests on verbal symbolism and the corresponding emphasis on verbal learning in Mr. Bereiter's program. The concentration throughout the experimentation on specific behaviors related to success in school offers valuable suggestions for the limited problem of his project. Many conferees, however, felt that larger generalizations about the linguistic behavior of boys and girls in other environments could not be based on such data without additional supporting evidence. For example, conversations of children in informal discussion might be compared with their language behavior in more structured situations.

Task Force members objected to Mr. Bereiter's assumption that they failed to recognize the urgency of the educational problems facing the disadvantaged. They pointed to their willingness to interrupt spring and summer plans to join the Task Force. The discussion indicated that the comments on urgency were directed less at the attitudes of Task Force members to the total problem than at the reluctance of many to sense the urgent need to accelerate crucial learning in programs for the disadvantaged.

Task Force members discussed the language spoken by the parents of disadvantaged children. Mr. Bereiter said that the parents of his children often use better language than their children are able to absorb. Such a family condition may or may not be characteristic of other disadvantaged children, but it suggests the importance to educators and social workers of finding ways to help parents help their own children.

Discussants were interested in the discovery that the children whom Mr. Bereiter studied do not seem in all ways to reveal the same language tendencies as do children of similar ages in other studies. Walter Loban suggested that linguistic deprivation takes many forms, that some children may be disadvantaged in dialect, some in vocabulary, others in cognitive processes and logic. He also urged that Mr. Bereiter's program be linked to experience designed to serve as a base for using language for thinking effectively and powerfully. Mr. Bereiter's experiments offer valuable insights to elementary teachers who mean to give direction to language. Naturally, teachers, unlike experimenters, will wish to integrate Mr. Bereiter's performance goals with the larger global elements of elementary curriculum. Some participants suggested that normative data, systematically collected, were needed to indicate the actual language behavior of the children before firm generalizations could be advanced.

Despite reservations about the applicability of some of the findings and methods of Mr. Bereiter's work to the normal preschool situation for disadvantaged children, conferees saw much value in specific experiments of this kind assisting educators to identify characteristics of disadvantaged children and approaches which provide remediation critical to success in school. The conferees felt that such projects seem less to provide model programs for emulation than ways of advancing general knowledge about the characteristics of disadvantaged learners of preschool age.

Group Identity and Educating the Disadvantaged

SOL TAX

For many years I have been interested in the general problem facing the Task Force—perhaps more so than most anthropologists. In addition to my regular work, which deals mainly with American Indians, I have been interested in the educational problems of people in relation to their urban environment. At the University of Chicago we have in our back-yard one of the great disadvantaged areas, Woodlawn. Many at the university have shown concern about the problems of the people in Woodlawn, but they have actually done little to help them. There are not too many people at the highest professional level in the behavioral sciences who actually work on the "firing line," so to speak, of the problems.

A few years ago, when notions of de facto segregation were relatively new, we assumed that school segregation was caused by factors beyond control and that no one could do anything about it. The Negro revolt properly questioned this assumption: it did not matter what the causes of segregation were; it mattered only that they be eliminated and that Negroes' education be improved. Pressure on the university faculty to work toward this end has mounted greatly, and there is increasing response.

The large private foundations in this country have been clearly most concerned with education. They have had other programs, dealing with economics and sociology, but their major effort has been in education. I remember a meeting at one foundation in which we talked about an elaborate program for taking preschool children from childhood through college and comparing them with children remaining with their families over a period of twenty years or so, to prove that children taken from a normal sample with Negro genes can accomplish anything achieved by other groups if given opportunities. We thought this experiment might end the argument about racial inferiority. It would not, of course, because the people who view life through prejudiced eyes would find some other way to argue racism.

Although this is not the only major problem facing our society today, it is important to put the disadvantaged into such social and economic condition that they may compete with others to the degree they want to compete. We have understood very little about how to do this, and we are now moving in a variety of trial-and-error directions. This is why the NCTE Task Force effort to pull everything together, to see what has been done in the last two years in one important area, may prove valuable.

My own research project, supported by a grant from the Carnegie Corporation, deals with one of the most difficult aspects of cross-cultural education. I have concentrated on the North American Indian, who was alone in this country when we took the continent from him. (The Negroes are a special case in that they did not select this continent themselves.)

One of the important characteristics of our ancestors who emigrated from Europe is that they were achievement oriented. In all of the generations since immigration from Europe began, American Indians have not come substantially closer to being what we think of as acculturated, or satisfied with their lot, or able to operate in our society. If one takes a map of North America and spots on it exactly where the Indians now live, he will discover that with the exception of parts of Oklahoma they all live where they originally did. Some Indian groups have disappeared. But those who remain are for the most part in their home territory. They may be in a very reduced part of their home territory, but you will still find them in Long Island, Connecticut, Massachusetts, Maine, and of course you will find them in the Southwest, California, and elsewhere. The remarkable thing is that they are a rapidly increasing population, not of people who only claim to be Indians, but of people who are culturally, socially, and very self-consciously Indian. Those who have wanted to become "white men" (a word they use to include Negroes as well) have become white men because of the pressures in our society and the opportunities that have been open. They are constantly told, "Come, shape up, get off the reservation, and do things," so that those who were the least inclined to do anything, or the least able to succeed on their own, have tended to join the general society.

Congress tries to continue this process—of getting the Indians off the budget, or our consciences, or whatever it is that they are on. Thinking "this can't go on forever," Congress always sees two ways of providing for the eventual assimilation. Either we do it the nice way, assisting and helping the Indian, or we do it impatiently, throwing him into the mainstream of society to sink or swim. There was a very short period during the New Deal when we tried to do it through the Indian culture and Indian language, assuming that if we once taught them to be literate in and to account for their own culture, they would become assimilated more quickly into American life. When the Indians showed no great appreciation—because they did not wish to be assimilated to begin with—our political leaders became impatient with this approach. They tried to throw Indians into the water to sink or swim, as they say, and as has been the chief problem with this method throughout history, Indians have neither sunk nor swum; they have floated. They remain as much of a "problem" as ever to the establishment.

From the Indian point of view, the major value is their own identity as Indians. They interpret any program that threatens their communities or their culture as threatening their very identity. Since no money is to be had from Congress or the state legislatures except on the assumption that the program is finally going to end the "problem," nothing constructive can possibly happen. I have learned to take for granted that there is no solution to the problem of the North American Indians unless one can change the attitudes of almost two hundred million Americans and their Congress. We must accept the fact that the American Indians are entitled by one means or another (for whatever rationalization the American people are willing to tolerate) to make a living *as Indians,* because this is the one opportunity that we took away from them.

Some Indians do manage to make a living as Indians. Through an accident of history, the Mohawk steel workers, for example, are successfully "adjusted" without being acculturated. Builders of high bridges over the St. Lawrence River found the Indians willing and especially able to become high steel workers, placing and riveting moving girders at dizzying heights. The Indians very quickly got the reputation of having different instincts and therefore being not afraid of heights (of course this turned out to be not true; perhaps they were more afraid than some others of being *thought* to be afraid). At any rate, the Mohawk Indians have become some of the best high steel workers we have. A skyscraper builder in Chicago, when he heard I knew something about Indians, repeated to me a myth which was very interesting. He said, "You know, those Indians won't go on a job until a white man has failed. Then you can get them to come." This, of course, is not true; they will go on any job that they want. But the myth has spread; the Indian has reconstructed the war path or hunting party. The men go off alone and earn enough money on any job so that they do not have to come to work the next day. They return to the reservation with enough money for their families for a while; then go off onto another job, and so on. They *do* go back to the reservation and they *do* marry their women at home. Their "home" while working could be under the

Williamsburg Bridge in Brooklyn where there are stores in which Indian foods are prominent; but they do not belong there.

Under the recent government relocation programs, as part of our program of assimilation, a few of the Indians came to the city and turned into "white men"; but vastly larger numbers do not turn into white men and remain Indian. It is almost impossible to find a relocated Indian who is well adjusted to the city. When the Indians were brought to the city, their family's transportation was paid, housing was found, jobs were found, and they were put in schools. They were expected to disappear as Indians. The people who came were often the ones least able to adjust well on the reservation, those for whom the city seemed the lesser evil. Their problems in the city are great. It is not surprising that they frustrate the government agencies and protect themselves by continuing to feel that they are in the city only temporarily to make a living. Poor as they may be, many go back to ceremonies on their reservations. This feeling that they can return to their communities seems important, as does the fact that they come together in small groups, with their own church, even though discouraged from doing so by federal government agencies.

Indeed such things often seem to be the only real things that make life in the city bearable for them. They are never able to make the kind of adjustment that we have always thought of immigrants making, for the obvious reason that all of our immigrants came from Europe or from Japan or from China where people were already achievement oriented, whether peasants or aristocrats, whether urban or rural.

One remembers from the book of Genesis how man had lived in a state of paradise for a while (obviously the food-gathering period of human history), and had become a smart aleck, and had begun to domesticate plants and animals. He thereafter had to earn his bread by the sweat of his brow. A farmer has to work; time becomes important; real estate becomes important, and inheritance becomes important. This is a revolution in which man begins to treat nature as something to be manipulated by man. *The American Indians never reached this stage,* but not because they were not smart enough to reach it. *They did not want it;* they rejected it; and they are still rejecting it.

We find that American Indians are characterized by a cultural difference that goes deeper than any cultural difference we are likely to encounter in any other group in this country. The Africans had a civilization beyond the small, intimate family tribal organization. The North American Indian, the Australian aborigine, and only a few other peoples in the world have maintained themselves in what we think of as a tribal state.

The people who are considered by our society to have gone farthest are the ones willing to leave home and family to seek further progress and to make something more of themselves. Our own religion, as we know, does not permit us to think of ourselves as being somebody; we have to *become* something. And beyond this is our whole notion of *responsibility,* our suggestion that everybody is responsible for his own soul. That notion of *becoming,* instead of simply *being,* is utterly foreign to Indians and is anathema, because you *become* something only *at the expense* of somebody. Every North American Indian that I know, regardless of his particular culture, is likely to think it impossible to progress or to be somebody else's boss in a work situation. An Indian does not order somebody else to do something; he is not authoritarian. He will not be tempted to get ahead of the next fellow economically. In the classroom it has often been noticed that when the teacher asks that the first child who finishes his problem raise his hand, the Indian child will not do so. From their point of view, *they would not know how to do it.* The idea is difficult for them to comprehend. In their community oriented culture, it is an immoral act to put oneself first. They are then, tribally or community directed in the extreme. Social harmony is the great value. Such is tribal life.

The problem in our project is to see whether, in this extreme tribal situation, one can still bridge the gap between the cultures educationally, for if one can do it there, it is possible for one to do it cross-culturally and in many other places. Our emphasis is simply on literacy. Since Indians are not competitive and since they are widely scattered and perhaps shy in a group, it seemed useful to experiment with programed work by correspondence, each person progressing at his own speed.

I started out the way most of us do, acting as though I thought that all the Indians were waiting for me to give them some nice gimmick to make them literate, that the whole world was waiting for the literacy program that I was planning. Since then I've studied the UNESCO and other basic education programs tried with little success all over the world, and I find that few if any have gotten beyond that primitive stage of my own thinking at that time. The only thing most of these programs worry about is the technique of how to do it. And so I have learned painfully to separate the problem of techniques from what you might think of as motivational factors or sociopsychological and economic factors.

In the past, many peoples have developed alphabets and universal literacy in the simple natural way common to the diffusion of cultural traits. Thus when a missionary supplied an alphabet, Gilbert Islanders all became literate in their own language. They are literate because they find it useful to write messages. People who are always traveling write letters. Centuries ago an important literature developed in Sumatra based on an alphabet derived from one in India. Today in the Philippines you find people called "primitive forest living peoples" who use this alphabet; they scratch messages on pieces of bamboo and send them. They are perfectly literate and have been for a long time. You discover that people, when they have any reasons to do it at all, find that literacy is really one of the simplest techniques, compared, for example, to weaving or the variety of skills that people must teach one another. Mothers everywhere teach their daughters the simple things. Many of our own children do not wait until they go to school; they learn to read and write over the shoulder of another child if the atmosphere permits. So we begin to ask, "What are the conditions under which people will themselves learn to read and write?" The basic question is thus one of proper conditions. If the conditions are right, we will go ahead and teach them. There may be technical as well as sociopsychological motivational conditions. There may be something involved in our own school system that inhibits some people from being able to get a decent start; there may be a clash between their own culture and ours.

We must assume that there is a reason for all human behavior. This is something that we have learned only recently. We assume, curiously, that the behavior of animals is wise, so that a bird building a nest in an unexpected place teaches us something new. But when we see a human do something a little different that we cannot interpret immediately, we think he is very foolish. We must take the view, heuristically, that every action by a normal human being has some positive reason for existing, and certainly if it is the action of a whole human group. Since there has been internal selection, and communication, there is no doubt that a community must have some positive reason for its actions. If some action seems foolish to us, it is because *we* do not understand the reasons, and it is we who are foolish when we act on the opposite assumption. The first rule that I have learned as an anthropologist is to assume optimistically that there is some positive reason for the behavior of any person or any community. Thus, nothing is to be treated negatively. We do not say that groups lack something or they would not do this; rather we recognize limitations on our own understanding of why each group acts in a particular way. But we know the group must have a reason for doing it in its way and try to discover the reason. But since we cannot say, ''Well, all right; I give myself ten minutes, and if I cannot discover it I 'll say they 're fools,'' the logical necessity is never to assume the negative and always assume the positive.

Therefore, when we come to think of reasons why people do not accept literacy, we have to think not that there is something wrong with them. Rather we must seek some positive reason either why they have rejected literacy (if they have had it) or why it is felt to be disfunctional in their situation. I take this as the major part of our study, then, rather than simply techniques.

Wahpeton Indian Students Use a Listening Center in Brigham City, Utah (Donald J. Morrow, Photographer)

We are working with Indians today at a field station in Tahlequah, Oklahoma, because this area seemed the very best place to study the most difficult problem. There is a history to the location. In 1819, Sequoia invented a syllabary for the totally illiterate Cherokees. It is an interesting story because he started out with hieroglyphics. After he had filled a house full of paper figuring out how to use the hieroglyphics, his wife became impatient and burned his work one day when he was out hunting. Then he said something like, ''Well, this can't be it; I can't remember all that work that I've done,'' and he developed the idea of doing it phonetically. At any rate, he invented an 85 character syllabary which linguists today say is as good as any which could be made. He tried it on his daughter by sending her a message. The scoffers were impressed. Within three years, 20,000 Cherokees were literate. A year or two later, they had a press and were printing a newspaper in Cherokee with some sections in English, perhaps for the white men in the vicinity. When they moved, or rather were *removed* to Indian territory, they took their press with them and printed for quite a while. They developed a school in Tahlequah which is still standing, reputed to be the first school west of the Mississippi River which taught Greek and Latin. Their nation lost its independence in a series of incidents which culminated in the establishment of Oklahoma as a state of the Union, and Congress officially deprived them of their tribal name. Meanwhile, however, they had become the most educated people in the early frontier territories. Yet today there are 10,000 Cherokees, in addition to Choctaws, and others in eastern Oklahoma who are among the most illiterate poor or disadvantaged in the United States.

We established our field station in Oklahoma then, for it was clear that something had happened from which we could learn. We want to find out what keeps them in their present condition, what the reasons are for the increase in illiteracy. One of the things that we have done is to begin by seeing how the Indians would react to the introduction of their own language. We manufactured type and have supported the Indians who are again printing a newspaper in Cherokee. Similarly, we have helped them to develop radio programs in Cherokee. The Indians have responded with enthusiasm, and a great many things seem to change. It is clear that in the next two or three years we will see whether blockage to change can be modified as they and their Oklahoma neighbors recognize their Indian identity. We found soon that businessmen wanted to advertise in Cherokee in the newspaper because there are 10,000 Cherokees who might give them business; similarly, the radio programs in Cherokee found people wanting to get advertising on it to appeal to these Cherokees, and the number of programs per week doubled. All of a sudden the Cherokees who were almost forgotten are becoming a community again. They are becoming interested and demanding schools and may, for all we know, begin to operate again as they operated at one time in other history.

As one looks over in some detail the problems that face us, one sees that there is something beyond a technique of education involved. Unless we define education very broadly to include all motivational factors and techniques, we must say it is important to distinguish the technical aspects of literacy training or education from the sociopsychological, cultural, and motivational aspects. The reason for treating the Indian softly is not that we necessarily believe in cultural relativism, although we do, but that we have seen that the other way just never works. If, after the government put pressure on Indians, saying, ''All of you people

211

are either going to shape up or you will not eat," they had all immediately shaped up, then there would be no problem. The point is that, such a policy has not worked, and I do not believe that it is ever going to work with any group which has its own notions of right and wrong. I don't believe that you can force feed a large community of people. We have had too many such cases, and we will continue to be unsuccessful unless we can "hook on to" something of their own that they want to do. It is not enough to say, "Well, there must be a cultural difference." What we need to know are the reasons why they act as they do.

In thinking of disadvantaged Negroes living under slum conditions, we must understand that many do not see the *function* of literacy, and hence respond poorly to education. It isn't going to substantially improve any individual's position in society to give him a fourth grade education. How much does he have to postpone present good for some very questionable future gain? Only when the real rewards are made very clear can we take advantage of motivational factors which are needed for success. These rewards cannot be made clear by preaching; a child in school cannot be told to learn something in which he is not interested on the grounds that "It will make a big difference to you in twenty years, although you're only four now." An education has to have a present reward for the child's family; it has to be functional. This is not to say that nothing should be done until the effort seems functional, that one should wait until all the socioeconomic factors are resolved. It may be that whatever is done will only work for the 10 or 20 percent of the people who do see the effort as functional. No one is arguing that you should not keep trying even wrong ways, because there are always some people who wrong-headedly make "wrong" ways right for them! It is always better to do something positive, if it can be done without creating more new problems than it solves old ones. If my watch is broken, I can throw it away because it will not work. Or I take it to a jeweler and give him a chance to identify the problem— a speck of dirt, only; or perhaps the mainspring; but even a mainspring may be replaced, once you know that is the trouble. From this point of view, it is never useful to say the watch is broken.

If one is able to discover some of the critical factors in working with the disadvantaged, the effort seems worthwhile. This seems to me what Carl Bereiter is trying to do. We have to treat his attempt as a pure research project, however, because it is dangerous to generalize from conditions provided children in a laboratory to those in a nonlaboratory situation. Some seem concerned that people will visit such projects and will mistakenly force similar conditions in situations where they will do more harm than good. What is important, it seems to me, is to get out of such research some essence that can be applied in all schools on a smaller scale. In contrast I am not sure that in my own research we can come out with anything quick, neat, and applicable. We are learning that it does no good to blame the pupil for resisting the educational process. We may find that his whole family situation is such that he has had no positive rewards from education. Remember that he lives in a smaller society where his ways are functional in his own terms. Dropouts are not negative; we treat them as negative because we don't understand them. In a pupil's own terms, he is not dropping out; he is rather adopting one of two alternatives. We do not know what it is that he is going to do, but we have to assume that every person faces alternatives in life. If you discuss these in the wrong terms, or in ways that simply crystallize opposition, as indeed has happened with the American Indian, then you are completely licked yourself. The important thing is to discover and work on the positive factors which caused people to behave as they have.

We have talked about children unable to understand simple logic; none of us can. We assume that a person is motivated or is not motivated, but with normal people, "not motivated" means merely the state of being motivated to do something else. We, however, do not treat it as positive alternative behavior but as negative behavior. The further we go in the direction of treating the uneducated or underprivileged in negative terms, the harder it will ever be to get them on the trail that we are hoping they will eventually follow. As soon as we say, "You are here. We are educating you for the first time. You have been nothing until now," a child who thought he was something, who thought his family was something, is immediately in a position where he may react negatively. When a whole group does this, they not only react negatively, but they may do it with picket signs. Today's protest seeks much more than good schools. Schools are only the immediate symbols; they really are seeking recognition as human beings. Every time we have a program of any kind in school that makes the opposite assumption, that assumes they are nothing, that is offered as the only positive alternative they have—every such program offers them nothing positive and probably interferes with the student's future education more than it helps him. The phenomena that Carl Bereiter describes in the children's own culture which clash with education are quite different from the things our school teachers are assuming. And as soon as children come up against this clash, they are rejected. They often *cannot* do what the teacher asks, things which seem to them, consciously or unconsciously, to denigrate their homes, their people, and their culture.

Negroes have already begun to face the difficult choice between equality and individuality. They began by asking for equal rights. When they get them, they will be much more like the American Indian and will want their own ways again and recognition of their own identity as a cultural group. This is already apparent in the emergence of groups like the Black Muslims. These groups, I think, are likely to grow through time. The more we equalize economic and other opportunities, the more it will be possible for the people to want their individual and cultural integrity recognized. There is a myth in this country that Negroes do not have a culture, that it was knocked out of them in the slave ships. Of course, this never has been as true as the myth makes it. Family affections especially are very strong. The genuinely lower class Negroes become terribly upset when we talk about there being something odd about their families. Their attitudes toward families are positive. They have a matrilineal extended family system, as good as or better than our own nuclear family in the opportunity it affords for a variety of people to take care of young children. We treat so many things as negative that would be seen as positive if they were only understood. Negroes in the North, I am told, are disturbed at the notion of being evicted from their homes. For hundreds of years the free home was one of the few things that they had—a place to live, even if it was slave quarters. The notion of home being a piece of property from which somebody could displace them really hits them hard. Such attitudes are very hard to discover and discuss because so many of the people that we talk to are already middle class or we would not be able to talk to them at all.

Discussion

Discussion concentrated on those aspects of the culture of the disadvantaged in conflict with assumptions widely held by teachers. When children recognize a clash between the values promoted in the classroom and those which are part of their own family and social group, they inevitably reject those taught at school. Not to do so is to reject their own culture.

When asked about the applicability of the notion of tribal or group identity to the Negro's search for civil rights, Mr. Tax expressed the opinion that as the Negro achieves increasing social, political, and economic equality, he will find himself forced to choose between further "equality" and his "individuality" or identity as a group. When this happens, Mr. Tax expected the Negro, like many other groups before him, to choose group identity. He felt that this will come about increasingly as educational opportunity is realized.

The French Lick conferees also concerned themselves with those ideas and points of view which seemed most threatening to the Negro. Degrading references to the Negro family unit seem to many Negroes far more severe than many teachers realized. Negroes tend to have strong feelings about family ties. Although the Negro family unit may differ considerably from that of the family unit common to the white majority culture, the family exists nevertheless. Loyalties to the family are deeply rooted, and the suggestion that anything is wrong with Negro family structure creates severe concern. The language which Negro children speak with their families is only one of several attributes of Negro culture which seem to be under attack in many schools. Teachers need to accept the language which Negro children bring to school, to recognize that it is a perfectly appropriate vehicle for communicating ideas in the Negro home and subculture. The teacher must encourage Negro children to learn a new English dialect, the informal English dialect of the school room, without making an attack on the dialect which children associate with their homes and their identity as Negroes.

Dialects, Education, and the Contributions of Linguists

JANET SAWYER

Because the report of the Task Force clearly emphasizes the need for linguistic training for teachers of English for the disadvantaged, I will not direct additional repetitive remarks to this end. Instead, I will concentrate upon several matters which have been of concern to me as the discussions and reports have progressed.

My first comment concerns two terms which have been used here. The terms are *language* and *dialect,* and the difficulty has arisen as we have attempted to label the type of language activity in which the teacher of the disadvantaged is engaged. Is the classroom teacher presenting a new dialect or a new language? Since some members of the group often said they were teaching a "new language" when referring to the teaching of native Americans, particularly southern Negroes who had moved to northern cities, some clarification of terms seems necessary. Within any language structure, variation of a minor nature is normal. In English, for example, we are aware of variations in the speech of Australians, Canadians, Englishmen, and Americans. In the United States we recognize at least four large dialect areas. We find, within any of these large areas, subdialects of a geographical nature. Now all of these dialects share the same basic sound system, grammatical system, and vocabulary. There are differences in the pronunciation of some of the vocabulary items. A few systematic sound differences set off various dialects from each other. There may be a few strikingly different items in the grammar. And there are often a large number of vocabulary items which are different. But none of these variations are great enough to cause speakers of various dialects of English more than momentary difficulty when they meet. And, for purposes of communication, each dialect is also equally valid.

No linguistic studies of the substandard dialects that we deal with in teaching the disadvantaged have revealed enough variation to justify calling any of these dialects different languages. There are pronunciation differences which are found to be characteristic of the speakers' places of origin. Southern Negroes, then, speak like southerners even after they move to northern cities. And such speech will persist in succeeding generations if the group continues to be isolated from the larger cultural community. Although the differences in pronunciation, grammar, and vocabulary are few in number, they are systematic and often occur frequently in everyday speech. What makes the English teacher's task difficult is the system behind the use of these variants. If a new dialect is to be mastered by the students, the teacher must help them to form new language habits, just as the teacher of a foreign language does. For this reason, some of the techniques of pattern drill used to teach a new language are useful, though the teaching of a new dialect is certainly not the same as the teaching of a new language.

My second comment is more directly related to the work of the Task Force in evaluating programs for teaching the disadvantaged. I am especially concerned about the contributions that the linguist can make to the planning of better programs and the adequate training of teachers. The group has discussed specific programs for teaching the disadvantaged at four levels: the adult level, the high school level, pre-school, and elementary school levels. In addition, we have dealt separately with the teaching of English as a second language to the culturally disadvantaged. Linguistic science can make a real contribution to the adequate preparation of teachers of both native and non-native speakers of English at the adult and high school levels. For example, the most detailed information about language structure, particularly English structure, is available to the teacher of English as a second language. Useful descriptions of hundreds of foreign languages make structural comparisons practical. Tapes, drill books, and fine texts for teaching English as a foreign language at any grade level are now at hand.

Dialect geographers have collected and are continuing to collect information on class dialects to assist the teacher who must teach a new social dialect at the high school or adult level. If the teacher makes the mistake of trying to teach these students an imaginary, artificial speech based on the frozen style that members of the English-speaking community use for formal writing, only two things can result, neither of which is desirable. Most of the students will reject this artificial dialect entirely; the others will master it and speak a pedantic, stilted style which will cut them off from social acceptance in the larger cultural community quite as much as a substandard dialect will. If such failure is to be avoided, teachers in the various communities must know how the prestige group of the community really speaks. The dialect geographer can supply this information.

217

A Volunteer Classroom Aide Reads a Story to Children in Wilmington, Delaware
(*Ebony* Magazine)

Certain features which are of prestige value in one community may be looked upon with horror in another. Let me illustrate with the example of a linguistic situation which I encountered in my study of the English of San Antonio, Texas. It involved the pronunciation of the ending of the present participles of verbs, pronounced *ing*, [iŋ] in some areas and *in* [in] in others. In San Antonio, a speaker of the prestige dialect could say *readin'* or *workin'* instead of *reading* or *working* if he were at home with his shoes off or if he were speaking to a garbage man or a janitor. But no educated speaker would say anything but *working* and *reading* in a formal speech situation. One of the churches hired a young minister from coastal Virginia, an area where the *in* pronunciation is preferred by the highly cultured prestige group. When this young preacher used this pronunciation in the pulpit, the ladies of the congregation were so shocked that they seriously considered sending a committee to discuss the matter with him. Obviously, a classroom teacher of the culturally disadvantaged in coastal Virginia would be foolhardy to object to *in* in *readin'* and *writin'*. But in San Antonio, a different situation obtains which must be duly recognized.

However, when we turn to the linguistics problems faced by the elementary school teacher and the preschool teacher of the disadvantaged, we find great differences. First of all, we have agreed that we are not going to concern ourselves with the teaching of a second dialect at this level. The purpose of this early language instruction is that of enriching the basic language system which the child already possesses. Linguists say that a child attains a mastery of his language between the ages of four and six. That is, he masters the sound system and the basic grammar and has an adequate vocabulary for communication. The school is concerned with the enrichment of this basic structure, and the addition of various style levels, particularly that style which is used for writing. But the members of the Task Force have suggested that the disadvantaged child of four or five is seriously retarded in his mastery of his language. It has even been suggested that such a child has no language, only a few words, and possesses no linguistic skill in using the English language for expressing relationships of any complexity. Some rightfully refute this notion as do many modern linguists. As we talked, however, I was also struck by the fact that a great deal of further research must be made in the area of child language learning, if we are to be of real service to the classroom teacher of the disadvantaged at this level. It is also clear that linguists alone cannot do such research any more than psychologists or sociologists can. Since any inadequacies in linguistic skill of four- and five-year-old disadvantaged children cannot be attributed to lack of intelligence, their failure to learn English as fast or as well as more fortunate members of our society must be due to differences in cultural values, social needs, home environment, motivation . . . and these problems must be tackled by teams of workers trained in cultural anthropology, linguistics, psychology, sociology, and elementary education. Since this level of instruction is obviously the most vital of all, it seems essential that questions such as those raised by this Task Force be given immediate attention.

Discussion

Conferees agreed on the importance of bringing together linguists, anthropologists, psychologists, and educators to consider the language problems of children. Too few current projects involve such resource specialists; an ever fewer number bring together such consultants at the same time so that project staffs may obtain the resultant cross-disciplinary stimulation.

One compelling need identified at the French Lick Conference is the identification of the language characteristics of children from different social and ethnic groups. These separate dialects need careful study at all educational levels. Until teachers understand better the linguistic behavior of children whose language seems to differ from standard informal English, progress in instruction will be retarded. Some conferees suggested that elementary teachers would profit studying methods of linguistic transcription so that they could gather their own basic data. Surely some study of phonetic sounds and orthographic representation is needed in preservice and inservice education programs if teachers are to be called to evaluate such adjustments of the English phonemic system as are offered for example in i.t.a. While recognizing contributions of i.t.a to wider reading by children and perhaps to writing programs as well, several conferees with linguistic training suggested that if teachers would study the English language more extensively, they would be less ready to accept such new developments as i.t.a. as the "only" answer to improving instruction in language and would recognize that the possibilities for variation in traditional orthography have not yet been fully exploited.

A Sustained Program of Language Learning

WALTER LOBAN

In preparing documents like this one you are preparing, it is common to fear being prescriptive. When you talk about practices and materials, it is true, you run the danger of offering a book of educational recipes which will encourage the teacher, like a housewife, to say, "I'll try this recipe," or "I'll do this one." On the other hand, I urge you to consider the opposite danger. Too many publications are heavy with principles never translated into classroom practice. To a good supervisor or teacher there is nothing more frustrating than to read theoretical pamphlets giving absolutely no idea of the principle translated into reality. For that reason I suggest you include some of the practices, materials, and content you have seen. If you are concerned that you will get a potpourri of recipes, you may wish to insert italicized questions in which you raise considerations or indicate the possibilities or dangers, so the reader will be raised to the highest level of thinking as he considers your publication.

You should also make very clear somewhere in the beginning of the publication that you are concerned with a large number of pupils who

Puppetry Stimulates Growth in Oral Language

speak many different kinds of social class dialects—the pidgin speaker in Hawaii, Cajun in Louisiana, Appalachian, as well as Spanish- and Oriental-speaking peoples who must learn a second language, the American Indian, and others—not just the Negro. Also you need to include some direct attention to the sociology of dialects, to the historical fact that language was one way a stable class society kept people in their classes. Language represents tremendous social power, and in any society the Establishment speaks one kind of dialect, the established standard dialect. You may wish to refer to other countries in which this is true about language. For example, the Yorkshire man rising to high political position in England has a language problem. The purely political and historical accident that Tuscan Italian became standard Italian, rather than Venetian or Sicilian, is another illustration of how standard speech is only another dialect. We need to remind ourselves often of the sociological relationship between poverty, with its waste of human potential, and language itself. Closed societies have always used language as one means of control. In a fluid society like ours, we try to diminish this ancient element of social control.

A Coordinated Program

At this conference, we have not yet considered sequence and articulation in relation to English and the disadvantaged learner. Yet if we are actually to help the disadvantaged use the prestige dialect, we will need a *sustained* program. Language instruction is not something to be accomplished separately by each division of a school system. There must be some kind of articulation, and we therefore need to use experiences so that instruction at each educational level reinforces and builds towards a common aim.

Pupils need to learn standard English in addition to the social class dialect they know, Cajun, Appalachian, or whatever it may be. (We are not here concerned with *regional variations* of English but with *social class variations.*) If such pupils do not learn a second kind of dialect, standard English, they will be forever prevented from access to economic opportunity and social acceptance. We can learn to grant full dignity to the child and to the language spoken in his home. At the same time, we must help him to acquire the established standard language so he can operate in society as fully as he may wish. He would, of course, be free to make the choice of not using his second dialect.

The research of Basil Bernstein in England and my own research on language development are pertinent here. The Cockney and the upper middle class British speaker have the same basic language, the same grammar. The difference lies, according to Bernstein,[1] in the extent to which Cockney fails to use the potential of the language. This is exactly what I found in my research in the Oakland, California, schools. In kindergarten and in subsequent years, the same grammar operated in the language of all the youngsters. But subjects from the lower socioeconomic groups do not use language with as full a range of potential as those from more favored groups. They can use the full potential, but if they are in the lower socioeconomic group they do not do so very often. By full potential, I mean using such syntactical devices as coordination or subordination to express a complex idea or using an appositive to reinforce or to extend the listener's understanding of what is being communicated. They do not use infinitives—not so much the infinitive alone as the infinitive phrase, the elaborated infinitive phrase, a much neater device than dependent, subordinate clauses for tightly coiling ideas. Gerund phrases, participial phrases, and infinitive phrases are usually indicative of a much tighter kind of thinking than is the long dependent clause. For instance, in the two sentences which follow the first version is better than the second:

Concepts evoked by the total situation may be relevant.
Concepts that are evoked by the total situation may be relevant.

Instead of, "The sparrows urged that Peter exert himself," the skilled speaker says, "The sparrows urged Peter to exert himself." In language research, various devices of subordination prove to be the mark of a person with the best control of the English sentence, the one who has the most to say and the skill to say it in skillfully compact forms.

People who live in the lower socioeconomic disadvantaged groups use language primarily for immediate concrete situations. For that reason, they are able to use many partial sentences. The tired father says to the older boy, "My slippers." He means, "Go get my soft shoes." The mother says to the daughter, "The table." She means, "It is time now for you to set the table." Children are making a lot of noise outside. The middle class mother would say, "Now you children know that Mrs. Jones has rheumatic spells every once in a while. She has pains in her shoulders, and at such times she's very unhappy and

---

[1] Basil Bernstein, "Language and Social Class," *British Journal of Sociology*, XI (1960), 271–276.

———, "Some Sociological Determinants of Perception," *British Journal of Sociology*, IX (1958), 159–174.

———, "Social Class and Linguistic Development: A Theory of Social Learning," *Education, Economy*, and *Society*, ed. A. H. Halsey, Jean Floud, and C. Arnold Anderson (New York: Macmillan [Free Press of Glencoe], 1961.)

easily upset. When children are running around making a lot of noise, it makes her even worse. Now children, how would you feel if you were Mrs. Jones? So, then, what must we do, children?'' The lower class mother says, ''Quiet!'' She may be just as kind and just as loving to her children as the middle class mother who has used the greater amount of language.

These less favored people do not often use language to examine the future. To cope with the present is enough of a problem for them. They do not go back to reexamine the past to see what lessons might be learned in the light of the past to foresee consequences of the future. Therefore, they have less occasion to use infinitives, appositives, gerunds, participles, and dependent clauses for amplification, embroidering, and extension of the subject-predicate relationships. They use short, brief sentences or partial sentences.

Furthermore, they are not in the habit of expressing subjective emotions and feelings, a very important possibility of language. It is not part of their culture to look at feelings and talk about them extensively. They indicate their feelings visually with shrugs, hands, bodies, eyes, and facial expressions much more than do middle class or upper class persons. And they are not frequently engaged in examining the nuances of ideas, looking at the very delicate possibilities or ramifications of an idea. Their lives are focused on the immediate, the concrete, the practical, the necessary. They use the same grammar, but they do not use the potentials of language, and their vocabulary and usage are different. In my own research,[2] the most important finding is not that disadvantaged children use the same basic grammatical patterns as others. Rather the significant difference is that those who have the greatest control and power over language have the largest repertoire of linguistic skills to extend and embroider and amplify their basic sentence patterns. These understandings provide necessary background to understand what should be done to enable people like the Cajun- or the pidgin-speaking child to use the full potential of language, including the established dialect.

In a sequential program, all disadvantaged children would begin earlier than others with experiences selected by virtue of their necessity for learning concepts and for amplifying the language (dialect) they already use. In preschool and kindergarten these disadvantaged children would have experiences in which they would talk as much as possible,

---

[2] Walter Loban, *The Language of Elementary School Children: A Study of the Use and Control of Language Effectiveness in Communication, and the Relations among Speaking, Reading, Writing, and Listening* (Champaign, Ill.: National Council of Teachers of English, 1963).

using the living, oral language. The purpose of this talk would be quite clearly to extend the length of the sentences they use. Much of it would occur in what the kindergarten teacher calls "unstructured activity," but I would like the teacher to know *why* she is having it. Children picking up magnets in schools become excited and talk a great deal. Children go out to see the baby sheep that have just been born; they talk tremendously! Or a boy says, "If he bes mah frien', ah don' meddle him." This is an "if-then" construction. Wonderful! Don't worry now about usage! Not this early in school.

What we want is to persuade disadvantaged pupils at this early age to talk as much as possible. Through grappling with ideas and the kinds of questions the preschool and kindergarten teacher asks, the child will begin to amplify and embroider in order to foresee consequences, to examine ideas, and to say, "if-then." In fact, the teacher *asks* questions, "What if we did this? Then what?" One teacher took the children to a dairy. At first she asked the usual perception questions, but then she began to maneuver more purposefully. "Mr. Johansen gave each one of us a free glass of milk. If he gave everybody a free glass of milk what would happen?" It is the "why" kind of question that will get the children to talk most fully. This means, of course, that we must educate the teachers, both in service and in preservice, as to the true nature of language. Many teachers still have an understanding of language equivalent to the medical knowledge possessed by a quack doctor. They worry about "may" and "can" and make the small child self-conscious about his indigenous language.

Now we face a critical problem: the children speak a social class dialect. In the kindergarten and in the earliest years of school, the emphasis should be upon the child's using *whatever dialect of the language he already speaks* as the means of thinking and exploring and imagining. Language is also more than a tool of thought. It is a way of expressing emotions and feelings. It is a way of adjusting to other people, of expressing solidarity with the human race. Language has many purposes among which one of the most important, and certainly the most important to the teacher, is the use of language as a means of developing the powers of reason. But it is not the only one. If the child speaks a dialect and says, "Them magnet's pickin' up the nails," we do not need to worry about "them magnet's" at this point. Let him say, "them magnet's." That usage will not interfere with the crucial cognitive processes. If we do not first encourage the child to use his own language in its full range, we may diminish his desire to use language in school. First of all, orally, he must develop and amplify sentences until he is using the full range of his mental and linguistic potential. It is much easier for him to do that in the dialect he already uses. (Do not worry that we intend to let him do this forever in school.) The preschool stage and kindergarten are much too early to press him to use standard dialect. Such teaching only confuses children, causing them to speak much less frequently in school.

However, if children do not soon begin to practice all of the phonemes in the English language, eventually they will not be able to make some of the phonemes as, for instance, Yugoslavs cannot make our ''v'' or ''w'' and North Americans have great difficulty with the Spanish ''r.'' Children must practice early. So in primary school, perhaps beginning with the first, second, and third grades (I am using grades only roughly; I am not concerned with grade placement; I would even hope that this could be in a nongraded school) when a child is six, seven, and eight, we should introduce a great many listening experiences which the pupil is to imitate. These would be taped, short little skits repeated twice, once in the dialect with which the child is familiar and once in the standard English. The purpose is to focus his attention upon *differences;* otherwise he will not hear them. They sound to him just as he says them; he must learn they are not exactly the same. One of the major tasks of the linguistically trained elementary school teacher is to focus the child's attention upon the linguistic distinctions presented in these skits, using language of both the established and the nonestablished dialects.

During grades 4, 5, and 6, we should introduce a barrage of language in different dialects, so pupils may become accustomed to the fact that there are many dialects they can imitate. Even small children imitate skillfully; this is why they pick up foreign languages so quickly. They should listen to Scotch, Australian, and New Zealand dialects, to pidgin, to Cajun, even to the Beatles. They should sing songs, recite rhymes, and engage in choral speaking in their own dialect and in the established dialect, trying to become flexible with all the many dialects that are possible, always with the idea that one should be able to imitate many different kinds of sounds.

In grades 4, 5, and 6, then, there would be an emphasis upon imitation and upon playing out short skits, drama, and creative dramatics. Drama is thus tremendously important in the theory of this articulated, sequential program. Often the drama would require puppets because children project themselves into puppets very easily. Simple little hand puppets presented on a stage made from cardboard boxes borrowed from the grocery store provide an incentive for children to write their own brief skits. Then they practice them, standing behind the stage. Thus they

Retelling a Story into a Tape Recorder in Los Angeles

carry out the puppetry while someone reads the parts. Throughout all this they would be imitating different dialects, but always with an increasing emphasis on the established standard English—one more tongue to imitate in the same way that Scotch or Irish dialects are imitated.

Never at any time throughout this elementary school period would we indicate to the child that there is the slightest thing wrong with his dialect, because we would not, in our own hearts, believe this. We need teachers who know that such dialects are essentially respectable and good, although the teachers realize these children must learn the dialect accepted by convention. There would never be any invidious comparisons, any criticism, at the preschool and primary school stage of the child's education.

However, before it is too late, teachers should begin to work on some of the more crucial items of usage by means of oral training. This would involve emphasis on usage *through the ear*. If "Him a good dog" exemplifies a crucial usage, the teacher in about grade 4 begins to say, "He is a good dog," and drills orally on case of pronouns—but does *not* employ grammatical analysis. Sometimes the teacher reads ten sentences aloud, explaining first which is standard dialect and which is not. The children listen to hear if the teacher expresses the usage in the established dialect. Often the pupils number from one to ten on a sheet and put a "plus" down if the teacher says an expression appropriately and a "zero" if the expression is not standard dialect. "See if the teacher can get every one in standard!" "I will try." Then I read: "(1) *He is a good dog.* (2) *She is my friend.* (3) *Him a happy fellow.*" and so forth up to 10 and the pupils listen to hear if I can handle the dialect (that is, standard dialect) correctly. But never would I indicate that there is anything bad about saying, "Him a good dog," or any other valid dialectal expression.

But the time comes when we face these pupils with the facts of social distinctions, and that time, to my way of thinking, is usually grade 5, 6, or 7. Teachers differ on the age for introducing this idea, but I see no point in telling children this earlier. Before they can really see the value of learning standard English, pupils need to understand the social consequences the world will exact of them if they cannot handle the established dialect. Grade 5, 6, or 7, therefore, would be the point at which I would select most carefully the teachers who had no snobbish attitudes about language, the scholar-linguist-humanists whom I could most safely entrust with the important task of explaining the sociological truth to these children. "Although the language your father uses is a perfectly good language and we have used it in this class, it is not the only way of speaking English. Have you ever noticed that the textbooks are printed in only one kind of dialect?" the teacher would say. "The day we went down to visit the juvenile court, the judges and lawyers all talked that standard language. When we had that speaker in assembly the other day and she told us about her work as a judge in the courts, even though she belongs to our same ethnic and racial group, she was using the same kind of standard English dialect you hear television announcers use. Now, here is something you need to know. Unless you can use that standard dialect as well as the one you speak, you will not be able to get certain kinds of jobs; that is the way the world is. Many business and professional people and many people who hire teachers and architects and clerks and stenographers just will not hire people who do not speak standard. And so, we must begin to handle this special standard dialect much better than we have been able to so far. We'll have to begin to work on it much more." Then from grades 6 through 12 I would try to eliminate as far as possible the use of social class dialect *in school.* The aim in school during these secondary years would be to help young people acquire this very important kind of dialect, this second language they need.

In acquiring the standard dialect, pupils must continue to amplify, embroider, and extend sentences. Thus, they should begin in grades 4, 5, and 6 a special kinesthetic method of sentence study. The teacher gives some of the children individual words printed on cards. These pupils come up to the front of the room where they arrange and rearrange themselves, determining how many possible ways they can make sentences with the words they are carrying. Then those not in front of the room practice saying the sentences aloud, using intonation patterns: Where do you drop the voice? Where do you pause? What words should we stress? Teachers may have other children waiting with extra cards, ready to come up in front to extend the sentences, to see how long they can make them, and then again how short they can make a sentence and still make sense: "What's wrong when we just have, *The great white horse. . . .* ? What's wrong with that? What do we have to do? More words, more words! What kind of words? All right—add them!" After they have done this, the next step is to provide smaller cards for seatwork; everybody rearranges his cards and works out different solutions and problems as a game. Next the pupils write compositions and with the opaque projector or some other projector, the teacher throws on the wall some of the papers for discussion. At other times a group of children may suggest better sentences as they work with each other's papers. Always, the teacher relates the study to the spoken language, to oral intonation, to pause, juncture, and all verbal signalling. From grade 7 on the activity would be in the established dialect, but in the early years we would accept "Him a good dog." We would be interested in seeing if the child could say, "Him a good dog *but with three fleas.*" We would be interested in amplification.

In addition to these strategies there should be much oral reading— by the teacher, through tapes and records and television, and by the pupils. We should restore the oral tradition to English instruction. In grades 7 through 12, I would use drill tapes and language laboratories in order to accomplish ear training that would alternate with dramatics, literature, discussion, and writing. The tapes would focus on usage, pronunciation, vocabulary, and idiom. Through the ear all of us learned to speak before we came to school. Only through the ear will any of us ever change our usage or pronunciation.

Today these disadvantaged people are demanding the rights and privileges other people have, and it is just and right that they should have them. If they are not belligerent and do not demand them, there is indeed something wrong about them. Their craven acquiescence would worry me much more than any justified belligerence. This change in our society has to happen if our society is to be healthy.

A democracy is always in process. We should become worried only when it is static or moves backwards. As long as there is process toward the ideal of equal human dignity, a democracy remains healthy. Because of the social revolution now taking place, we can be encouraged about the durability of this society. Already we note a shift of mind in education. This conference, an historic occasion for the National Council of Teachers of English, is one of the many events which will change American education. If it is difficult to move ahead when there are many problems, we should remind ourselves that the mature person would not, even if he could, alter the fact that life is a struggle. We are Faustian men, in Western Culture, and we do not believe that repose is a good thing.

Discussion

The sustained program of language experiences recommended by Mr. Loban elicited considerable discussion, including the observation that the proposals were not unlike some being considered by the Detroit Public Schools. In Detroit, however, planned instruction starts with the preschool level.

Conferees at French Lick agreed that restoration of the oral tradition to instruction in English is vital if disadvantaged children are to learn to communicate ideas either in speech or in writing. Oral approaches developed for teaching English to speakers of other languages seem to provide ways of introducing oral practice in standard English through the use of tape recordings, self-contained audiovisual units, and language laboratories. San-su C. Lin, who had just completed a study of the use of language laboratories in teaching English to nonstandard speakers, warned that the repetitive practice characteristic of many such language laboratory programs was in itself insufficient to change language habits of native speakers unless reinforced by classroom oral experiences in the communication of ideas.

Several members of the Task Force questioned the desirability of delaying presentation of the "facts of life" about language until the seventh grade. Mr. Loban admitted that his suggestions for grade placement were crude and said that he personally favored nongraded schools. He suggested that some matters pertaining to the nature and complexity of language might be introduced earlier provided that teachers delay any attempt to explain all of the social intricacies of language operation when the topic is first introduced to small children.

Discussion of the importance of developing greater teacher awareness of the cultural and social varieties of English led to an exploration of the potential value of grouping school children by dialect groups for the purpose of instruction in English. Mr. Loban said he would be willing to group children in this way for instruction in language, provided they are grouped in other ways during the remainder of the school day. Program administrators can obtain from sociolinguists information about the characteristics of ethnic groups and the potential effects of dialect grouping.

The French Lick Conference decided that it is crucial to find concrete classroom applications of knowledge being accumulated by sociologists and linguists. Unless the educator, the sociologist, and the linguist pool their insights and work together as they seek additional information on the language learning of the disadvantaged, today's opportunity to make great strides in developing successful new educational programs could be dissipated and ultimately lost.

Part IV

POINTS OF VIEW

Social Dialects and the Disadvantaged
LEE A. PEDERSON

Language, Intelligence, and the Disadvantaged
SAMUEL A. KIRK

Points of View

Basic to the work of the Task Force were certain key understandings concerning the nature of disadvantaged learners and approaches which may be employed to assist them. To provide a context for discussing such insights, the Task Force invited consultants attending the Chicago conference to review critical aspects of research in linguistics and psychology of importance to those planning educational programs for the disadvantaged. The following papers, prepared as background material for the Task Force, are presented here because they summarize certain aspects of research which need to be considered carefully by the profession. Lee Pederson reviews current studies of American dialects with reference to the inner cities. Samuel Kirk discusses experimentation indicating the positive effects of intensive educational programs on the learning of disadvantaged preschool children.

Social Dialects and the Disadvantaged

LEE A. PEDERSON

My invitation to attend this conference included a request that I prepare a paper on "The problems of language learning of culturally disadvantaged children and youth, with emphasis on those aspects of the overall problem with which observers in this project might be especially concerned."[1] In reviewing the roster of Task Force members, I find the names of some who have at their fingertips more information on the overall problem than I could gather in six months and the names of others who have more practical experience in teaching the culturally disadvantaged than I will ever have. Under these circumstances, it seems best to rely upon the research and experience of these authorities rather than compete with them. I will, therefore, outline the problems as they have already been defined, emphasize those aspects that I know best, and then welcome extensive discussion.

There are several important aspects of the overall problem which should be of interest to the observers in this project;[2] these are (1) problems of language underdevelopment, (2) problems of social dialectology,[3] and (3) problems of investigation. The first of these involves problems that were defined several years ago and certainly ought to be the concern of all projects presently underway. The second set of problems covers those that were discussed at the Bloomington Conference last summer and which will interest planners of all future

---

[1] When this paper was written, *culturally disadvantaged* was taken to mean anyone who is prevented, for whatever reason, from participating fully in the dominant culture, i.e., usually white middle class. This definition excludes the genuinely upper class who do not choose to participate fully in the bourgeois culture, but it does include such interesting social structures as the one described to me by Raven I. McDavid, Jr., in which Negroes at Institute, West Virginia, exclude from their more advanced and sophisticated culture those whom they label hillbillies.

[2] When this paper was written, it was assumed that the observers would be concerned with the problems of language learning as well as the programs to solve them. For that reason, considerable attention was given to field procedures, which may not be of primary importance to the observers but which should be brought to the attention of the teachers of the culturally disadvantaged.

[3] Raven I. McDavid, Jr., "American Social Dialects," *College English*, XXVI, 4 (January 1964), 254–260.

programs, especially those aimed at language learning difficulties in urban centers. The final set includes four broad areas of concern for language observers.

In May and June of 1962, the problem of "Improving English Skills of Culturally Different Youth" was discussed at a conference sponsored by the U. S. Office of Health, Education, and Welfare, Department of Education.[4] One of the papers read there was a research proposal by Alexander Frazier, Director of the Center for School Experimentation, The Ohio State University.[5] Frazier discussed the problem in terms of "language underdevelopment," and his three definitions of language underdevelopment provide an outline of the problems and research adopted at the 1962 conference under these three headings:

1. *True Verbal Destitution*, characteristic of some whose opportunities for using language may have been so circumscribed that they truly have less language than other children.

2. *Full but Nonstandard Development*, characteristic of some whose language includes broad departures from socially accepted norms.

3. *Unconceptualized Experience and Underdeveloped Language*, characteristic of some whose background in certain aspects of experience valued by the school has been so restricted that they may have had no occasion to verbalize meanings and, consequently, may appear impoverished in their language.[6]

Although behavioral scientists and researchers might become impatient with the language and heuristic observations of some of the participants in that conference, those reports seem especially useful in planning further investigation. Observers in this project should find them interesting because many reflect the attitudes of classroom teachers; linguists find them valuable because they offer hypotheses to be tested by systematic study.

Most investigations of verbal destitution have concentrated on the speech of the mentally ill and the mentally handicapped. Before considering those studies specifically concerned with the culturally disadvantaged, it is interesting to note that between 1920 and 1960 the northern Negro had, in addition to his linguistic problems, the high-

---

[4] Arno Jewett, Joseph Mersand, and Doris V. Gunderson (eds.), *Improving English Skills of Culturally Different Youth*. OE-30012, Bulletin 1964, No. 5 (Washington: U.S. Department of Health, Education, and Welfare, Office of Education, 1964).

[5] Alexander Frazier, "A Research Proposal to Develop the Language Skills of Children with Poor Backgrounds," *ibid.*, pp. 69–79.

[6] *Ibid.*, pp. 70–74.

est rate in the United States for commitment for mental illness, and Allison Davis has justly indicted the big city on both counts.[7]

In a report on her study of the speech of entering freshmen at a Negro college, Eunice Newton had identified three areas of verbal destitution:

1. *Limited Vocabularies*, chiefly derived from the Old English and Middle English wordstock;
2. *Impoverished Use of Descriptive and Qualifying Words*;
3. *Inability to Comprehend Figurative Language.*[8]

Marjorie Smiley, Director of the Office of Instructional Research at Hunter College, summarized the findings of several other investigations as follows:

> The verbal deprivation of lower class children begins, as all language learning begins, with their early experiences in speech. A 1948 study by Irwin of the development of speech in infancy reports that, while initial development was age-related only, development during the second year revealed social class differences. In a more recent study of lower class children's speech development, Templin reports that sentence length and complexity of sentence structure are related to socioeconomic level. The Institute of Developmental Studies, under the direction of Dr. Martin Deutsch, currently investigating the language patterns of lower class children, notes that they are ''poor in their use of verbs.''[9]

And it has been argued by Werner Cohen that to describe such language ''merely as dialect, though it may be this as well, is to miss the fact that the simplifications in linguistic structure characteristic of lower class speech make it almost impossible to frame intellectual concepts.''[10]

Apart from the studies mentioned above, research and recommendations concerning the second kind of ''language underdevelopment,'' namely, ''Full but Nonstandard Development,'' were limited to comments by Ruth I. Golden of the Detroit Public Schools and Walter Loban of the University of California at Berkeley. In discussing ''Ways to Improve Oral Communication,'' Mrs. Golden noted that many of her culturally disadvantaged students . . . use such structural deviations as ''he have,'' ''they is,'' ''he taken,'' and ''that's mines,'' add-

---

[7] Allison Davis, ''Society, the School, and the Culturally Deprived Student,'' *ibid.*, p. 12.

[8] Eunice Shaed Newton, ''Verbal Destitution: The Pivotal Barrier to Learning,'' *Journal of Negro Education*, 29 (Fall 1960), 497–499.

[9] Marjorie Smiley, ''Research and Its Implications,'' in Jewett, Mersand, and Gunderson, p. 39.

[10] Werner Cohen, ''On the Language of Lower-Class Children,'' *School Review*, 67 (Winter 1959), 435–440, as summarized by Frazier, *op. cit.*, p. 72.

ing the *s* sound, but saying, "ten cent," omitting the *s*. They may substitute *f* for the *th* as in *bofe, I* for *e* in *pInny*, the low front vowel *ae* for *aI* to confuse *rat* with *right,* and use a great many nonstandard expressions.[11]

In reporting the findings of a study of 338 children in the kindergarten and first six years of elementary school, Loban made the following observations:

> For the Negro child with a southern background, using the verb *to be* appropriately proved to be twelve times as troublesome as for the northern Caucasian subjects. Confusion of present with past tense impressed one as another difficulty to be attacked in the middle grades as well as earlier. By noting the incidence of southern Negro's errors in relation to those of the northern Caucasian, one can locate those deviations that require the greatest help in the schools with a number of Negro children similar to this group. For instance, the use of the nominative pronoun for the possessive (Mary took *she* book home) showed a larger difference between southern Negro and northern Caucasian than *hisself* and *himself.*
>
> Analysis of the nonconventional statements of the total sample for all seven years of this study showed subject-predicate agreement to be the major source of difficulty. That sensitivity to the conventions of standard English is related to skill in language was seen in the significant differences on conventional usage. The high group was significantly superior to the random group and the low group significantly below the random group. The results were significant at the 1 percent level; this finding occurred in various ways throughout the study.[12]

Loban also made these observations concerning the elements within the structural patterns:

> Although differences in structural patterns were not potable—with the exception of partials and linking verbs—very important differences did show up in the dexterity with which subjects used elements *within these structures.* The nominals, whether in subject or object position, and the movable elements showed marked differences when low and high groups were compared. This held true consistently for any syntactical nominal structure. It was assumed from this that predication, when it was studied, would show similar marked differences.[13]

Loban summarized those differences as follows:

1. In the movable elements of sentence patterns, the high group consistently showed a greater repertoire of clauses and multiples (movables within movables).
2. For subject nominals, the low group depended almost exclusively on nouns and pronouns. The high group used noun clauses, infinitives, and verbals.

---

[11] Ruth I. Golden, "Ways to Improve Oral Communication," in Jewett, Mersand, and Gunderson, p. 104.

[12] Walter Loban, "Language Ability in the Elementary School: Implications of Findings Pertaining to the Culturally Disadvantaged," *ibid.,* pp. 63–64.

[13] *Ibid.,* p. 66.

3. For nominals used as complements, both groups used nouns and pronouns with the same frequency, but the high group invariably exceeded the low group in the use of infinitives and clauses.[14]

Frazier's aforementioned research proposal dealt specifically with the third kind of "language underdevelopment," "Unconceptualized Experience and Underdeveloped Language." Although Frazier's experiment is, apparently, not yet completed, several interesting points (which may well prove useful to the observers in the present project) are made in defining his position. These are:

1. Language is a product of the process of conceptualization or thinking things out. The young child learns his language through imitation and a continuous testing out of what he thinks he knows. He can learn only those words and ways of dealing with experience that words represent and which he hears.

2. One learns with his native language many ways of dealing with experience that are culturally defined. The child incorporates in the language he learns certain kinds of discriminations that represent the qualities, objects, and processes that are deemed to have importance.

3. Groups in a population may differ in the variety and complexity of their frameworks for conceptualization, and these differences are reflected in their language. The young child learns to think with whatever language he learns from those around him. Naming, comparing, defining, judging, and generalizing will all necessarily be done within whatever limits exist in the minds and vocabularies of his older associates.

4. Children brought up in a disadvantaged group may be more handicapped than other children by having less language to think with in approaching school sponsored experiences. A child may be able to make highly differentiated verbal responses to some aspects of his experience that are highly valued by his family (such as types of crops, values of different fertilizers, and degrees of kinship) but may lack the framework for thinking and the words to use in dealing with more remote or "less important" matters.[15]

At the conference on Urban School Dialects and Language Learning held at Bloomington, Indiana, in August 1964, reports were made on several projects which are closely related to the problems outlined in 1962.[16] Most of these were preliminary surveys by linguists who were engaged in investigation of urban social dialects. The goals, techniques, findings, and implications for future research in the New York and Chicago projects indicate developments in social dialectology and suggest areas of interest for the present project.

---

[14] *Ibid.*

[15] Frazier, *op. cit.*, p. 75.

[16] The proceedings of the Bloomington Conference are printed in Roger W. Shuy (ed.), *Social Dialects and Language Learning* (Champaign, Ill.: National Council of Teachers of English, 1965).

Studies of variable elements in New York City speech have been undertaken (under the direction of William Labov of Columbia University) to describe the sociolinguistic structure of the local speech community. Using a sample already constructed for a sociological survey of 100,000 residents of the Lower East Side, Labov was able to concentrate his attention upon the linguistic habits of more than 1,000 informants. Although he found the Atlas materials, notably the dissertation of Mrs. Frank,[17] useful, he established new procedures to isolate socially significant variables and to examine these on the basis of contextual styles. His inquiry into differences in an informant's reading style and use of careful or casual speech offers an important consideration for all investigators of social dialects. Labov argues convincingly that it is not enough to draw conclusions from data without close consideration of the context in which the forms were elicited. His interviews included sections intended to encourage the casual style, e.g., discussions of childhood rhymes and another on dangers of death. The careful style was encouraged by the reading of a text, pronunciation of isolated words, and comparison of minimal pairs. In isolating the contextual styles, Labov uses several "channel cues," which include laughter or changes in tempo, breathing, volume, or pitch. Another important innovation in his technique is the analysis of subjective evaluations of linguistic variables by the informants themselves. That information is used to classify the linguistic variables into three basic categories:

indicators, which show social variation but usually not stylistic variation, and have little effect upon the listener's judgment of the social status of the speaker;

markers, which show both social and stylistic variation, and have consistent effects upon the conscious or unconscious judgment of the speaker's status by the listener;

stereotypes, which are the overt topics of social comment in the speech community, and may or may not correspond to actual linguistic behavior.[18]

The next phase in the New York project is the analysis of Negro and Puerto Rican speech. The aims of this phase are listed under two headings:

1. To determine the socially significant variables in English structure which separate Negro and Puerto Rican speakers from the rest of the New York speech community.

---

[17] Yakira H. Frank, "The Speech of New York City" (Unpublished Ph.D. dissertation, University of Michigan, 1948).

[18] William Labov, "Stages in the Acquisition of Standard English" in Shuy, op. cit.

2. To define those structual and functional conflicts of the Negro and Puerto Rican vernaculars with standard English which may interfere with the acquisition of reading skills.[19]

This project is already underway, and the speech of thirty-six Negro adults has been studied in detail. Plans have been made to interview fifty delinquent Negro boys, who have been sentenced to terms in state institutions, and twenty-five Puerto Rican boys with the same status.[20]

The findings in Labov's first study are reported in detail in his Columbia University dissertation, "The Social Stratification of English in New York City" (1964).[21] From these findings he presented a paper at Bloomington entitled "Stages in the Acquisition of Standard English,"[22] in which he discussed linguistic variables in the context of urban speech and identified six stages in the acquisition of spoken English:

1. The Basic Grammar (achieved under the influence of the parents);
2. The Vernacular (achieved in the neighborhood, ages 5 to 12);
3. Social Perception (achieved with wider contacts, ages 14 or 15);
4. Stylistic Variation (achieved in the first year of high school);
5. The Consistent Standard (never achieved by some);
6. The Full Range (never achieved by many).[23]

Labov also lists three obstacles to the acquisition of standard English:

1. Cultural Isolation;
2. Structural Interferences (e.g., phonological differences in the native dialect);
3. Conflicts in the Value System (e.g., attitudes toward teachers and peers).[24]

Under the direction of Raven I. McDavid, Jr., Alva Leroy Davis, and William M. Austin, the project in Chicago has been concerned primarily with large-scale inventorial research of social indicators (or variables) in the speech of Negroes and in-migrant Poor Whites. The phonological basis for this survey was established in my dissertation "The Pronunciation of English in Metropolitan Chicago: Vowels and Consonants"[25] and that study, like the other work completed in Chi-

---

[19] William Labov, "A Proposed Study of Negro and Puerto Rican Speech in New York City." Photocopied.

[20] *Ibid.*, p. 4.

[21] William Labov, "The Social Stratification of English in New York City" (Unpublished Ph.D. dissertation, Columbia University, 1964).

[22] Labov, in Shuy, *op. cit.*

[23] *Ibid.*

[24] *Ibid.*

[25] Lee A. Pederson, "The Pronunciation of English in Metropolitan Chicago: Vowels and Consonants" (Unpublished Ph.D. dissertation, University of Chicago, 1964).

Using a Listening Center in Miami, Florida

cago, was made along the lines of traditional Atlas methodology with considerable modification for urban research. The Chicago survey distinguishes the phonological variables found among the neighboring counties, the lower urban classes, and the characteristic Negro speech. Among the speech patterns distinguishing the neighboring counties from the characteristic forms of city and suburban residents are Midland and Southern forms and relics, many shared with the Negroes in the city, but none usually found among the speakers of the dominant Caucasian dialect. The social indicators of the lowest urban classes, however, though some are shared with the Negroes, were always found in Caucasian speech, especially the high-back vowels in *whore* and the stopped consonants in *either, mother,* and *father.* The Negro speech forms proved to be the most interesting, with ten phonetic and thirty-six phonemic differences identified.

To include those features which were indicative of age, education, or both, the tripartite classification of informants in the Atlas records was extended. Here, instead of listing them as

    I. Little formal education,
    II. Better formal education (usually high school),
    III. Superior education (usually college),[26]

the classification was extended to ten types to include:

1. A superior level of education, specifically a college degree with formal or informal graduate level studies or reading, and extensive social contacts.
2. A high level of education, specifically a college degree with less postgraduate studies or reading and fewer social contacts than Type 1.
3. A college degree, specifically exposure to four years of higher education.
4. A superior high school education, perhaps intellectually superior to Type 3, but heavily dependent upon written authoritarian sources for vocabulary development and ''preferred pronunciations.''
5. A good high school education.
6. A high school education, specifically exposure to four years of secondary schooling.
7. A superior elementary school education, perhaps intellectually superior to Type 6, but characterized by uncultivated speech.
8. A good elementary school education.
9. An alert uneducated informant.
10. An uneducated informant.[27]

With the speakers of the dominant dialect thus defined and with many social indicators identified, the next phase of the Chicago Project included the interview of fifty informants: thirty Negroes and twenty Poor Whites. Raven I. McDavid, Jr., and William M. Austin drew the following tentative conclusions from that data:

1. Vocabulary reflects cultural experience and can be expected to change as people become adjusted to city living. The survival of certain humble ethnic words in ethnic neighborhoods, of whatever kind, is traditional; it may even be reinforced by a feeling of ingroup solidarity.

2. Grammar reflects social and educational advantages. Grammatical differences between middle class and lower class speech are easily identified. They are

    [26] Hans Kurath *et al., Handbook of the Linguistic Geography of New England* (Washington: American Council of Learned Societies, 1939), p. 44.
    [27] Pederson, *op. cit.*

most striking in areas (such as the southeastern and south central states) where sharp differences of caste and class have long been recognized. Since the Negroes of the Chicago slums are normally from the lower class or the lower caste of such regions—whether born there or in Chicago—it is to be expected that their speech would show strong divergencies from the grammatical norms of middle class Chicago, and that in turn middle class Chicagoans would identify as ''Negro Grammar'' features that are widely distributed in uneducated southern speech of both races. The existence of these divergent grammatical forms has long been recognized in the schools; the traditional treatment, however, has been in terms of lapses, errors or deviations, with no recognition that they are part of a regular system. Future educational programs should be developed in terms of substituting for the grammatical system of lower class southern speech that of middle class Chicago white speech—at least for those economic and social situations where grammatical norms are important.

3. In pronunciation, differences between middle class and lower class white speech or between middle class and lower class Negro speech are much less easy to detect than differences between the speech of white Chicagoans and southern Negroes. Moreover, the fact that middle class white Chicagoans often identified as a southern Negro the southern white control speaker suggests that for middle class white Chicagoans any palpably southern pronunciation is automatically registered as Negro, rural, and uneducated though the speaker in question is city bred and the most highly educated of the group whose speech was sampled. This kind of identification suggests that any educational application of this project should take two directions:

a) Since for the moment the strong southern pronunciation of the Chicago lower class Negro constitutes a social handicap, it would be desirable to teach Chicago middle class pronunciation to the children of this group, beginning with nursery schools. Such teaching should be informal at the beginning, in any effort to provide a substitute for the characteristic language learning process where children arriving from various communities pick up the local idiom from older children in their neighborhood. Since the normal situation will operate only after genuinely integrated residential patterns are established, teachers in this artificial situation must recognize a discrepancy between the ''target pronunciation'' in the schools and the home pronunciation—and avoid stigmatizing the latter. The aim is *functional bidialectalism*, with the children able to switch codes as the occasion demands.

b) At the same time, as a part of education in human understanding, it would be desirable to include in the school English program, from a rather early period, something about the nature of languages, the origin of dialects, and the variety of cultivated pronunciations to be found in the United States. Some textbooks already provide this kind of information, and several series of illustrative recordings are either in progress or planned.[28]

---

[28] Raven I. McDavid, Jr., and William M. Austin, ''Preface'' to the report on the cooperative project in social dialects by University of Chicago and Illinois Institute of Technology.

These findings, then, in New York and in Chicago, not only enlarge our understanding of linguistic behavior but also recommend the inclusion of social dialect investigation for any large-scale approach to the problem of language learning among the culturally disadvantaged. As structural linguistics provides a methodology for rigorous analysis of formal features in the measurement of communication skills, so dialect investigation provides a methodology for the study of linguistic variables within their sociolinguistic context. The application of these methods is the subject of the third part of this paper.

From the standpoint of language, the observers in this project have at least four broad areas of concern. These are:

1. The people involved in the learning situation,
2. The range of the inquiry,
3. The methods of observation,
4. The criteria for evaluation.

After it has been established who the culturally disadvantaged are and what degrees of cultural disadvantage fall within the range of this survey, it will be necessary to identify the intellectual, social, and psychological characteristics of the students and their teachers and, if possible, of the friends, relatives, and others with whom the subject participates within the speech community. At a maximal level of thoroughness, this would involve investigation into the background of every student and teacher.

It is also important to consider differences in problems, as well as in linguistic structures, among different age groups. William Stewart of the Center for Applied Linguistics[29] has concerned himself with differences in what he calls "little boy" and "big boy" speech, and both Labov and I have pointed out differences which separate the adolescent Negro from the rest of his speech community.

For the second area of concern, the range of the inquiry, the observers in this project will probably be most interested in communication skills: effective speech, writing, and reading. The first step in such investigation will probably be inventorial. This will involve a listing of significant departures from middle class white speech (if this is the dominant dialect) as noted by both the teacher and the observer in terms of phonological, morphological, lexical, and syntactical variables. These variables, then, must be considered in terms of two fundamental questions:

---

[29] William A. Stewart, "Urban Negro Speech: Sociolinguistic Factors Affecting English Teaching," in Shuy, op. cit.

1. What are the specific ethnic, social, and regional variables in the particular situation?

2. What correspondences are apparent between the linguistic systems of the culturally disadvantaged student and his written performance?

If possible, each of these skills should be observed in situations which evoke both the casual and careful styles. It is as important to know how the student communicates under a minimum of pressure as it is to know how he performs for his teacher.

Several other aspects of the communication process are so obvious that they might not be given the attention they deserve. For example, there are distinct differences between the cognitive operations involved in speech (or writing) and those in reading. The former is essentially an encoding process; the later, a decoding process. Although it is important to remember that speech is primary, the relationship of the spoken word to each of these skills is distinctly different. Another common oversight in the linguistic approach to composition is a failure to distinguish between conversational speech and written (or oral) composition. Apart from the stylistic differences, there are important functional and formal differences between these modes of discourse. Most speech occurs in the form of dialogue with two or more participants actively cooperating at the structural, paralinguistic, kinesic, proxemic, and haptic levels. Written composition is almost always a monologue and is always done without the aid of vocal qualifiers, physical movement, shifting proximity, or bodily contact. The performer here is entirely on his own, as well as deprived of the use of these four important communication systems.

The third area of concern, the methods of observation, includes at least five techniques that have been used by fieldworkers and linguistic analysts. Each of these approaches provides different kinds of information, and each has its place within the plan of the present object.

1. *Free Conversation.* Charles C. Fries [30] established the corpus for his study of English structures with fifty hours of telephone conversation, and more recently Elizabeth Bowman based her investigation of the minor and fragmentary sentences in a corpus of spoken English on tape recorded conversations among the members of a family.[31] This technique offers a wider range of linguistic data than any of the other

---

[30] Charles C. Fries, *The Structure of English: An Introduction to the Construction of English Sentences* (New York: Harcourt, Brace and World, Inc., 1952).

[31] Elizabeth Bowman, "The Minor and Fragmentary Sentences in a Corpus of Spoken English" (Unpublished Ph.D. dissertation, University of Chicago, 1963).

methods, and, with the exception of sound film, is the closest approach to the actual language. This approach is especially valuable for inventorial investigation and is useful for comparative studies.

2. *The Atlas Interview*. After the free conversation has been observed, variables can be measured by eliciting response to a questionnaire. The interviewer provides a minimum of suggestion and encourages responses without giving the informant a choice among several forms.[32]

3. *The Check-list*. This method has been most successful in lexical surveys, notably in Wenker's German Atlas,[33] in Atwood's studies in Texas,[34] Allen's in the Upper Midwest,[35] and Shuy's in Illinois.[36] This technique is something like the multiple choice quiz, narrowing the range of responses but providing for a large number of informants at one time.

4. *Reading Texts*. Both C. K. Thomas [37] and Allan Forbes Hubbell [38] have made good use of the text method. Using something like "Grip the Rat," an interview can elicit pronunciations of identical syntactical forms in very careful spoken English.[39] A tape recorder is strongly recommended in this situation also.

5. *Written Texts*. As the great historical grammars of Jespersen, Poutsma, Kruisinga, and others were established through close analysis of literary texts, investigators in this project could do much the same kind of work with the not-so-literary student themes.

An extensive investigation of the language learning problems of the culturally disadvantaged should make use of all of these methods, emphasizing whichever techniques are the most productive in the collection of data and the most effective in the analysis of the variables.

Finally, in determining the criteria for evaluation, several sources ought to be considered. These range from theoretical essays on gram-

---

[32] See Kurath, *op. cit.*

[33] See Walther Mitska, *Handbuch Zum Deutschen Sprachlatas* (Marburg: N. H. Elwort, 1952).

[34] E. Bagby Atwood, *The Regional Vocabulary of Texas* (Austin: University of Texas Press, 1962).

[35] Harold B. Allen, "The Linguistic Atlas of the Upper Midwest," *Orbis*, I (May 1952), 89–94.

[36] Roger W. Shuy, *The Northern-Midland Dialect Boundary in Illinois*, *Publication of the American Dialect Society*, 38 (November 1962).

[37] C. K. Thomas, *The Phonetics of American English* (New York: Ronald Press, 1958).

[38] Allan Forbes Hubbell, *The Pronunciation of English in New York City: Consonants and Vowels* (New York: King's Crown Press, 1950).

[39] William Labov also made use of this technique in his aforementioned studies.

mar and usage to field investigations in linguistic geography. Since no regional dialect has established itself as distinctly prestigious, every situation will involve problems that are related both to generally accepted standards of correctness and to the dominant dialect of the community under consideration.

First, close attention must be given to those standards of correctness observed by the teacher and the observer, whether those standards are derived from a consensus of usages, a historically established authority, or the mystical intuition of the transformationalist. In addition to such important theoretical statements on the subject as, for example, Jespersen's "Standard of Correctness"[40] and Joos's *Five Clocks*,[41] the research of the Usage Committee of the American Dialect Society coordinated by Gerald Udell might also be consulted. It might also be good to compare our attitudes on this problem with those of the teachers and their students in the classroom. Everyone knows that something must be done to modify the attitude of the student who regards standard English as a sissy style, but not enough has been said about the teachers themselves. What is to be done about the compulsive middle class reactions of many Caucasian teachers or the hypercorrective tendencies of the upward mobile Negro?

And, second, since each situation will involve problems peculiar to the local culture, it will be necessary to review the research already done in American English in any given area. Several urban surveys have been made, providing descriptions of the dominant dialect. The coordination of research projects is as important to investigation as is the application of these findings to pedagogy. Since the present project should be especially helpful in relating linguistic research to the problems of language learning, it is to be hoped that this work will make full use of the experience and results of past investigations.

---

[40] Otto Jespersen, "Standards of Correctness," *Mankind, Nation and Individual from a Linguistic Point of View* (Bloomington, Ind.; Indiana University Press, 1964). First published in 1946, three years after Jesperson's death.

[41] Martin Joos, *The Five Clocks, International Journal of American Linguistics*, 28 (April 1962), 2.

Language, Intelligence, and the Educability of the Disadvantaged

Samuel A. Kirk

A difficult problem in education is that we must provide for individual differences. Consequently we have to consider three factors which form the basis for individual differences in children. The first of these is genetic; the second is prenatal; and the third is the physical, social, and psychological environment which begins after birth. As for the first factor, genetics, we know we cannot do anything about a person's genes, at least at the present time. Similarly, we cannot do very much about defects that occur during and immediately after pregnancy; however, there are some things we can do about them. By this I mean that the effects of genetics are not so static that environment cannot impinge upon the organism. Indeed, it is this postnatal environment that must be the primary target of education.

For an example, we do know that there are certain variations in genes, errors of metabolism that occur in children, and chromosomal abnormalities about which little can be done. There is a concept in genetics, however, called the *norm of reaction* or reaction range, which allows for modifications of the inherited genes by such things as mutations effects *in utero,* paranatal influences, and life experiences. Thus in the area of language and intelligence there could be a range, the extent of which we can only surmise. The original, inherited potential of an individual, aside from environmental influences (both biological and cultural), may not have been fixed but has a wide range of reaction to varying influences. Similarly, even the organism which results from genetic, prenatal, and paranatal influences probably has a reaction range within which variation may result from life experiences. Perhaps we should say that an individual has an I.Q.—not of 80 or 60 or 120—but of 80 to 120 or 120 to 160, and that how the individual develops after birth is dependent on the interaction of the organism with the environment. So this individual may have an I.Q. of 80 with a poor environment or 120 with a good environment. I think that is the kind of range within which we operate culturally, educationally, or environmentally.

I do not like the term "cultural deprivation" because it is not well defined and is not a diagnostic term. Once I had psychologists test children in low socioeconomic areas. They tapped on doors and asked the mothers if they had children under six who could be tested. Most of the children had low I.Q.'s. But occasionally one of the psychologists would come in and say, "You say they are low in intelligence because they are low in socioeconomic standing, but out of one of the worst homes in town there is a four-year-old boy with an I.Q. of 125." That happened a number of times, so I went out and visited one of those homes. I found a Negro boy, 4 years old, whose mother was working and whose grandmother lived in the home. All the grandmother had done since the boy was born was to play with that boy. Apparently she gave him a tremendous amount of stimulation. She wasn't educated, she was not even particularly intelligent, but her mental ability and her language were well above that of the four-year-old boy. With the stimulation that his grandmother gave, he developed good communication and intelligence, and from a home we would call "culturally deprived" he was able to achieve an I.Q. of 125.

I think we ought to talk about intellectual and language deprivation rather than socieconomic or cultural deprivation because there is not a one-to-one correlation between the two. I once worked with a set of twin girls, aged five. They came from a home that would not necessarily be called culturally disadvantaged—perhaps lower middle class. The father was economically stable. The mother was very religious and had signs around her house that read "God does not swear." "God does not cheat." "God does not talk out loud." (As a matter of fact, God did not do anything the mother didn't like.) It was a very restrictive home. These two little girls could not move without surveillance and restrictions. We examined both of them; one had an I.Q. of 87, the other an I.Q. of 76. One was left handed; the other was right handed. One had a speech defect; one was more verbal than the other. So we took the girl who scored lowest into a preschool and trained her, leaving the other at home. At the age of 6 or 6½ they both entered the first grade, and we followed the two girls for four years. After initial testing, at which time the one with the preschool experience (who was more defective initially—left handed, speech defect, etc.) was doing normal work with a normal I.Q. and reading in the fourth grade. The other one was in the fourth grade, reading at about second grade level. During the one year between ages 5 and 6 (particularly because of the greater opportunity for the mother's restrictiveness to affect the second girl), a great difference between the two girls occurred. This was a case of intellectual and language deprivation but not necessarily socioeconomic or cultural deprivation. I do not know whether we should make these differentiations or not, because one can go into an area that we call low socioeconomic and still find some children quite high and some quite low. And it may not be entirely due to genetic differences.

There are two things to present from our research, relating partially to the problem. The first consists of studies of preschool education with these children. The question is, ''Can we change the intellectual and language abilities and later adjustment of children from lower socioeconomic groups by the intervention of some sort of stimulation outside the home such as that of a good nursery school?'' I will present some data on this problem and then move into another topic called the ''Communication Process.''

The first is an experiment with some children all under five—averaging about 4½ years of age. Among them we found four children who were so neglected in their homes that the social agencies had to remove them and place them in ''foster homes.'' Usually these foster homes were not of the highest type, but at least there was someone who would take the child for the $60 a month provided by Family Service. We also placed these four children in the special preschool. We examined them on many intelligence tests and rated them according to a composite evaluation—not just an I.Q. These four children all increased significantly in their rate of development. One went up as much as 30 points in I.Q.—all of them went up at least 10 points. This is a situation in which we intervened rather drastically, taking the youngsters out of the home and placing them in foster homes (usually lower middle class homes) and also adding the stimulation of a preschool from 9 a.m. to 3:30 p.m. each day. This procedure increased the rate of development for all four children, as shown in Table I.

We also had eight other families in town, all on public assistance, very deprived economically and intellectually. These eight families had a lot of children—twenty-six children under age 6. We placed twelve of these children in a preschool (Experimental Preschool Children, Table I), sending a taxi to the home to bring them to the school in the morning, and returning them to the home by taxi at 3:30. The other fourteen were twins (including the twin mentioned earlier) or siblings of the twelve in the experimental group. We included as sibling controls those who were either a year younger or a year older than the twelve in the experimental group. We followed these children from age 4½ to age 8. At 8, after they had been in the public schools

TABLE I

Development of Children in Foster Homes plus Preschool, and Comparison of
Experimental Preschool Group with Siblings and Twin Controls
Living in the Same Home

	Foster Home plus Preschool Education		Experimental Preschool Children		Twins and Sibling Controls	
	N = 4		N = 12		N = 14	
	No.	Ratio	No.	Ratio	No.	Ratio
Increased in rate of development	4	1.0	8	2/3	2	1/7
Held original rate of development	0	0.0	3	1/4	7	1/2
Decreased in rate of development	0	0.0	1	1/12	5	5/14

for a year or two, various measures showed that of the twelve children,
eight had increased their rate of development significantly, three had
remained the same, and one had dropped. These are children who attended the preschool but remained in their own homes, as contrasted
with the other four who were placed in the foster homes and attended
preschool.

Of the twin and sibling controls, two did increase their rate of development while staying at home, seven held their rate of development,
and neither rose nor lowered significantly. Five dropped in rate of
development. All of the final evaluations were made at approximately
the age of 8.

The results presented in Table I indicate that environmental intervention (such as a foster home and preschool) at a young age yields
very good results. When you intervene with a preschool but leave the
children at home, you get positive but less marked results. When you
do not intervene at the preschool level (even though the children enter
school at the age of 6), they tend to either hold their own or drop in
rate of development.

To evaluate the effect of preschool experience on the rate of development of young children in an institutional setting, we also organized a preschool for fifteen three- to five-year-olds in a state institution for mentally retarded children. Another twelve were left in
the wards. It will be noticed from the graphs in Figure 1 that between
ages 4½ and 8, on the Binet test, the Kuhlmann test, and the Vineland
School Maturity test, those who attended the preschool increased in
I.Q. and S.Q. significantly. The children who remained in the wards
and then later went to school tended to drop in I.Q. Six of the fif-

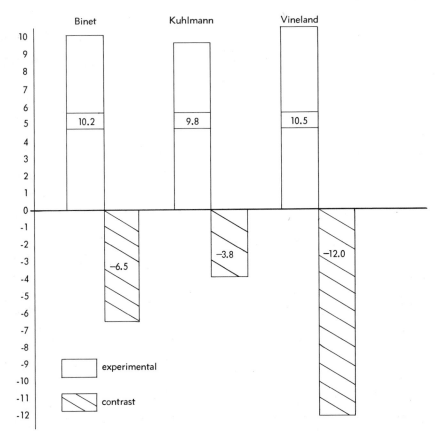

FIGURE 1

IQ and SQ Change Scores of Experimental and Contrast Groups

teen experimental children were paroled. And out of the 6 who were paroled, two became normal. One of them is graduating from high school this year and has been accepted at a state university. In terms of I.Q., as shown in Figure 1, the data show that the experimental group went up 10.2 I.Q. points on the average, while the control group dropped 6.5 on one test. Such differences are considered significant.

Figure 2 shows graphically the effect of introducing stimulation at different ages. The first bar represents a study made by Skeels in 1939 in Iowa. He found a group of 25 low I.Q. children below the age

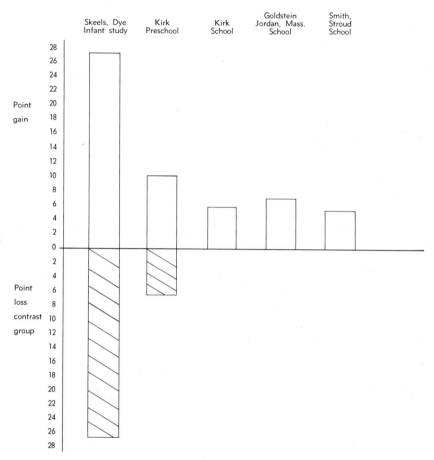

FIGURE 2

Changes in IQ Scores When Training Is Initiated at Different Age Levels

of 3 in an orphanage of 200 children. He took half of this group, 12 children, at ages 1 and 2½ years (average age 19 months) and placed them singly or in pairs in separate wards of an Iowa institution for mental defectives where they were placed with older, mildly defective girls. He said to the older mentally defective, adolescent girls, "Here is your baby. Stimulate him. Teach him to walk, teach him to talk, and play with him." The girls competed with respect to which child talked first, walked first, and what they learned to do. Two years later, they examined the 12 children committed to the institution for mental defectives. These children showed an average increase in I.Q. of 27.5 points, and most of them were paroled from the institution and placed in foster homes.

The children who remained in an unstimulating orphanage environment dropped in I.Q. 26 points. Although the average I.Q. of this contrast group had been 86.7 as compared to an average initial I.Q. of 64.3 for the experimental group, their average I.Q. dropped to 60.5 after two years, whereas the I.Q. of the group receiving individual stimulation rose to 91.8.

This study was published in 1939 and received tremendous criticism. It was thought to be impossible; tests at that level were unreliable; it was a fake. Terman and McNemar at Stanford made some statistical studies and said that the statistics were wrong. Dr. Goodenough said sarcastically that according to this, all we have to do is to send our children to an institution for the feeble-minded to be raised by feeble-minded girls and their I.Q.'s would go up. Anyway, the study was criticized so drastically that Skeels, Dye, Skodak, and others working in this field kept quiet for a long time.

Recently, however, the question has again received attention. Dr. Skeels has made a long-term follow-up study of his twenty-five children. But he did not follow them up in the usual way by sending letters. Twenty-one years had elapsed since the time he had last seen the children. So he decided that he would have to do it personally and has spent several years finding all twenty-five subjects. Of the group that remained in the orphanage, 50 percent are now in public institutions. One had died. The average school attainment for the twelve children who had remained in the orphanage was third grade, while the average grade of the experimental group was twelfth grade. After twenty-one years and much criticism, Dr. Skeels was vindicated.

My experiment (the second bar in Figure 2) started with children a little older (average age 4½) in institutions and in communities. You will remember that I likewise found an increase in I.Q. among the children in preschools and a decrease in those who remained at home or remained in the institution wards. But you will notice that the difference between the extent of effect on Skeels' children aged 1½ and that on children aged 4½ is quite marked.

We have had three other studies with children 6 years of age and older. We find that when the deprived retarded child enters school at the age of 6, he does have an acceleration of about 6 or 7 I.Q. points according to intelligence tests. But when the improved environment is provided after age 8 is reached, we find increases are difficult to obtain.

The moral of this story is that, in language and intellectual ability, the greatest development in intelligence and language probably occurs between conception and age 3 or 4. And then when one works with children at age 4, something can be done but not as much as at an early infant stage. At age 6 something can be done but not as much as can be accomplished at age 4. Less and less can be accomplished as the children grow older as far as acceleration in intellectual development is concerned.

These data are confirmed in a study by Benjamin Bloom whose recent book on stability in human characteristics (physical, intellectual, and academic) draws the same conclusion—that 50 percent of the variance in intelligence takes place between conception and age 4, 30 percent between 4 and 8, and 20 percent after age 8. So what I am trying to say is that the bulk of evidence, biologically, psychologically, and socially, would indicate the earlier we introduce meaningful stimulation, the more we can hope to produce a change in language ability and intellectual characteristics.

Learning Disabilities

In addition to children with low intelligence, there are many children in our schools who have been delayed in learning to talk, who do not develop language facility, or who have great difficulty in reading, spelling, writing, or mathematics. It is said that there are children who are not deaf but cannot hear, who are not blind but cannot see, or who are not mentally retarded, but cannot learn. Such children have been classified as having learning disabilities.

In the past, extreme learning disorders of children have been the concern of the medical profession, since such disorders in adults have resulted from brain injuries after the functions had been acquired. As a result, children with these developmental disorders have been referred for neurological examinations, although generally there is no medical treatment for such abnormalities if they are found. From an educational point of view, the question of brain injury or a predisposition to malfunction because of a genetic determiner is usually of secondary importance. The important problem is a behavioral assessment of the child which leads to a remedial program designed to remove or ameliorate the disability.

There are currently a number of approaches to the training of disabilities in children. One example of behavioral assessment which leads to remediation is the analysis of psycholinguistic disabilities in children on which the staff at the Institute for Research on Exceptional Children has been working for a number of years. Although the system has been described in previous publications (Kirk and McCarthy, 1961; McCarthy and Kirk, 1961; Bateman and Kirk, 1964), a brief and condensed explanation will be given here.

The communication model, presented in Figure 3, includes three dimensions (a) *levels* of organization (a meaningful or representational level as well as a more automatic, nonmeaningful level); (b) *channels* of communication by which stimuli are received and responses made (including only the more common visual-motor channel and auditory-vocal channels); and (c) *processes* by which communication takes place (the receptive process of "decoding," the expressive process of "encoding," and an intermediary process which has been labeled "association"). The interaction of these three dimensions makes necessary nine tests to isolate the effect of each factor on the child's communicative functioning.

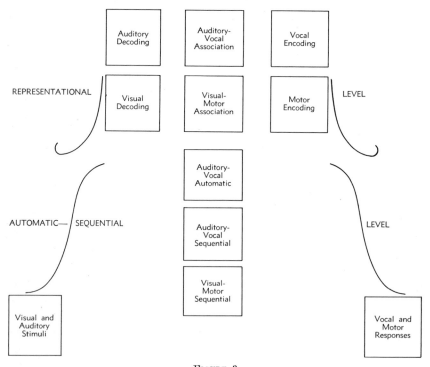

FIGURE 3
A Model of the Communication Process

Tests were constructed to isolate each of the nine factors in Figure 4 so that abilities and disabilities in the communication process may be identified. These tests were standardized on 700 normal children between the ages 2 and 9.

The meaning of each test in Figure 3 is presented below:

1. *Auditory decoding* measures the child's ability to understand spoken language.
2. *Visual decoding* measures the child's ability to understand visual objects without the use of vocal response.
3. *Auditory-vocal association* measures the child's ability to associate verbal symbols.
4. *Visual-motor association* measures the child's ability to relate visual objects.
5. *Vocal encoding* measures the child's ability to express himself vocally.
6. *Motor encoding* measures the child's ability to express himself in motor gestures.
7. *Auditory vocal automatic* measures the child's ability to respond in automatic or grammatical terms.
8. *Auditory vocal sequential* measures the child's auditory sequential memory, such as digit repetition.
9. *Visual motor sequential* measures the child's memory for sequential visual symbols.

The theoretical background of this construct of the communication process will not be elaborated here, since this has been discussed elsewhere. It will suffice to say that discrete tests were constructed for each of the nine abilities. The scores on the Illinois Test of Psycholinguistic Abilities can be drawn on a profile so that intra-individual differences among abilities can be analyzed.

The value of such a procedure is its diagnostic uses for isolating the disabilities that require remediation. This procedure differs from that of an omnibus intelligence test which results in an M.A. and an I.Q. from which a classification is made. An I.Q. of 75, for example, tells the examiner that the child is retarded in general intelligence, but does not tell the teacher where his deficits lie so that amelioration may be effected. An analogy is found in reading examinations. The survey type reading achievement test informs the examiner of the level or the grade at which the child is reading. It does not inform the teacher about the specific difficulties the child may have in the reading process. Diagnostic reading tests are administered after the

Results of Remediation

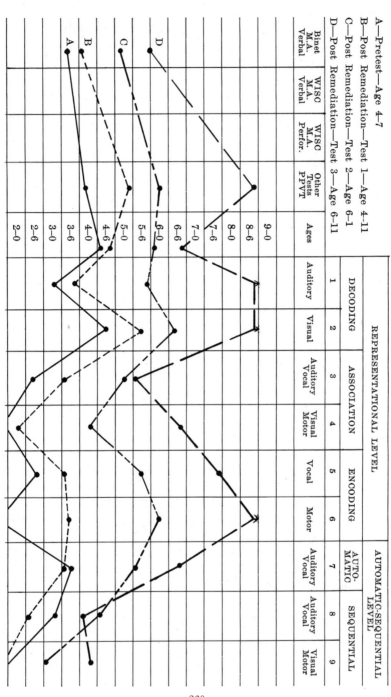

A—Pretest—Age 4-7
B—Post Remediation—Test 1—Age 4-11
C—Post Remediation—Test 2—Age 6-1
D—Post Remediation—Test 3—Age 6-11

FIGURE 4

260

survey test for the latter purpose. The Illinois Test of Psycholinguistic Abilities serves a similar purpose.

Several examples of such a diagnosis are illustrated below, together with the results of remediation.

Figure 4 presents a profile of the test data on John. This boy had shown noticeable delay in talking and walking, and at age 4 he had been excluded from a nursery school because of suspected retardation and social immaturity. His developmental history indicated that he crawled at 18 months and walked at 23 months. He used two-word combinations at 3 years instead of the usual age of 2 years. The medical examination was negative. At age 4-4 he obtained an I.Q. of 79 on the Stanford Binet.

Profile A represents the first examination of John at age 4-6. It will be noted from the profile that auditory decoding (1), visual dicoding (2), auditory vocal automatic (7), and auditory vocal sequential (8), represent his abilities. He scores low, or below norms of age 2, on association (3,4), encoding (5,6), particularly motor encoding (6), and the visual motor sequential test (9). These deficits indicate the areas in which John needs remediation.

Remediation was given this boy in the home, four times a week for four months. It consisted of exercises in motor encoding, development of visual-motor association, and visual sequencing. At the end of four months he was reexamined. Profile B represents the first posttest and shows progress in many areas and particularly in motor encoding. He was then tutored for eight months (summer session intervening) and examined one year later. Profile C represents the results of the third examination. It should be noted that marked gains were made in the areas of disability: visual-motor association, motor and vocal encoding, and in visual sequencing. The other areas developed at or above the rate expected in normal growth.

Individual tutoring continued sporadically. In addition he was enrolled in a kindergarten with an experienced rhythmic and sensorimotor program. In this program he attended fifteen half-hour sessions over a period of five weeks.

The group training was geared to activities pertinent to body image, sensori-motor integrity, and psycholinguistic abilities. Activities were presented in nine of the twelve movement areas suggested by Barsch's Movegenic Theory (1963):

a) visual dynamics (see and move)
b) auditory dynamics (hear and move)

c) dynamic balance (balance both sides of body)
d) spatial awareness (awareness of one's body in space as a reference point)
e) tactual dynamics (feel and move)
f) body awareness
g) rhythm (movement to well-defined rhythmic patterns)
h) unilateral and bilateral movement (move one side of body or two sides)
i) flexibility (ability to change tempo, movement patterns, mood, etc.)

At the termination of this program, John had five one-hour psychodrama sessions. At the beginning of training he appeared withdrawn and unmotivated to move or play roles. Encouragement was used as a motivational factor by allowing for small successes in simple activities, progressing to more difficult movements. His attitude changed from one of withdrawal to that of active participation. (Painter, 1964).

At the termination of this program John was again reexamined. Profile D in Figure 4 shows surprising acceleration in auditory decoding (1), visual decoding (3), and in his area of greatest deficit, motor encoding (6). At this point his scores were higher than his chronological age. Auditory and visual sequencing, not touched in training during the latter period, now remain the greatest deficits. In addition to the test scores, parents and teachers reported considerable improvement in this boy's abilities and in his succesful participation in activities with other children. His last I.Q. at age 6-8 was 86 on the Binet, and his mental age on the Peabody Picture Vocabulary Test was 8–10, confirming the scores at that level on auditory and visual decoding.

The next case I will discuss concerns Tommy, a ten-year-old boy in the fourth grade, who was referred for examination because of his difficulty in responding vocally and in writing. His classmates accepted him as a boy "who didn't talk." The teacher reported that in a discussion he raised his hand in class but when called upon did not respond or responded in one word sentences. One teacher reported that it seemed as though he wanted to say something but could not. Counseling was tried with the boy without success.

Psychometric examinations ranged from an I.Q. of 73 on the Goodenough Draw-a-Man-Test to 118 I.Q. on the Wechsler Verbal Scale (excluding the vocabulary test) and 129 on the Peabody Picture

Vocabulary Test. On reading, arithmetic, and language achievement tests he was scoring at the third grade level.

Figure 5 presents the profile of Tommy on the Illinois Test of Psycholinguistic Abilities. It will be noted from the final profile that this boy is extremely deficient in both vocal and motor encoding but near the top of the norms in most of the other tests.

Helping Preschool Children in Honolulu

Results of Remediation of an Expressive Disability

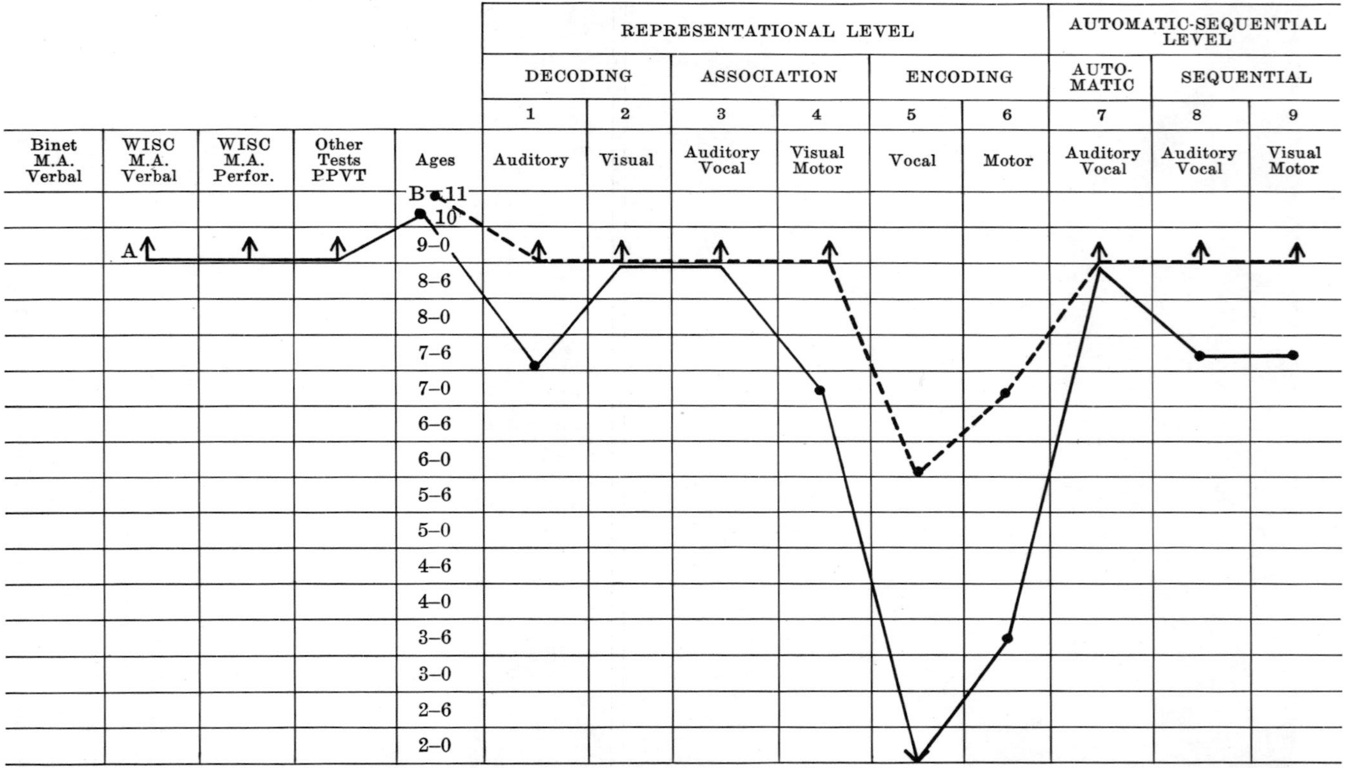

FIGURE 5

264

An effort was made to elicit vocal and motor responses from this boy in the classroom and also in a tutorial situation. The classroom teacher made an effort to assist him in vocal response by telling him a part of the sentence so that he could repeat it and complete it. The tutor, with the aid of the program learning laboratory, programed through a computer lessons that could be accomplished on a typewriter. Here again he was given sentences which he could read orally, then sentences with a letter of a word missing, then sentences with a word or words missing. In addition a tape recorder was used to record his vocal responses, which he could play back by pressing a lever.

Profile A showed quite clearly a boy of normal intelligence but with a severe vocal and motor encoding disability, a typical case of "expressive aphasia." Profile B shows the results of the post-test a year later, at the age of 11. It will be noted that he made over three years' progress in encoding. The teacher currently reports that the boy has made marked improvement and that he is expressing himself in class to an extent not previously expected.

These and similar cases illustrate a clinical approach to the amelioration of learning disabilities in children, some of whom had been merely classified as mentally retarded. This is decidedly a different approach to the education of some of these children

It does not in any way replace the emphasis on the three R's and social adjustment for these children. It does, however, introduce another dimension, namely the attempt to train aptitudes instead of only achievements. It can be another dimension of education and can relate to the educability of intelligence as measured by modern intelligence tests.

The basic approach of this method employs behavioral analysis and behavioral treatment. It is not necessary to determine whether or not a child has a central nervous system involvement. It is necessary to determine the behavioral or functional abilities and disabilities, and to organize learning techniques that will ameliorate the behavioral deficits. Remediation in this context does not assume that biological structure or function is being changed or altered. It assumes that the child has potentialities in certain areas that have not been developed, due possibly to a biological defect but also to an avoidance of the activity because of early failure. A child who has some difficulty in expressing himself verbally will tend to avoid verbal interaction and substitute a motor method of expression. Or, if he has some difficulty in visual interpretation, he may rely on auditory reception for information. As the child grows, the discrepancy between ability in areas that are comfortable and those that are not becomes greater. Special training on the deficits tends, therefore, to develop functions that should have developed earlier.

REFERENCES

Barsch, R. "Project M.O.V.E. as a Model for Rehabilitation Theory." Paper presented at American Psychological Association Convention, Philadelphia, Pennsylvania, 1963.

Descoeudres, Alice. *The Education of Mentally Defective Children.* Translated by E. R. Rom from 2nd ed. Boston: D. C. Heath & Company, 1928.

Itard, J. M. G. *The Wild Boy of Aveyron.* 1894. Translated by G. & Muriel Humphrey, 1932 (reprint). New York: Appleton-Century-Crofts, 1962.

McCarthy, J. J., and S. A. Kirk. *The Illinois Test of Psycholinguistic Abilities, Experimental Edition.* Urbana: University of Illinois Press, 1961. (a)

———. *Examiner's Manual, The Illinois Test of Psycholinguistic Abilities, Experimental Edition.* Urbana: University of Illinois Press, 1961. (b)

Montessori, Maria. *The Montessori Method.* 1894. Translated by Anne S. George, 1912 (reprint). New York: Schocken Books, 1964.

Painter, Genevieve. "The Effect of a Physical and Sensory-Motor Activity Program on Perceptual-Motor-Spatial Abilities of Kindergarten Children." Unpublished Master's dissertation, University of Illinois, 1964.

Skeels, H. M., and H. B. Dye. "A Study of the Effects of Differential Stimulation on Mentally Retarded Children, *Proceedings of the American Association on Mental Deficiency,* 44, 1 (1939), 114–136.

Discussion

QUESTION: DOES ORAL LANGUAGE AID LEARNING?

The Russian School of Psychology talks about the verbal control of behavior, or the regulation of behavior by verbal control. This means that an individual can do things if he can say them. The experiments which they use to prove this are rather simple experiments in which a child is told that when he sees a red light he is to press a button, and when he sees a green light he is not to press the button. They used this experiment for different ages of children with different intelligence levels. They find that a child can learn the procedure much faster if when the red light comes on, he says, "Press," and when he sees a green light he says, "Don't press." When the words *press* and *don't press* are spoken, the children learn the procedure faster than they do without the verbal control. There is evidence from other experiments that oral response increases the speed of learning.

QUESTION: IF, AS YOU SAY, EARLY EDUCATION IS MOST PROFITABLE, WHY HAVE WE NOT EMPHASIZED EDUCATION AT THIS AGE?

When we work with children ages 4, 5, and 6, we obtain general increases in I.Q.'s; when we work with children 10 and 11 years old we do not obtain any great increases in I.Q.'s. The Russians have developed créches in which they work with children 6 months and above. We have to realize that what children can accomplish in English IV in high school depends a lot on what was done in the lower age levels.

We have established a tradition of compulsory education at ages 6 and 7. One can ask the question, ''Why 6, why 7? Why not 8?'' Why is it that we happen to establish ages 6 or 7 for compulsory education? Is it sacrilegious in some places to send children to school earlier because that is the province of the home? I think it is time we ask why compulsory education does not begin at 5, or 4, or 3, or 2. It might be profitable with some groups to have compulsory education at 2 years. In intellectually and linguistically deprived children, there seems to be a lack of development and conceptualization not because of the children's restricted environment, but because the environment is not varied sufficiently. There is not enough variety of experiences. I am inclined to think that we will have to make radical changes in the preschool period, especially for children from disadvantaged homes. We probably have to take some of these children out of their homes at 8 a.m. and keep them in school until 6 or 8 p.m. We should probably also work with mothers at the same time.

QUESTION: CAN WE EDUCATE THESE YOUNG CHILDREN IN LARGE GROUPS?

One difficulty occurs when a group of children with different dialects are brought together. The children play with each other and their many language deficits interact. The teacher alone is not going to be able to change these children, because a child tends to function like his peer group. A normal child in a class of the mentally retarded becomes more like the mentally retarded. Perhaps the best thing for these children is to put them in a high socioeconomic preschool class. Perhaps the other children can teach them more than the teacher can. I think we are going to have to establish preschools in a very intensive manner. We will need to have many more adults in a class than are found in the first grade or kindergarten class. Not one teacher to forty children, but one teacher to four or five children.

A Boy in a Detroit, Michigan, Reading Class Receives Individual Help

Part V

GENERAL RECOMMENDATIONS

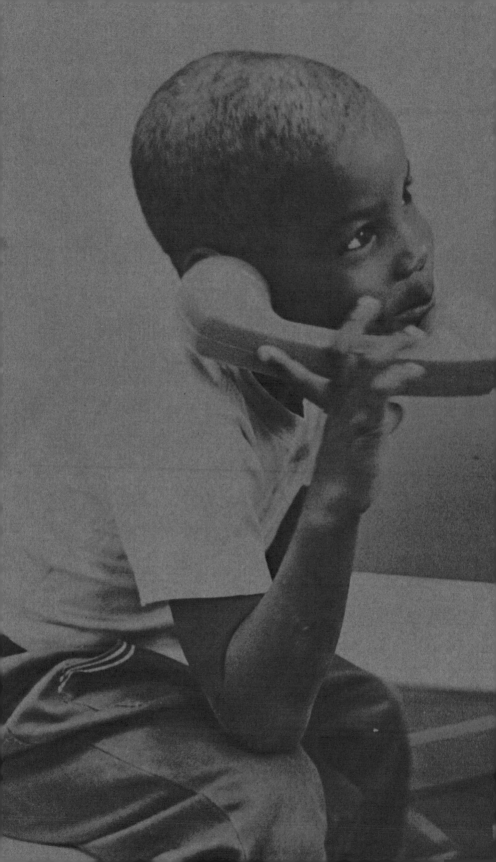

General Recommendations

The Task Force of the National Council of Teachers of English, after its four month nationwide study of projects and programs for the disadvantaged, proposes ten general recommendations for the future establishment and operation of such projects and programs. The recommendations are not offered as solutions but as guidelines for solving problems currently besetting national and regional efforts to adapt the system of education to the special needs of the disadvantaged.

1. Leaders in all parts of the country report the need for increased cooperation and communication among educators concerned with the disadvantaged. Most college and university researchers, agency officials, and project directors seem to be working in near isolation; many community agencies and organizations concerned with the problems of education work independently of local school systems, and school systems make few attempts to examine or coordinate with their work the efforts of nonschool enterprises.

The NCTE Task Force recommends that every reasonable measure be taken to establish, especially at the local level, lines of communication and bonds of cooperation among persons, organizations, and institutions working with the disadvantaged.

University researchers and project directors with local school and agency officials need to discover ways of mutually increasing their effectiveness, through cooperation in research projects, testing discoveries, and disseminating information. Schools cannot hope to achieve maximum success if they fail to secure community backing; neither will community agencies achieve permanent gains if they ignore the schools.

At the university level, linguists, sociologists, psychologists, economists, and educators need to explore ways of bringing the resources of their individual disciplines to bear on the problems of cultural, social, and educational disadvantage.

Above all, for maximum professional productivity, the various national clearinghouses of information on the disadvantaged should be notified of the work being done at all levels, whether action programs or research experiments.

2. Many disadvantaged children and adults speak a nonstandard English dialect. Every speaker of English is a speaker of a dialect,

whether it is characteristic of New England, New York City, sub-urban Chicago, rural Georgia, Harlem, or Oakland, California. The unfortunate and unavoidable fact is that some of the English dialects are so unique as to prevent speakers from participating fully in social structure, in prosperity, in the distinct culture, or in the democracy of the United States. Our educational enterprise has as one important function the preparation of every citizen for full participation. And to the extent that a man's dialect denies him this privilege, the school must help him overcome that disability. Teachers everywhere recognize that social and economic mobility requires that a person be able to speak an "established" dialect, or standard informal English. However, no one seems to be certain what to do, when to do it, or how to go about it.

The NCTE Task Force recommends that children be permitted to operate in the dialect of their community at the lower levels of elementary school education, and that direct instruction in the use of standard informal English be begun no earlier than the intermediate elementary grades.

During the early stages of development in school, children must become acquainted with language in general, with its uses in thinking and communicating; many of these experiences must be provided through the dialect which they already speak. As children gain experience in listening to and understanding informal English, especially through contact with teachers, school programs can gradually begin to teach standard informal English.

This does not imply, of course, that children not be exposed to standard English dialect or that classroom personnel speak the local dialect. It implies that actual instruction in the use of standard English is more appropriate and effective after children have experience listening to and understanding it from television, radio, and, especially, the teacher.

3. The lack of planned attention to oral pattern practice, to communicating ideas aloud, and to planned experiences in listening is a serious deficiency in many programs. Rigidly structured reading programs, without oral experiences using new vocabulary and sentence patterns, seem unlikely to achieve lasting growth.

The NCTE Task Force recommends that oral language receive greater stress in language instruction for the disadvantaged at all levels of education, from preschool through adult.

Only as progress is made in the use of oral language will there be substantial improvement in reading and writing. The interdependence of these language skills has been demonstrated both in research and in practice. All forms of drama, from puppetry to formal acting, and the oral tradition of literature need to be given greater emphasis in schools.

4. Literature rests on a shaky foundation in programs for the disadvantaged. In some areas, because literature in traditional textbooks is too difficult or too remote, it has been dropped altogether. In others, books written for younger children are pressed into service with adolescents who might know the words but who understandably reject the ideas. In still other programs, basic literacy is so urgent a goal that the entire focus is on learning to read expository and factual materials for skill development and for information. Perhaps the most uncreative solution has been to use conventional and inappropriate materials *anyhow*, because eventually they will or should be "good" for the students.

The NCTE Task Force recommends that at all levels of instruction the English curiculum for disadvantaged students include appropriate imaginative literature chosen and presented with these students in mind.

Implementing this recommendation makes necessary two sets of choices: the materials and modes of presentation. At the preschool and primary levels, reading aloud by teachers trained in oral interpretation or by recorded artists offers an important way of extending horizons, enriching cultural backgrounds, and calling attention to imaginative and figurative uses of language so untypical of many dialects in lower socioeconomic groups. As the children mature and the thematic or "substantive" content of literary materials becomes more significant, so too does the choice of materials. Although oral reading by the teacher should never stop altogether, it does not itself surmount the difficulties inherent in, say, *Silas Marner, Ivanhoe,* or *Franklin's Autobiography.* For independent, silent reading, the choice is even more crucial. In this age of the paperback revolution, of a widely expanding body of attractive literature for children, of increased funds available to purchase materials or excellent recordings of literature, of annotated booklists available from such organizations as the National Council of Teachers of English and the American Library Association, no program can find any excuse other than inertia for not providing imaginative literature for disadvantaged children. Perhaps more than anything else, the disadvantaged learner needs to find his own identity and to relate himself to the larger social community. Where better than through literature can students learn to rise above themselves and to extend the range of their intellectual and emotional powers?

5. Many administrators discussed with Task Force members the problems of attracting the best possible teachers to schools for disadvantaged. The design and institution of a new program is only half a solution unless it is staffed by teachers who can put it into effective action. Existing policies of teacher assignment make it impossible in most areas of the country for administrators to recruit and assign teachers to individual schools.

The NCTE Task Force recommends that policies of teacher placement be revised where necessary to enable school principals and project directors to play a direct role in recruiting teachers for positions in schools for the disadvantaged.

According to many administrators, the tendency for qualified teachers to shun positions in disadvantaged areas is gradually diminishing

Boys in a Wilmington, Delaware, School Read the Day's Announcements (*Ebony* Magazine)

in the face of heightened interest in the disadvantaged and in new curriculum practices and administrative policies within the schools. Curriculum innovations, adapting traditional programs to the special needs of the disadvantaged, and increased teacher freedom to develop and test new approaches are reported to have a significant positive effect on teacher attitudes.

6. Many school programs are inadequately financed. The federal government's annual expenditure of an average of $5,900 to provide remedial experiences for each Job Corps dropout stands in marked contrast to the annual expenditure of $400 to $700 per pupil characteristic of most public school systems, or even to the $3,000 to $3,500 required annually to educate boys and girls in many prestigious private schools and academies. As much as $70 per student may be spent for teaching materials in the federal program; whereas in New York, one of the nation's most affluent states, some districts budget as little as $6.95 per pupil on teaching materials and no district expends more than $53.36.[1]

The NCTE Task Force recommends that greater financial support be given to school programs for the provision of ample materials and personnel.

Surely the heavy expenditure in the Job Corps program can be justified, particularly in terms of the ultimate economic saving to our society if a high percentage of such young men who might otherwise become wards of society can be made sufficiently self-supporting. But a substantial increase in expenditures in many school programs would make available learning materials, staff members, smaller classes, and more individualized instruction, all of which would contribute to the success of many school programs and perhaps ultimately reduce the need for the extensive postschool reeducation that federal programs are providing now.

7. Too few administrators and teachers seem aware of the help already available in print. Task Force members seldom found copies of professional periodicals like *Elementary English* and the *English Journal* available in schools or offices. Professional libraries for teachers seemed to be undeveloped in many school buildings. Local leaders were often unaware of professional associations in their states, much less in the nation at large. The absence of information about projects, programs, and research noted throughout the report is due partly to

[1] From an address by Senator Robert F. Kennedy, Albany, New York, March 1, 1965.

the failure of local project directors, school administrators, librarians, and the teachers themselves to secure many of the reports already available (such as those listed in the Appendices).

The NCTE Task Force recommends that administrators and project directors develop deliberate programs to make available to teachers reports on new research and experimentation.

In addition, directors of research or of experimental programs must assume greater responsibility for keeping the profession informed about their work. Whether through special reports or articles in professional publications, researchers need to provide continual information on their findings, their hypotheses, and their current activities.

8. Teachers interviewed by Task Force members were almost unanimous in agreeing that their preservice academic preparation was inadequate for the task they now have in the education of disadvantaged students. Not only do they feel that teacher education programs ignore the special problems of educating the disadvantaged, but that even when teacher education programs do include training for work with the disadvantaged, they generally fail to help teachers translate theoretical principles and findings into practical information that can be used in the classroom.

The NCTE Task Force recommends that both preservice and inservice teacher education programs develop courses dealing with the application of current educational theory to classroom teaching, especially in the study of language.

Preservice programs have the responsibility of developing an understanding of the disadvantaged in society and in formal and informal systems of education. Preservice programs also have the responsibility of informing prospective teachers of English about learning and language—about the structure of English, for example, about dialects, sentence patterns, intonation patterns, and language development in general. Such programs must also inform teachers about the implications of such theory for classroom instruction. Preparation for teaching English specifically to the disadvantaged may require more extensive programs of inservice education than are today available. Institutes and workshops sponsored by districts or universities can make a major contribution.

9. An excellent elementary school program may be followed by unrelated or mediocre junior high program. Much that a child may achieve in a special program at one level may be lost as he moves on in school, making any gains only transitory.

The NCTE Task Force recommends that the problem of developing adequate structure and continuity throughout all levels of school, from preschool through twelfth grade, be the responsibility of the school district.

The sequence of language experiences outlined by Walter Loban in his final comments at the French Lick Conference is worthy of careful consideration as a means of establishing continuity in the total school experience. (See Part III.) It is, however, the responsibility of the district administration to bring individual school administrators and teachers together to discuss present programs and to plan future ones. Such a meeting, if it is a regular and recurring event, would go far to insure maximum efficiency in the use of school money, personnel, and facilities.

10. Every major investigation of the teaching of English that has been conducted in recent years concludes that teachers know far less about the nature and structure of language and about language learning than is minimally essential for effective teaching. This study is no exception. Task Force members report that few teachers at any level of education, from preschool to adult, possessed even an elementary understanding of the nature of a nonstandard English dialect, for example. Even fewer teachers seemed to possess a working knowledge of the English grammars currently being developed. Too many teachers admit that they are awaiting the appearance of a single "linguistic" textbook which will teach them and their pupils whatever is needed to be known about language. No single book will ever satisfy the need. A knowledge of the structure and operation of language, of the language development of children, and of the social and cultural varieties of language cannot be acquired overnight. An understanding of language—like an understanding of literature, reading, or composition—can be acquired only gradually through sustained study and experience. Fortunately, an increasing number of programs for preparing elementary teachers and secondary teachers of English are emphasizing the importance of studying language. Most summer English institutes supported by the National Defense Education Act devoted at least one third of their programs to language study. The emphasis is long overdue. A teacher who knows little about oral language development, dialects, the relationships of reading and language, and the interaction of language and thinking stands little chance of becoming an effective teacher of English to the disadvantaged student. Further, a teacher without a basic knowledge about language cannot

even read intelligently the professional journals that are available to the teacher of English.

The NCTE Task Force recommends that teachers of the disadvantaged possess at least a working knowledge of developments in structural and transformational grammar, in social dialectology, in psycholinguistics, and in language and cognitive development.

Teachers must use every means at their disposal to obtain this essential knowledge: through NDEA institutes, local college or university extension or summer courses, inservice workshops, or self-initiated reading programs. Not until a teacher gains knowledge of the basic concepts of language and the principles of language learning will he fully realize their importance. The Task Force recognizes that for teachers the complications of furthering their academic training are many; there are considerations of family, finances, and immediate commitments. However the question is not one of convenience; it is one of capability.

Members of other professions continue their education in order to specialize. Similarly, teachers who specialize in teaching the disadvantaged need to continue their study in the areas of their students' greatest needs: language competence (in one or two dialects or one or two languages), reading proficiency, and cognitive development. The specialist teacher will thus equip his students with a full use of the English language and a rich appreciation of the literature written in it.

Part VI

APPENDICES

A.
Selected References on Educating the Disadvantaged

B.
Selected References on Language Learning

C.
Annotated List of Selected Bulletins and Materials

D.
Index to Programs, Projects, and Participating Schools

E.
Members and Consultants of the Task Force

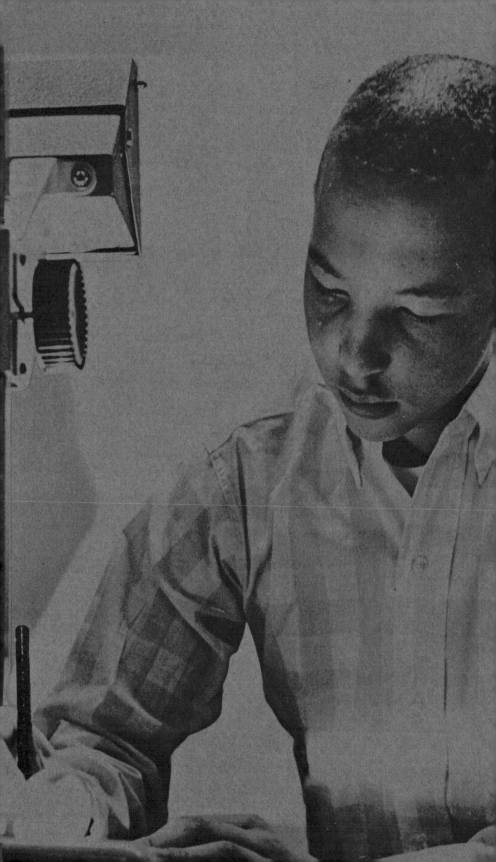

A. Selected References on Educating the Disadvantaged

Bloom, Benjamin S., Allison Davis, and Robert Hess. *Compensatory Education for Cultural Deprivation*. New York: Holt, Rinehart and Winston, Inc., 1965.
Report of the Research Conference on Educational and Cultural Deprivation at the University of Chicago; generalizations on education and the disadvantaged with specific policy implications; includes an annotated bibliography on education and cultural deprivation.

Burchill, George W. *Work-Study Programs for Alienated Youth, a Casebook*. Chicago, Ill.: Science Research Associates, 1962.
Descriptions of nine work-study programs at the secondary level which combine classroom and job experience; useful for schools planning or evaluating similar programs to prevent the alienation of certain youths from their society.

Clark, Kenneth B. *Dark Ghetto*. New York: Harper and Row, Publishers, 1965.
An analysis of the Negro power structure and the debilitating effects of the ghetto on the individual; includes a discussion of the problems of education in such areas.

Conant, James B. *Slums and Suburbs*. New York: McGraw-Hill Book Company, Inc., 1961.
Contrasts the people and problems of education in city slums with those which are typical of wealthy suburbs; includes proposals for improving education in both areas.

Crosby, Muriel. *An Adventure in Human Relations*. Chicago: Follet Publishing Company, 1965.
The reactions of the teachers, the students, and the community of Wilmington, Delaware, to a three-year project designed to improve the schools through the development of appropriate curricula and in-service teacher education, and to involve community agencies in the problems of educating the disadvantaged.

Davis, Allison. *Social Class Influence Upon Learning.* Cambridge, Mass.: Harvard University Press, 1948.

A classic statement on the differences in social class values and their effects upon motivation and achievement in education.

"The Disadvantaged," *Publications Bulletin.* New York: Anti-Defamation League of B'nai B'rith.

A bulletin published by B'nai B'rith listing books, pamphlets, and articles judged to be important to understanding both the problems of educational segregation and cultural disadvantage. This bulletin may be ordered from The Anti-Defamation League of B'nai B'rith, 315 Lexington Avenue, New York, New York 10016.

The Disadvantaged Child: A Program for Action. Trenton: New Jersey Education Association, 1964.

Specific programs for improving the education of disadvantaged children; special emphasis on the recruitment and training of teachers for schools in which there are large concentrations of disadvantaged youth.

Educational Policies Commission. *Education and the Disadvantaged American.* Washington, D. C.: National Education Association, 1962.

A policy statement reviewing the problems in the education of the disadvantaged and ways in which to meet them.

Friedenberg, Edgar Z. *The Vanishing Adolescent.* New York: Dell Publishing Co., Inc., 1959

A discussion of the pressures and fears of our culture which are destroying adolescence, placing the adolescent in the role of a rebel subject to the censorship of both his peers and his teachers.

Harrington, Michael. *The Other America.* Baltimore: Penguin Books, Inc., 1962.

A critical study of the problems and the people who make up the "other America" of cultural deprivation and poverty.

May, Edgar. *The Wasted Americans.* (Signet Books.) New York: New American Library of World Literature, Inc., 1964.

A study of America's welfare program; how it is now working and how it should work.

National Council for Effective Schools. *A Tentative Summary Report for an Effective School Program in Urban Centers*. Chicago, Ill.: American Federation of Teachers, March 1965.

Includes specific recommendations about integration, personnel, class size, materials, and community involvement in education in the large urban center.

Passow, A. Harry (ed.). *Education in Depressed Areas*. New York: Teachers College, 1963.

Series of fifteen papers presented at a 1962 Conference on Curriculum and Teaching in Depressed Urban Areas; covers schools, teachers, programs, and the sociological and psychological aspects of education in depressed areas.

"Poverty and the School," *Educational Leadership*, XXII (May 1965)

An entire issue devoted to the problems of education in areas of great poverty and deprivation.

Programs for the Educationally Disadvantaged. U. S. Office of Education, Bulletin 1963, No. 17. Washington, D. C.: U. S. Government Printing Office, 1963.

A collection of papers presented at the May 1962 Conference on Teaching Children and Youth Who Are Educationally Disadvantaged; reports practices and methods specifically designed for use with such children.

Promising Practices from the Projects for the Culturally Deprived. Chicago, Ill.: The Research Council of the Great Cities Program for School Improvement. (228 North LaSalle Street, Chicago, Illinois)

An extensive summary of successful programs, with evidence for claims which are made.

Quick, E. J. (ed.). *New Opportunities for the Culturally Disadvantaged*. Toronto: The Canadian Education Association, 1964.

A report by Canadian educators on programs for the culturally disadvantaged in fifteen large cities of the U.S.; includes an analysis of the problems of compensatory education in Canada, and practices from the U.S. programs which might prove useful there.

Riessman, Frank. *The Culturally Deprived Child.* New York: Harper and Row, Publishers, 1964.

An attempt to develop new approaches to the education of the deprived child, emphasizing the positive aspects of his culture; includes a critical evaluation of the Higher Horizons program and recommendations for further action.

Rivlin, Harry N. "Teaching and Teacher Education for Urban Disadvantaged Schools," *The Journal of Teacher Education,* XVI (June 1965), 135–186.

Reports by teachers and administrators from inner cities, giving their own experiences and methods in the education of teachers for disadvantaged students.

Sexton, Patricia C. *Education and Income.* New York: The Viking Press, 1961.

A study of school inequalities and the relation of educational opportunities to income and social class; argues for special attention to the education of low income and slum children to help them overcome their environmental handicaps.

Silberman, Charles E. *Crisis in Black and White.* (Vintage Books.) New York: Random House, Inc., 1964.

A study of the Negro problem as it exists in our great urban centers; recognizes that to change the status of the Negro will require other great changes in the fabric of American life.

The Society of the Streets. New York: The Ford Foundation, 1962.

A summary of Ford Foundation's projects dealing with problems of cultural deprivation and the disadvantaged.

Stauffer, Russell G. (ed.). *Language and the Higher Thought Processes.* Champaign, Ill.: National Council of Teachers of English, 1965.

A collection of articles from the April and May 1965 issues of *Elementary English* dealing with the relation of language to thought and the development and operation of this relationship; includes discussion of recent research and implications for classroom teaching.

Training the Hard-Core Unemployed: A Demonstration-Research Project at Virginia State College, Norfolk Division. Washington, D.C.: U. S. Government Printing Office, 1964.

A program which has demonstrated that even members of the "hard-core" of unemployed can be trained to be productive members of society within a relatively short period of time.

U. S. Bureau of Indian Affairs. *Education for Cross-Cultural Enrichment.* Washington, D. C., The Bureau, 1964.

A collection of articles from *Indian Education* representing almost thirty years of writing about the education of the American Indian; most discussions are applicable to other minority groups. Also, *Education for Cultural Change,* 1953, and *Education for Action,* 1944.

B. Selected References on Language Learning and the Disadvantaged

Allen, Harold B. *Readings in Applied English Linguistics* (2nd ed.). New York: Appleton-Century-Crofts, 1964.

An interesting book throughout, but particularly relevant are Part IV, "Linguistics and Usage," and Part V, "Linguistics and the Teaching of Grammar and Composition."

————. "Suggestive Notes on Language Instruction in a Summer Institute for Elementary Teachers," in *Source Book on English Institutes for Elementary Teachers*. Champaign and New York: NCTE and MLA, 1965.

Concise but comprehensive discussion of the nature of language with particular reference to the needs of elementary teachers, including attention to social varieties of American English.

Arnold, R. "Why Juan Can't Read," *Commonweal*, 76 (April 1962), 110–112. Reply with rejoinder, P. J. O'Grady, June 1, 1962.

Discussion of the conflicts which exist between the teacher and the world he presents in the classroom, and the slum child and the world with which he is faced out of school.

Bernstein, Basil. "Some Sociological Determinants of Perception," *British Journal of Sociology*, IX (1958), 159–174.

Discussion of the differences in the mode of expression of working class as opposed to middle class children, and the implications for measuring perception and verbal performance.

————. "Language and Social Class," *British Journal of Sociology*, XI (1960), 271–276.

An analysis of the descriptive orientation of the modes of expression of the lower working class as opposed to the more abstract, subjective orientation of the middle class.

————. "Social Class and Linguistic Development: A Theory of Social Learning," in *Education, Economy and Society*, ed. A. H.

Halsey *et al.* New York: The Macmillan Company (Free Press of Glencoe), 1961.
Discussion of the central role of language in socialization and the different linguistic codes associated with social class membership.

Cohen, Werner. "On the Language of Lower-Class Children," *School Review*, 67 (Winter 1959), 435–440.
Concise discussion of some major differences between nonstandard and standard dialects, and steps toward a pedagogical position based more on moral neutrality than snobbishness.

Crosby, Muriel. "Identifying Oral Language Relationships," in *Children and Oral Language*. Champaign, Ill.: ACEI, ASCD, IRA, and NCTE, 1964.
Role of oral language in personal and social development and in thinking, with special reference to problems of disadvantaged children.

Cutts, Warren G. "Reading Unreadiness in the Underprivileged," *NEA Journal*, April 1963.
Suggestions for approaching English language instruction for the underprivileged based upon principles of teaching a foreign language; with emphasis on language teaching in kindergarten and the first grade.

Deutsch, Martin. "The Role of Social Class in Language Development and Cognition," *American Journal of Orthopsychiatry*, XXV (January 1965).
Report of a study on differential rates of language acquisition and cognitive development among children of various social, ethnic, and economic groups; includes implications for school programs.

Engelmann, S. E. *Cultural Deprivation—Description and Remedy.* In manuscript, but available for $.50 from Institute for Research on Exceptional Children, College of Education, University of Illinois, Urbana, Illinois.
Analysis of the nature of the language deficit that characterizes disadvantaged children, and a recommended approach for overcoming this deficit with preschool children.

"English and the Disadvantaged Student," *English Journal*, LIV, 4 (April 1965).

Special issue including six articles on teaching English to disadvantaged students.

Finocchiaro, Mary. *Teaching English as a Second Language.* New York: Harper and Row, Publishers, 1958.
Suggestions for teaching English as a second language based on experience with non-English speaking children and adolescents in New York schools.

Golden, Ruth I. *Improving Patterns of Language Usage.* Detroit, Mich.: Wayne State University Press, 1960.
A study of nonstandard language expressions and their effects on the socioeconomic level of the speaker. Available from NCTE, 508 South Sixth Street, Champaign, Ill. 61822.

Gotkin, Lasser. ''Cognitive Development and the Issue of Individual Differences,'' reprinted from *Programed Instruction,* 1963, and available from the Institute for Developmental Studies, New York Medical College.
A report on programing problems with a special section on problems in programing for disadvantaged students.

Hayes, Alfred S. (ed.). *Literacy.* Washington, D.C.: Center for Applied Linguistics, 1965.
Recommendations from a work conference on literacy sponsored by the Agency for International Development; includes discussion of current literacy research, recommended research projects, and guidelines for establishing literacy programs.

Higgins, V. Louise. ''Approaching Usage in the Classroom,'' *English Journal,* XLIX (March 1960), 181–186.
A discussion of the basis for a linguistic approach in the classroom. Premises include accepting the teacher as arbiter of usage and the social and psychological situation as decisive in determining usage.

Hogan, Robert F. ''A New Kind of Change, a New Order of Growth,'' *The English Leaflet,* Spring 1965.
A brief discussion of the implications for teaching usage, drawing on recent findings in sociolinguistics and dialectology. Published by New England Association of Teachers of English.

Holbrook, David. *English for the Rejected*. New York: Cambridge University Press, 1964.

Addressed primarily to teachers and administrators; humane description of the nature and the needs of the disadvantaged and extensive discussion of methods and approaches in training for literacy.

Jewett, Arno, Joseph Mersand, and Doris Gunderson. *Improving English Skills of Culturally Different Youth*. Washington, D.C.: U.S. Department of Health, Education, and Welfare, 1964.

Papers from a conference on educating the disadvantaged, including research reports, descriptions of projects, and recommendations for further action.

Kelly, W. M. "If You're Woke You Dig It: With Phrases and Words," *N.Y. Times Magazine*, May 20, 1962, pp. 45–46.

A discussion of words and phrases heard in large Negro communities such as Harlem.

Lin, San-su C. "An English Program for Students Handicapped by a Local Dialect," *CLA Journal*, 7 (December 1963), 141–148.

Interim report on research project at Claflin College describing procedures used to teach standard English to speakers of nonstandard dialects, with considerable stress on an oral-aural approach.

————. *Pattern Practice in the Teaching of Standard English to Students, with a Non-standard Dialect*. New York: Bureau of Publications, Teachers College, Columbia University, 1965.

Final report of a cooperative research project at Claflin; experiments in the use of pattern practice techniques and materials to help southern Negroes master the standard English dialect; includes classroom and language laboratory materials.

Loban, Walter. *The Language of Elementary School Children*. NCTE Research Report No. 1. Champaign, Ill.: NCTE, 1963.

First report of a longitudinal study of language development, including detailed analysis of social class differences in acquisition of language skills.

————. *Problems in Oral English*. NCTE Research Report No. 5. Champaign, Ill.: NCTE, in press.

Second report from longitudinal study on language development in children; concerned with the most crucial and frequently occurring departures from standard English and the implications for teaching; based on samples of children's language from kindergarten through grade 9.

McDavid, Raven I., Jr. "American English Dialects," in *The Structure of American English*, ed. W. Nelson Francis. New York: The Ronald Press Company, 1958.

Survey of dialect differences in American English and the social, geographical, economic, and other forces that underlie these differences.

—————. *American Social Dialects*. Champaign, Ill.: NCTE, 1965.

Reprints of articles: "The Cultural Matrix of American English," from *Elementary English*, January 1965; and "American Social Dialects," from *College English*, January 1965.

Malmstrom, Jean. *Language in Society*. New York: Hayden Book Companies, 1965.

Although addressed to high school students, a helpful introduction to social dialects for adults; illustrations and exercises may help students to understand dialect differences in their school and community.

—————, and Annabel Ashley. *Dialects* USA. Champaign, Ill.: NCTE, 1963.

An introduction to dialect study for high school students sponsored by the NCTE Commission on the English Language. The text is partially based on scholarly work of Raven I. McDavid and on classroom activities tested in Portland, Oregon, schools.

Newton, Eunice Shaed. "Verbal Destitution; The Pivotal Barrier to Learning," *Journal of Negro Education*, 29 (Fall 1960) 497–499.

Description of the verbal patterns characteristic of college freshmen from disadvantaged areas, and discussion of implications for instruction.

Ozmon, Howard A., Jr. "A Realistic Approach to the Writing of Children's Textbooks for Deprived Areas," *Elementary English*, XXXVIII (December 1960), 534–535.

Contends that teaching deprived children is difficult enough without complicating the problem with books that are uninteresting to the child and unrelated to his life.

"Reading Instruction for Disadvantaged Children," *The Reading Teacher*, March 1965.

Several reports of research and curriculum projects and special inservice programs for teachers or reading; special issue of the magazine.

Root, Shelton L., Jr. "Institute Study in Literature for Teachers of Culturally Disadvantaged Children," in *Source Book on English Institutes for Elementary Teachers*. Champaign and New York: NCTE and MLA, 1965.

Consideration of the role that literature can play in the lives of disadvantaged children, and a sequence of inservice activities that will prepare teachers better to capitalize on the potential of literature.

Sableski, Julia A. "A Selective Annotated Bibliography on Child Language." *The Linguistic Reporter*, VII, 2 (April 1965).

Useful, informative annotations on twenty-eight recent studies by educators, psychologists, and linguists in the area of language acquisition.

Shuy, Roger (ed.). *Social Dialects and Language Learning*. Champaign, Ill.: NCTE, 1965.

Papers and summaries of discussion from interdisciplinary conference; summarizes the state of dialect research techniques and findings, and relates these to problems of teaching English.

Slager, William R., and David P. Harris. "The First NDEA Institutes in English as a Second Language," *College English*, XXVI (April 1965), 559–562.

Summary of a report commissioned by the U. S. Office of Education to evaluate pilot TESOL institutes; includes descriptions of work in linguistics, methodology (including demonstration classes), cultural background, and practical language training.

Stewart, William A. (ed.). *Non-Standard Speech and the Teaching of English*. Washington, D.C.: Center for Applied Linguistics, 1964.

Three articles dealing with similarity and essential differences between teaching standard English as a second dialect and teaching a second language; with a study of dialect differences in Chicago; and with approaches to teaching English.

C. Annotated List of Selected Bulletins and Materials

Many bulletins, materials, and program descriptions were reviewed by the Task Force. Some were collected in programs visited by observers. Others were submitted directly to the Champaign offices of the National Council of Teachers of English. To assist those interested in the teaching of English to the disadvantaged, the Task Force prepared the following selected list of such materials. Only noncommercial materials are included. Complete addresses of most projects are presented in the *Index to Programs, Projects, and Participating Schools* which immediately follows in this report. To indicate the level of interest, each item is coded as follows:

1—Preschool
2—Elementary
3—Secondary
4—English as a Second Language
5—Adult
6—Teacher Education
7—Project- Administration and General

ABCD—BOSTON SCHOOL DEPARTMENT PRE-KINDERGARTEN PROGRAM. Boston Public Schools, Boston, Massachusetts. (ABCD—Action for Boston Community Development) (1)

> A detailed outline of the First Day's Program; includes essential routines that are taught in the initial stages of the preschool experience.

ABCD—BOSTON SCHOOL DEPARTMENT PRE-KINDERGARTEN PROGRAM. Sample Lessons, Spring, 1964. Boston Public Schools, Boston, Massachusetts. (1)

> There are four lessons: (1) *Language*—unit on circus words and concepts. (2) *Auditory Discrimination*—lesson on development of loud and soft concepts. (3) *Visual Discrimination*—unit on recognition of color, combining color names with language development. (4) *Muscular Coordination*—lesson on development of muscular coordination through cutting and pasting activities.

ABCD PRE-KINDERGARTEN PROGRAM—AN INTERIM REPORT ON THE BOSTON SCHOOL DEVELOPMENT. Boston Public Schools, Boston, Massachusetts. (1)

> A report discussing the procedures and problems of organizing their pre-kindergarten program and suggestions for experiences which have proven successful for teachers in the program.

ALICE LINN AND HER BROTHER IN OAKLAND, AND ACCOMPANYING EXERCISES. Oakland Public Schools, Adult Education Department, Oakland, California. (5)

A series of lessons in writing, vocabulary, spelling and syntax which form a story about two people in Oakland, California.

APPRAISAL OF THE CITY SCHOOLS READING PROGRAM. Detroit Public Schools, Division for Improvement of Instruction, Language Education Department, Detroit, Michigan. (2,7)

An evaluation of the program in terms of interest appeal, oral reading, and word recognition.

AURAL-ORAL ENGLISH GUIDE FOR TEACHERS OF NAVAJO BEGINNERS. Navajo Agency, Window Rock, Arizona. (2)

Question and answer exercises for use in developing grammar, intonation, verb agreement, and sentence patterns.

BASIC EDUCATION AND ACCULTURATION. Job Opportunity Center, Inc., Denver, Colorado.

The objectives and tentative outline of a program to train unemployed adults to take a useful place in society.

BASIC GOALS FOR ELEMENTARY CHILDREN. Publication Service, Haskell Institute, Lawrence, Kansas, Bureau of Indian Affairs, Department of the Interior. (2,6)

Goals for elementary programs with extensive suggestions for achieving them; designed for Indian children but useful with any group.

BENEFITS FORGOT. Oakland Public Schools, Adult Education Program, Oakland, California. (5)

An adaptation of Honoré Morrow's story complete with questions asking for factual recall, simple analysis, and vocabulary study.

BICULTURAL, LINGUISTIC CONCEPTS IN EDUCATION. E. Roby Leighton and Associates, 2934 E. Cushman Drive, Tucson, Arizona. (4,6,7)

A handbook of suggestions for teachers interested in the education of Spanish and Indian speaking students.

BILINGUAL READINESS DURING EARLIEST SCHOOL YEARS. Hunter College of the City of New York, New York. (2,4)

A description of a Cooperative Research Project to assess the effect on bilingual readiness of two language groups being present in the same classroom.

CALIFORNIA YOUTH AUTHORITY COURSE OF STUDY OUTLINES. Department of Youth Authority, 401 State Office Building #1, Sacramento, California. (7)

A description of the programs in state correctional schools.

THE CARDOZO PROJECT. Cardozo High School, Washington, D.C. (3)

This 22 page description contains interesting evaluations by returned Peace Corps volunteers of literature units taught in grades 9–12.

COMPARISON OF READING APPROACHES IN FIRST GRADE TEACHING OF EDUCATIONALLY DISADVANTAGED CHILDREN. The Research Foundation of the City University of New York, 33 West 42nd Street, New York, New York, Albert J. Harris. (2,6)

Description of a Project supported by the Cooperative Research Program, U.S. Office of Education, studying four methods of teaching reading to the disadvantaged.

COMPENSATORY EDUCATION, STUDY REPORT—NUMBER FOUR. 1964 Series, Chicago Board of Education, Chicago, Illinois. (7)

Extensive discussion of the problem, the educational implications, present programs; with recommendations for the future.

THE COMPENSATORY EDUCATION PROGRAM. Preschool Department Guide for 1964–1965, Fresno City Unified School District, Fresno, California. (1)

This 55 page publication contains an outline of the program for preschool children and the daily schedule of work; outline of experiences for development of number concepts, reading readiness, and sensory training and for parent participants, with descriptions of those activities in which they are involved.

A COMPREHENSIVE CURRICULAR AND EVALUATIVE MODEL FOR PRESCHOOL PROGRAMS DESIGNED FOR EDUCATIONALLY (CULTURALLY) DISADVANTAGED PRESCHOOL CHILDREN. N. S. Metfessel, and J. T. Foster, Center for the Study of Educationally (Culturally) Disadvantaged Youth, Los Angeles City Schools, Los Angeles, California. (1,7)

This project analyzes traditional and a creative approach to preschool teaching in terms of their objectives, success, and theoretical orientation.

COURSES OF STUDY FOR SPANISH S (Bulletins 20-Ss-1-3 revised). Dade County Public Schools, Miami, Florida. (2,3,4)

Courses of study printed in Spanish and English for elementary, junior, and senior high students who are native speakers of Spanish.

DEVELOPMENTAL READING—A HANDBOOK OF AIDS, SKILLS, AND TECHNIQUES FOR TEACHING READING IN FOUR MAJOR CONTENT FIELDS. Compiled by M. S. Wilson and H. Hedrick, Division of Secondary Education, Los Angeles City Schools. (6)

Although this publication covers four subject areas (English, social studies, mathematics, and science), the English section is very specific about illustrative methods and devices.

DIVISION OF INDIAN EDUCATION. State Department of Public Education, 425 Arizona State Building, Phoenix, Arizona. (4,7)

This department has several excellent guides on teaching English as a second language; designed for Indian children but useful with any disadvantaged group.

EDUCATIONAL IMPROVEMENT PROGRAM — INTEGRATED LANGUAGE ARTS YEAR I. Philadelphia Public Schools, Philadelphia, Pennsylvania. (2)

Guides to planned experiences for the urban child.

ENGLISH SEQUENTIAL PATTERN DRILLS FOR SPANISH-SPEAKING STUDENTS. Intermediate levels, Tucson Public Schools, District No. 1, Tucson, Arizona. (4)

A 122 page booklet for improving the ability of Spanish-speaking students to handle the basic oral patterns of English.

GATEWAY ENGLISH. Marjorie B. Smiley, Project Director, Project English Curriculum Development Center, Hunter College of the City University of New York, New York. One of the USOE Project English Curriculum Centers. (3,6)

STORIES IN VERSE. An anthology of 22 ballads, including ''John Henry,'' ''Big Bad John,'' ''Barbara Allen,'' ''Billy Boy,'' and others; grade 7. (Teacher's manual is separate.)

COPING. An anthology of short stories and verse about people with problems and how they cope with them; grade 7. (Teacher's manual is separate.)

WHO AM I? An anthology of 16 stories, poems, and plays dealing with differences in personality and behavior which tell us who we are; grade 7. (Teacher's manual is separate.)

A FAMILY IS A WAY OF FEELING. An anthology of 24 stories, poems, and lullabies dealing with the affections and troubles which bind individuals together in family; grade 7. (Teacher's manual is separate.)

DEVELOPING ORIGINAL MATERIALS IN READING. A manual of practical suggestions for junior high school teachers about the preparation of materials to supplement commercial materials. Examples of teacher-made materials are included.

IDENTIFICATION. This guide contains stories, written and adapted by teachers, in which students are cast as characters; includes lesson notes and descriptions of techniques.

BOOKLIST I. An annotated list of approximately one hundred books selected as a classroom library to supplement grade 7. Selections of books take into consideration many factors; for example, many of the books have Negro or Puerto Rican characters and urban settings.

GENERAL GUIDE FOR URBAN STUDY PRINTS. New Haven Public Schools, New Haven, Connecticut. (7)

This guide for the use of photographs and prints of local points of interest and the urban environment is valuable to schools seeking to make the best use of their city location. The guide uses a language-experience approach.

GENERAL MATERIALS used in an Institute for Developmental Studies workshop, April 25–30, 1965, New York Medical College, New York, New York. (6)

These materials include suggestions for kindergarten enrichment checklist, lists of educational toys, home activities for children, activities for children and parents, techniques with games.

HANDBOOK. Division of Elementary Schools, Board of Education of the City of New York, New York. (2,6,7)

A 260 page description of the objectives, special projects, and activities of the elementary program of the city system.

HIGHER HORIZONS BULLETIN, Vol. 3, No. 1, January 1965. Higher Horizons Office, Board of Education of the City of New York. (2,3,7)

Bulletin highlighting several New York schools (both elementary and secondary) in the Higher Horizons Program.

HIGHER HORIZONS BULLETIN: LANGUAGE ARTS MATERIAL FOR THE ACADEMIC IMPROVEMENT TEACHERS. Higher Horizons Office, Board of Education of the City of New York. (2,7)

This includes sections on independent activities, skills inventories, the basal readers, the elementary school library, and other activities for the elementary classroom.

HINTS FOR REGULAR CLASSROOM TEACHERS AND SPECIAL TEACHERS HAVING NON-ENGLISH PUPILS. Bureau of Adult Education, Hartford Public Schools, Hartford, Connecticut. (6)

An excellent, informal manual for teachers who must cope with non-English speaking children.

HOMEWORK HELPER PROGRAM. Mobilization For Youth, Inc., 271 East 4th Street, New York, New York. (6,7)

Outline of tutor training session and follow-up materials.

IRCD BULLETIN. Yeshiva University, 150 West 56th Street, New York, New York. (7)

A publication of Yeshiva's Information Retrieval Center on the Disadvantaged, a clearing house for information concerning problems, theory, research, programs and practices, materials, and other developments in the field of compensatory education. Bimonthly, available by subscription.

INITIAL TEACHING ALPHABET PROGRAM. Lehigh University and Bethlehem Area Schools, Bethlehem, Pennsylvania. (2,6,7)

Research program based on the Pitman Initial Teaching Alphabet. A teacher's manual and a workbook accompany each of the seven readers; also some fifty or more supplementary readers and a child's alphabet book.

JOB APPLICATION FORMS. Materials Development Unit, Mobilization For Youth, Inc., 271 East 4th Street, New York 9, New York. (3,5)

For dropouts, adults, job corps, junior high and above. Series of five workbooks and a pocket dictionary to teach how to fill out forms.

JOHN F. KENNEDY PRESCHOOL PROGRAM. Dade County Public Schools, Special Programs, Miami, Florida, April, 1965. (1)

The publication identifies the design of the program, the staff, and its responsibilities; includes purposes of the study, program outline, inservice training, and discussion of observations and use of volunteer aides.

LEARNING TO TEACH IN DIFFERENT SCHOOLS. BRIDGE Project Staff, Department of Education, Queens College, Flushing, New York. (6)

A 65-page booklet describing graphically how three young teachers reacted to teaching youngsters in one junior high. The format makes this booklet very valuable for teacher training and inservice.

LESSONS IN ENGLISH. Bulletin A-100, Oakland Public Schools, Department of Adult Education, Oakland, California. (5)

A series of exercises in vocabulary and simple language patterns.

A LINGUISTIC APPROACH TO BEGINNING READERS FOR BILINGUAL CHILDREN. Dade County Public Schools, Miami, Florida. (2,4,6)

A report on the May 1965 conference in Detroit about the Miami Linguistic Reader Series; attempts to harmonize principles of linguistics with the conventional approach to the teaching of reading.

MATERALS DEVELOPMENT UNIT. Mobilization for Youth, Inc., 271 East 4th Street, New York, New York 10009. (7)

Lists materials being developed by MFY for use with disadvantaged children. Includes original material and adaptions of commercial materials for use with disadvantaged.

MERCED CITY SCHOOLS. Merced, California. (2,4,7)

Assorted materials on their language program, compensatory education, and Junior First Grade for students whose home background has not prepared them well for school.

ORIENTATION CENTER PROGRAMS FOR IN-MIGRANT TRANSIENT CHILDREN. Milwaukee Public Schools, Milwaukee, Wisconsin. (2,3)

This program serves children who are new to the city or transient within the city, offering intensive remedial help before assignment to regular classrooms.

THE PERCEPTION AND GUIDED DEVELOPMENT OF INTELLECT IN FIRST GRADE CHILDREN. Mobilization for Youth, Elementary Reading Clinic, New York City. (2,6,7)

Project seeks to develop tests to more accurately assess the intellectual development and progress of the elementary school child.

PERRY PRESCHOOL PROJECT PROGRESS REPORT. June, 1964. Ypsilanti Public Schools, Ypsilanti, Michigan. David Wickart, Project Director. (1,7)

A project report with accounts of a cognitively oriented program, home visits, teacher-structured experiences, and parent group meetings.

297

PILOT PROJECT IN COMPENSATORY EDUCATION. A Report to the State Advisory Committee on Compensatory Education, San Diego City Schools, San Diego, California. (7)

The publication includes a discussion of the problem as it exists nationally, statewide, and locally. Goals, ways and means, evaluation, basic assumptions, procedures, results, conclusions and examples.

PLANNING FOR DEVELOPMENTAL READING AS A SCHOOL-WIDE PRACTICE, DEPARTMENT BY DEPARTMENT. Wilson and Hedrick, Lincoln High School, Los Angeles, California. (6)

Although this dittoed publication covers all subject areas, the language arts section is very specific about illustrative methods and devices.

PRELIMINARY REPORT, TULARE CITY SCHOOLS PRESCHOOL PROJECT, Tulare, California, March 1, 1965. In cooperation with the Rosenberg Foundation. (1)

A description of the Tulare preschool program including the selection of children, the design and testing, the parent involvement and a brief discussion of experiences in several areas of the curriculum.

THE PREPARATION OF TEACHERS FOR SCHOOLS IN CULTURALLY DEPRIVED NEIGHBORHOODS (THE BRIDGE PROJECT). Queens College of the City University of New York, Flushing, New York.

The reports of a cooperative research project seeking to better define the problems of educating the disadvantaged and to better prepare teachers to meet them.

PRESCHOOL ADULT EDUCATION PROGRAM. Oakland Public Schools, 1025 Second Avenue, Oakland, California. (1,5)

An outline of the goals, organization, and program for preschool adult education; includes a commercial bibliography.

PRESCHOOL CURRICULUM. Oakland Public Schools Interagency Project, 1025 Second Avenue, Oakland, California. (1)

A detailed outline of the preschool program in Oakland Public Schools. Materials are listed and their use is described. Each curriculum area is outlined to some degree. Sample lesson plan included.

PRESCHOOL EDUCATIONAL PROGRAMS. Detroit Public Schools, Detroit, Michigan. (1)

A preventative program focused upon the early years of development; and designed to provide for maximum growth of the child who lacks meaningful environmental stimuli and simultaneously may be bombarded by a variety of random, unrelated stimuli that may cause regression or screening out. A part in the program is group work with the mothers of the children.

PRESCHOOL EDUCATION TENTATIVE OPERATIONAL GUIDELINES, May 28, 1965. Economic Opportunities Services, Cincinnati Public Schools, Cincinnati, Ohio. (1)

A program outlined in four general areas of physical, social, emotional, and intellectual development. A sample daily program is included and special opportunity provided for language development. The appendix includes lists of equipment for classroom activities.

PRESCHOOL INSTRUCTIONAL PROGRAM FOR NON-ENGLISH SPEAKING CHILDREN. Texas Education Agency, Austin, Texas, Bulletin No. 642, March, 1964. (1)

A 132 page publication providing an extensive description of the program for teaching non-English speaking children at the preschool level. An instructional aids section is helpful; includes ways to improve students' pronunciation, language patterns, rhythm and tone.

PRESCHOOL INTERAGENCY PROJECT. Oakland Public Schools, 1025 Second Avenue, Oakland, California. (1)

Equipment sources (a list of sources of equipment with necessary details of address) and Preschool Equipment (manipulative material).

PRESCHOOL MONTHLY SUPPLEMENTS FOR TELEVISION. Dade County Public Schools, Miami, Florida. (1)

A series of supplements for fifteen minute television presentations; includes guide sheet for classroom and copy of content to be presented, such as poems, finger plays, and stories. Possible materials for the lesson are listed in the supplements.

PRESCHOOL PARENT AIDE PROGRAM. Oakland Public Schools, 1025 Second Avenue, Oakland, California. (1,7)

Includes goals of the program, the qualifications, training, and responsibilities of persons involved, and a detailed treatment of the role of the parent aide. An evaluation of the program suggests several points for consideration.

PRESCHOOL PROGRAM. Oakland Public Schools, 1025 Second Avenue, Oakland, California. (1)

Goals of the program include development of positive readiness toward learning in preschool children and overcoming environmental deficiencies. A parent program seeks to increase parental skills, and understanding of the values of education increase their ability to help educate their children; included is a daily schedule, an outlined research proposal calendar, and a bibliography follows the first section.

PRESCHOOL PROGRAM—PROPOSED OUTLINE FOR PRESCHOOL EDUCATION FOR LOW SOCIO-ECONOMIC LEVELS. Division of Instructional Services, Los Angeles City Schools, November, 1964. (1)

A brief description of the preschool project at 102nd Street School in Los Angeles; includes general objectives of the program and a charting of skills and experiences for preschool children. Specific materials, equipment, and trips are included as they relate to development of skills and experiences.

PRESCHOOL PROGRAM—OAKLAND PUBLIC SCHOOLS INTERAGENCY PROJECT. Guides for Use of Manipulative and Language Promoting Materials. 1025 Second Avenue, Oakland, California. (1)

A six-page bulletin containing sixteen suggested activities for use of language promoting materials. Objects, such as puppets, playhouse materials, letters, books, puzzles and picture cards, are included. Guidelines for developing good language in children are also suggested.

PRESCHOOL PROGRAMS. Division of Instructional Service and Division of Elementary Education, Los Angeles City Schools, Los Angeles, California. (1)

A description of two preschool projects; includes two outlines, a child growth and development chart for ages two to five, and a chart of characteristics and developmental tasks of the four-year old—with suggested activities and field trips, necessary materials and equipment; also, includes outline of classification of objectives as noted by Metfessel and Foster (USC).

PRESCHOOL TEACHERS. Oakland Public Schools, 1025 Second Avenue, Oakland, California. (1)

A detailed outline on the role of the teacher and her responsibilities to the Adult Education Classes. A bibliography of books for teacher use and background for preschool teaching is included.

PROGRAMS FOR THE EDUCATIONALLY DISADVANTAGED. Los Angeles City Schools, Los Angeles, California. (1,2,7)

Preschool and elementary programs designed to promote social adjustment and provide compensatory education. Interesting suggestions for urban schools.

PROGRAMS FOR POTENTIAL DROPOUTS. Study Report Number Three, 1964 Series. Board of Education of the City of Chicago, Chicago, Illinois.

The report of a study by a citywide committee which describes Chicago's programs for potential dropouts and makes recommendations for expansion and improvement.

PROMISING PRACTICES FROM THE PROJECT FOR THE CULTURALLY DEPRIVED. The Research Council of the Great Cities Program for School Improvement, 228 North LaSalle Street, Chicago, Illinois. (7)

An extensive summary of successful programs, with evidence for claims which are made.

PROVIDING OPPORTUNITIES FOR DISADVANTAGED CHILDREN. Colorado State Department of Education, Office of Instructional Services, Denver, Colorado. (7)

A guide to planning programs which recognize the special problems and cultural heritage of the disadvantaged.

REACH—AN EXPERIMENTAL COURSE IN READING AND SPEECH FOR JUNIOR HIGH SCHOOL. Detroit Public Schools, Schools Center Building, Detroit, Mich. (1)

A complete course outline with suggested materials for teaching reading and speech skills.

READ, WRITE, AND SPELL. Massachusetts Council for Public Schools, Inc., Boston, Massachusetts. Charles Drake, editor. (5,6)

A series of teacher and student manuals presenting an organized structural approach to reading, writing, and spelling that takes into account the possible existence of a perceptual-motor problem.

READING BULLETIN # 2. John Marshall High School, District # 8, Chicago, Illinois. (3)

Contains a semester's outline for a reading class and sample test materials and exercises.

REPORT OF EVALUATION OF FIRST GRADE READING AND LANGUAGE DEVELOPMENT PROGRAM. Stonehurst Elementary School, Oakland, California. (2)

Study of special techniques for the teaching of reading at the kindergarten level, including opaque projectors, tape recorders, and other materials.

A REPORT ON THE LATE AFTERNOON ELEMENTARY SCHOOL CLASSES CONDUCTED AT THE BUNDY SCHOOL. Washington Public Schools, Washington, D.C. (2,7)

A program for boys excluded from regular classes because of their disruptive behavior.

REPORT ON THE SUMMER INSTITUTE FOR TEACHERS OF ENGLISH AT PREDOMINANTLY NEGRO COLLEGES. Summer, 1964. Indiana University, Bloomington, Indiana. (6)

This report contains program descriptions and the evaluation of courses as well as a description of the general administration of the program.

THE ROLE OF THE FIELD TEACHER AND FIELD ASSISTANT. Oakland Public Schools, 1025 Second Avenue, Oakland, California. (1)

An outline including a description of the job for the field teacher and field assistant; also involves a time schedule. The bibliography is extensive and relates to child growth and development.

SUMMARIES OF PROJECTS IN THE EDUCATION WAR ON POVERTY. Model School Division, Washington Public Schools, Washington, D.C. (2,3,7)

This program is concerned with raising the educational level of disadvantaged children in the inner city.

SUMMARY DIGEST OF THE INTERAGENCY SCHOOL PROJECT. Oakland Public Schools, Interagency Project, Oakland, California. (7)

Discussion of project which ranges from K-12, and brief description of operations now in progress.

A TEACHER'S GUIDE: NON-ENGLISH SPEAKING PUPILS. Division of Curriculum and Instruction, Milwaukee Public Schools, Milwaukee, Wisconsin. (4)

A listing of understanding, speaking, reading, and writing situations used in developing language patterns at all grade levels. The bibliography includes audiovisual materials and techniques for placing children.

TEACHING ENGLISH AT BOYS' TRAINING SCHOOL. Daniel Fader, Department of English, University of Michigan, Ann Arbor, Michigan. (3)

Recommendations for establishing a program in English at the W. J. Maxey Boys' Training School—and related materials; the program includes integration of writing in all subject areas, use of newspapers, magazines.

UNIVERSITY OF TEXAS COOPERATIVE RESEARCH PROJECT. Austin, Texas. (2,4,7)

Policy statements and sample units from a project concerned with Spanish-Americans with limited English.

VOLUNTEER TUTORIAL SERVICE IN THE CINCINNATI PUBLIC SCHOOLS. Cincinnati, Ohio. (2,3,6,7)

This report contains a description and evaluation of the tutorial program for elementary and 6 junior high schools. (Revised September, 1965.)

WILLOW MANOR SCHOOL LANGUAGE DEVELOPMENT PROJECT REPORT. Oakland Public Schools, Oakland, California. (2,7)

This program emphasizes oral language and planned experiences.

THE WORK ORIENTED CURRICULUM, PHASE III. Montgomery County Public Schools, Rockville, Maryland. (3)

Descriptions of units which use an audiovisual approach to prepare students for the social and vocational demands of the world of work; supplementary list of audiovisual aids with annotations and evaluations.

THE WORK ORIENTED CURRICULUM, PHASE IV, BULLETIN 190. Montgomery County Public Schools, Rockville, Maryland. (3)

Follow-up units to the Phase III curriculum designed to facilitate the transition from school to job and insure effective job performance.

D. Index to Programs, Projects, and Participating Schools

The following index has been prepared as a guide to the many projects, schools, and individuals who have allowed their own efforts to be examined, either through visits or contributions of their printed reports, by members of the Task Force staff. The index is organized by city and state, with local superintendents and other appropriate officials listed for those projects administered through the public school system; private or independent efforts have separate entries preceding the list of public school system projects. The areas of major concern are indicated to the right of each project by the following symbols:

1 preschool
2 elementary
3 secondary
4 English as a second language
5 adult
6 teacher training and education.

All projects visited by members of the Task Force staff are marked with an asterik to the left of the listing. For schools which were involved in more than one project, the full address and appropriate personnel are given under the first project only, though the school is noted under all projects in which it was involved.

ARIZONA

Tucson

ROBERT MORROW, *Superintendent of Schools*

THOMAS LEE, *Assistant Superintendent*

IRIS MULVANEY, *Coordinator of Language Arts*

DOROTHY TALBERT, *Intermediate Supervisor*

MRS. JEWELL TAYLOR, *Primary Supervisor*

*HUMANITIES APPROACH TO ENGLISH; 3

Pueblo High School
3500 South 12th Avenue
Florence Reynolds, Acting Principal

*LINGUISTIC APPROACH TO REMEDIAL LANGUAGE; 3
Wakefield Junior High School
400 West 44th Street
Frank Ott, Principal

*HIGH HORIZONS; 3
Safford Junior High School
300 South 5th Avenue
William Corcoran, Principal

303

*LANGUAGE EXPERIENCE
APPROACH; 2

Holladay Elementary School
1110 East 33rd Street
  Gerald D. Sogert, Principal

*MIAMI MATERIALS; 2

Richey Elementary School
2209 North 15th Avenue
  Helen Henry, Director
  Anna Henry, Principal

*UNGRADED PRIMARY AND
BASAL INDIVIDUALIZED
READING; 2

Pueblo Gardens Elementary School
2210 East 33rd Street
  Mrs. Beulah Lavin, Principal

Winslow

*LEUPP BOARDING SCHOOL; 2
U.S. Bureau of Indian Affairs
Star Route
  Lee A. Brewer, Principal

CALIFORNIA

Berkeley

*SPAN PROJECT OF THE
GRADUATE INTERNSHIP
PROGRAM IN TEACHER
EDUCATION; 3,6

1610 Tolman Hall
University of California
  Clark Robinson, Director
  Mrs. Ruth Mandelbaum, Assistant
  Director

*BERKELEY HIGH SCHOOL; 3
Berkeley, California

Calexico

CARL L. VARNER, *Superintendent of
Schools*

*TEACHING ENGLISH AS A
SECOND LANGUAGE PILOT
PROJECT—MIAMI LINGUISTIC
READERS; 2,3
P. O. Box 792

Carl L. Varner, Director
Mrs. Edith Donlevy, Assistant
Director

Dool School
Encinas and Sherman Streets
  Mrs. Edith Donlevy, Principal

Jefferson School
7th and Andrade Streets
  H. Tannehill, Principal

Calexico Union High School
1000 Encinas
  W. Slade, Principal

Carlsbad

HARRIS TAYLOR, *Superintendent of
Schools*

PROJECT HEADSTART; 1
*ENGLISH AS SECOND
LANGUAGE; 2,3

Carlsbad Union School District
801 Pine Street
  Juan Solis, Director

Jefferson Elementary School
Carlsbad Union School District
  Juan Solis, Principal

Fresno

MR. DANN, *Superintendent of Schools*

MR. MENER, *Assistant Superintendent*

MRS. MAXWELL, *Supervisor of English*

*COMPENSATORY EDUCATION;
1,2,3,4,5,6

305 East Belgravia Street
  Arthur S. Carlson, Director
  Evelynne Walker, Assistant
  Director

Edison High School
540 California Street
  Mr. Solo, Principal

Kirk Elementary School
2354 Lily
  Mr. Parker, Principal

Preschool
305 East Belgravia
  Mr. Carlson, Principal

Teilman Elementary School
11 South Teilman
  Mr. Gaston, Principal
Reed Clegg High School
Welfare Department
  Furn Coe, Principal

Los Angeles

JACK P. CROWTHER, *Superintendent of Schools*

LOUISE WOOD SEYLER, *Deputy Superintendent*

EVERETT B. CHAFFEE, *Associate Superintendent*

BERNICE M. CHRISTENSON, *Supervisor of Elementary English*

VIRGINIA BELLE LOWERS, *Supervisor of Secondary English*

ROBERT J. PURDY, *Associate Superintendent of Elementary Education*

ROBERT E. KELLY, *Associate Superintendent of Secondary Education*

ROGER HYNDMAN, *Supervisor of Senior High English*

GORDON TRIGG, *Coordinator of Youth Opportunities*

ROBERT MAULLER, *Head Start and Compensatory Education, Elementary*

WALTER LANSU, *Reading Specialist, Special Programs, Secondary Education*

*PROJECT ''TEACH''; 6
School of Education
California State College
5151 State College Drive
  Lyle Hanna, Director

*COMPENSATORY EDUCATION; 2,4
Hammel Street School
438 North Brannick Avenue
  Frieda Mayers, Principal
Main Street School
129 East 53rd Street
  Elizabeth Culley, Principal

Malabar Street School
3200 East Malabar Street
  Jacqueline Hartwick, Principal
99th Street School
920 East 99th Street
  Richard Clower, Principal
102nd Street School
1916 East 102nd Street
  John Doyle, Jr., Principal

*DIVIDED PRIMARY DAY; 2,4
Hammel Street School
Malabar Street School

*EXTENDED DAY; 2,4
Hammel Street School
Malabar Street School
99th Street School
102nd Street School

*PRESCHOOL CLASSES
Hammel Street School
Main Street School
99th Street School
102nd Street School

*RECEPTION ROOM; 2
102nd Street School

*REMEDIAL READING AND LANGUAGE; 2,4
Hammel Street School
Malabar Street School

*SATURDAY SCHOOL; 2,4
Malabar Street School

*BASIC READING; 3
David Wark Griffith Junior High School
4765 East 4th Street
  Truman Case, Principal
John Adams Junior High School
151 West 30th Street
  William Zazueta, Principal
Thomas Jefferson High School
1319 East 41st Street
  Donald Skinner, Principal

305

Abraham Lincoln High School
3501 North Broadway
  George Ingles, Principal
Los Angeles High School
4600 West Olympic Boulevard
  John Holt, Principal

*NON-ENGLISH SPEAKING AND
FOREIGN SPEAKING; 3,4
David Wark Griffith Junior High
School
Abraham Lincoln High School
Los Angeles High School

*READING IMPROVEMENT; 3
David Wark Griffith Junior High
School
John Adams Junior High School
Thomas Jefferson High School
Abraham Lincoln High School
Los Angeles High School

*POWER READING; 3
David Wark Griffith Junior High
School
Abraham Lincoln High School
Los Angeles High School

*SCHOOL COMMUNITY
OPPORTUNITY PROJECTS IN
EDUCATION—READING; 3
John Adams Junior High School
Abraham Lincoln High School

*SCHOOL COMMUNITY
OPPORTUNITY PROJECTS IN
EDUCATION—AFTER SCHOOL
LIBRARY; 3
Thomas Jefferson High School
Abraham Lincoln High School

*STUDENT ACHIEVEMENT
CENTERS; 3
David Wark Griffith Junior High
School
Thomas Jefferson High School

*VOCATIONAL EDUCATION; 3
Thomas Jefferson High School
Abraham Lincoln High School

*NEIGHBORHOOD YOUTH
CORPS; 3
Thomas Jefferson High School
Abraham Lincoln High School
Los Angeles High School

Merced

RUDOLPH RIVERA, *Superintendent of
Schools*
SIDNEY G. MOSES, *Assistant
Superintendent*

*TEACHING SPANISH TO
SPANISH SPEAKING PUPILS,
TEACHING ENGLISH TO NON-
ENGLISH SPEAKING PUPILS;
2
555 West 22nd Street
  Sidney G. Moses, Director
  Maude Edmonson, Assistant
  Director
  William DeSimone, Assistant
  Director
Galen Clark School
632 West 13th Street
  Gather B. Haynes, Principal
Tenaya School
760 West 8th Street
  William DeSimone, Principal
Margaret Sheehy School
1240 West 6th Street
  John Cripe, Principal

Oakland

STUART S. PHILLIPS, *Superintendent
of Schools*
EDWARD COCKRUM, *Assistant
Superintendent (Elementary Section)*
ELMER STOLTE, *Assistant
Superintendent (Secondary Section)*
VIRGINIA REID, *Supervisor of English
(Elementary Section)*
JEAN WILSON, *Supervisor of English
(Secondary Section)*

*INTERAGENCY PROJECT; 1,2,3,5
1025 Second Avenue
  Andrew J. Viscovich, Director

306

Willow Manor School
1501 Campbell Street
  John Picchotto, Principal

Clawson School
3240 Peralta Street
  Charles Cline, Principal

James Madison Junior High School
400 Capistrano Drive
  Norman Shapiro, Principal

Castlemont High School
8601 MacArthur Boulevard
  George Cherry, Principal

Stonehurst Elementary School
  Colin Fern, Principal

*ADULT DAY SCHOOL; 5
6901 Foothill Boulevard
  Henning Edlund, Director

Richmond

RICHMOND HIGH SCHOOL; 3
1250 23rd Street
  Terry Borton, Teacher of English

San Andreas

*FRICOT RANCH SCHOOL FOR
BOYS EDUCATIONAL
PROGRAM; 2
Fricot Ranch School
  Thomas M. Lewis, Principal

San Diego

RALPH C. DARLARD, *Superintendent
of Schools*

DON L. CHAMBERLIN, *Administrator,
Inservice Education*

*PILOT PROJECT—
COMPENSATORY EDUCATION;
2,3
San Diego City Schools
4100 Normal Street
  William H. Stegeman, Director

Kennedy Primary School
San Diego Public Schools
  Lowell C. Ballard, Principal

Emerson Elementary School
3575 National Avenue
  George Montello

Memorial Junior High School
2884 Marcy Avenue
  Frank B. Thornton, Principal

San Francisco

*MISSION ADULT HIGH
SCHOOL; 5
3750 18th Street
  Albert Silverstein, Principal

San Quentin

VIRGIL HOLLIS, *Superintendent of
Schools*

STANLEY FRIESE, *Assistant
Superintendent*

*LITERACY TRAINING. FOR
ADULTS; 5
San Quentin Prison
  H. J. Hastings, Director of
  Education

Bayview Schools

California State Prison
  George Renworth, Principal

Tulare

MAX COCHRAN, *Superintendent of
Schools*

THELMA GOMEZ, *Assistant
Superintendent*

*PRESCHOOL PROGRAM; 1
Tulare City Schools
600 North Cherry Avenue
  Thelma Gomez, Director
  Glena Crumal, Assistant Director

Lincoln School
909 East Cedar Street
  Glena Crumal, Principal

Frank Kohn School
500 South Laspina
  Harold McKeown, Principal

COLORADO
Denver

KENNETH E. OBERHOLTZER,
Superintendent of Schools

ROY A. HINDERMAN, *Assistant Superintendent*

JERRY REED, *Supervisor of English*

*JOB OPPORTUNITY CENTER, INC.; 5

1360 Speer Boulevard
James Galvin, Director
Tom Espie, Assistant Director
Marilyn Weir, Supervising Teacher

CONNECTICUT
Hartford

KENNETH L. MEINKE, *Superintendent of Schools*

ROBERT M. KELLY, *Assistant Superintendent*

*MDTA BASIC EDUCATION; 4,5

Hartford Board of Education
249 High Street
Richard F. Kelly, Director

Hartford Adult Schools
Bureau of Adult Education
249 High Street
Richard F. Kelly, Principal

New Haven

LAURENCE PAQUIN, *Superintendent of Schools*

*URBAN EDUCATION STUDIES PROJECT; 1,2,3,6

Board of Education
200 Orange Street
Elizabeth S. Wright, Director of Curriculum

Preschool Project Headquarters
31 Webster Street
Adelaide Phillips, Supervisor

Curriculum Assistance Program
Conte Community School

Wooster Square
Elena Smith, Chairman

Higher Horizons Program
Strong Elementary School
69 Grand Avenue
Beverly Keener, Supervisor

Dialects Project
Hillhouse High School
480 Sherman Parkway
Alice Hogan, English Department Chairman

Special English Project
Bassett Jr. High School

DISTRICT OF COLUMBIA
Washington, D.C.

CARL F. HANSEN, *Superintendent of Schools*

EDITH A. LYONS, *Assistant Superintendent, Elementary*

JOHN D. KOONTZ, *Assistant Superintendent, Secondary*

MRS. CHARLOTTE K. BROOKS, *Supervisor of English*

LOUIS KORNHAUSER, *Director, Language Arts Program*

*ITA READING PROJECT; 2

Bruce Elementary School
Kenyon Street and Sherman Avenue, N.W.
Mrs. Alma F. Felder, Principal

*LANGUAGE ARTS PROGRAM; 2

John F. Cook Elementary School
P Street between North Capitol and First Street, N.W.
Mrs. Jeanne W. Hargrave, Principal

Langston Elementary School
P Street between North Capitol and First Street, N.W.
Mrs. Marjorie P. Savage, Principal

Seaton Elementary School
I Street between Second and Third Streets, N.W.
Bradford A. Tatum, Principal

Thomson Elementary School
Twelfth and L Streets, N.W.
  Robert A. Hiltz, Principal

Walker-Jones Elementary School
First and L Streets, N.W.
  Mrs. Wilhelmina B. Thomas,
  Principal

*LINGUISTICS APPROACH; 3

Banneker Junior High School
Georgia Avenue and Euclid Street,
N.W.
  Elmer F. Mitchell, Principal

*MODERN SCHOOL SYSTEM;
1,2,3

Preschool Center
Galbraith Methodist Church
1113 Sixth Street, N.W.
  Esther Carter, School Manager

Shaw Junior High School
Seventh and Rhode Island Avenue,
N.W.
  Oliver R. Rogers, Jr., Principal

*PEACE CORPS PROGRAM; 3

Cardozo High School
Thirteenth and Clifton Streets,
N.W.
  Randall Evans, Principal

Banneker Junior High School

*TEAM TEAHING; 3

Bakus Junior High School
5171 South Dakota Avenue, N.E.
  Harry L. Chasey, Principal

*TELE-TRAINER PROGRAM; 3

Banneker Junior High School

*TREANOR COMPOSITION
METHOD; 2

Myrtilla Miner Elementary School
615 Fifteenth Street, N.E.
  Mrs. M. Otwiner DeMond,
  Principal

*WORDS IN COLOR; 2

Davis Elementary School
Forty-Fourth Place and H Streets,
S.E.
  Norman S. Anthony, Principal

Other Schools Visited:
  Boys' Junior-Senior High School
First and I Streets, S.W.
  Fred J. Aranha, Principal

H. D. Cooke Elementary School
Seventeenth and Euclid Streets,
N.W.
  Winston E. Turner, Principal

Bundy Elementary School
429 O Street, N.W.
  Charles E. Carter, Principal

Armstrong Adult Education
Center
First and O Streets, N.W.
  Elliott W. Lucas, Principal

Dunbar Senior High School
First and N Streets, N.W.
  Howard P. Bolden, Principal

DELAWARE

Wilmington

  *ELEMENTARY EDUCATION; 2

PAUL E. SMITH, *Superintendent*

MURIEL CROSBY, *Assistant
Superintendent*

  Wilmington Public Schools
  1400 Washington

FLORIDA

Coral Gables

  *TEACHER EDUCATION
  PROJECT; 6

  University of Miami
    Dr. Sidney Besvinick, Director

Miami

JOE HALL, *Superintendent of Schools*

JOHN BAHNER, *Associate
Superintendent*

ELIZABETH WHITE, *Supervisor of
English*

  *FORD FOUNDATION
  BEGINNING READING FOR
  NON-ENGLISH SPEAKING AND

CULTURALLY
DISADVANTAGED STUDENTS;
2,4

Lindsey Hopkins Building
1410 N.E. Second Avenue
  Pauline M. Rajos, Director
  Ralph F. Robinett, Assistant
  Director

Coral Way Elementary School
1950 S.W. 13 Avenue
  Lee Logan, Principal

Riverside Elementary School
221 S.W. 12 Avenue
  Edith A. Chase, Principal

Allapattah Elementary School
4700 N.W. 12 Avenue
  George E. Bowker, Principal

*JOHN F. KENNEDY
PRESCHOOL PROGRAM; 1

Lindsey Hopkins Building BPI
1410 N.E. Second Avenue
  Howard D. McMillan, Director

Buena Vista Elementary School
3001 N.W. Second Avenue
  Rea E. Cook, Principal

Allapattah Elementary School

Little River Elementary School
514 N.W. 77th Street
  John Gardner, Principal

*JUNIOR AND SENIOR HIGH
SCHOOL LEARNING
LABORATORIES; 3

Lindsey Hopkins Building BPI
1410 N.E. Second Avenue
  Gilbert Johnson, Director

Miami-Jackson Junior-Senior
High School
1751 N.W. 36th Street
  Donald A. Burroughs, Principal

Brownsville Junior High School
4899 N.W. 24th Avenue
  Ida R. Ratcliffe, Principal

Robert E. Lee Junior High School
3100 N.W. Fifth Avenue
  Otto Stradley, Principal

Plant City

J. Crockett Farnell, *Superintendent
of Schools*

Denton L. Cook, *Assistant
Superintendent*

Charles Isom, *Supervisor of English*

*REMEDIAL READING
PROJECT; 3

Marshall High School
P. O. Box 1630
Maryland Avenue at Church Street
  E. Lutrell Bing, Director
  Hattie Teddleton, Assistant
  Director

ILLINOIS

Chicago

Msgr. William McManus,
*Superintendent of Chicago Catholic
Schools*

Rev. William Goedert, *Assistant
Superintendent*

Sr. M. Francis Raphael, O.P.,
Supervisor of English

*REMEDIAL READING
PROJECT—CREATIVE
WRITING; 2

Saint Clara School
6423 South Woodlawn Avenue
  Sister M. Loverna, Director

Saint Martins School
320 West 59th Street
  Sister M. Ethelbert, Principal

Benjamin G. Willis, *Superintendent
of Schools*

Evelyn Carlson, *Associate
Superintendent*

Thaddeus Lubera, *Associate
Superintendent*

*LANGUAGE LAB READING
PROGRAM; 2,3

Chicago Public Schools, District 8
2935 West Polk Street
  Mrs. Sophie Reiffel, Supervisor,
  District 8

Roentgen Vocational Guidance and
Education Center
15 South Homan Avenue
  Martin Gabriel, Principal
Marshall Senior High School
3250 West Adams Street
  John P. Byrnes, Principal
Manley Elementary School
2935 West Polk Street
  Joseph J. Zbornik, Principal

INDIANA
Indianapolis
  RESEARCH AND TEACHER
  TRAINING; 6
  Board of Fundamental Education
  146 East Washington Street
    Karl F. Schwengel, Principal

KENTUCKY
Louisville
  MICHARD VAN HOOSE, *Superintendent*
  A. J. BEELER, *Curriculum Coordinator*
  *JEFFERSON COUNTY PUBLIC
  SCHOOLS; 2,3
  Jefferson County Public Schools
  506 West Hill Street

LOUISIANA
New Orleans
  PRE-FRESHMAN PROGRAM
  Dillard University
  Lou LaBrant, Director

MARYLAND
Baltimore
  LAURENCE PAQUIN, *Incoming
  Superintendent of Schools*
  EDITH V. WALKER, *Assistant
  Superintendent*
  SUMMER INSTITUTE FOR
  TEACHERS OF
  DISADVANTAGED YOUTH; 2,6

Morgan State College
Hillen Road & Cold Spring Lane
  Regina M. Goff, Director
*COMPOSITION PROJECT; 3
Patterson High School
  Elsa Graser, Coordinator
*EARLY SCHOOL ADMISSIONS
PROJECT; 1
Baltimore City Department of
Education Annex
2519 Charles Street
  Mrs. Catherine Brunner,
  Coordinator
O'Donnell Heights Elementary
School
O'Donnell & Gusryan Streets
  Dallas Smith, Principal
Lexington Terrace Elementary
School
Lexington St. and Myrtle Avenue
  Henry West, Principal
*DEPARTMENT OF
EDUCATION; 3
2 East 25th Street
Baltimore, Maryland
  Sidney N. Chernak, Assistant
  Superintendent

Rockville
  HOMER O. ELSEROAD, *Superintendent
  of Schools*
  JOHN A. PERMENTER, *Assistant
  Superintendent*
  KATHERINE B. GREANEY, *Supervisor
  of English*
  *WORK ORIENTED
  CURRICULUM; 3
  Montgomery County Board of
  Education
  Washington Center
    Samuel M. Goodman, Director
    Mrs. Lois Parker, Curriculum
    Coordinator for Work Oriented
    Curriculum

Northwood Senior High
University Boulevard, West
Silver Spring, Maryland
　Harold R. Packard, Principal

Springbrook Senior High School
Valleybrook Drive
Silver Spring, Maryland
　Thomas P. Marshall, Principal

MASSACHUSETTS

Boston

*ADULT LITERACY PROJECT; 5

Massachusetts Council of Public
Schools, Inc.
16 Arlington Street
　Mrs. Annette C. Krebs, Director
　Mrs. Edna Koretsky, Coordinator

Blue Hill Christian Center
Blue Hill Avenue
Arlington Street Church
285 Boylston Street
South End Settlement House
48 Rutland Street
St. Stephen's Episcopal Church
419 Shawmut Avenue

WILLIAM H. OHRENBERGER,
Superintendent of Schools

MARGUERITE G. SULLIVAN, *Deputy
Superintendent*

*PRE-KINDERGARTEN AND
DEVELOPMENTAL READING;
1,2

Boston School Committee
15 Beacon Street
　Frances Sullivan, Director of
　Kindergartens, Boston Public
　Schools
　Catherine M. Maney, Coordinator,
　Boston Public Schools and ABCD
　Programs

J. J. Williams Pre-Kindergarten
School
15 Groton Street
　Hugh O'Regan, Principal

Whittier Pre-Kindergarten School
1158 Tremont Street
　Catherine H. Mahoney, Principal

David A. Ellis School
(Developmental Reading)
302 Walnut Avenue
Roxbury, Masachusetts
　William McCarthy, Principal

*OPERATION COUNTERPOISE; 2

15 Beacon Street
　Marguerite G. Sullivan, Director

D. A. Ellis School

Sarah Greenwood School
189 Glenway Street
Dorchester, Massachusetts
　Mary Flaherty, Principal

Christopher Gibson School
16 Ronald Street
Dorchester, Massachusetts
　Dorothea Callahan, Principal

Ellis Mendall School
164 School Street
Jamaica Plain, Massachusetts
　Marry Brennan, Principal

Lewis Junior High School
131 Walnut Avenue
Roxbury, Massachusetts
　Francis X. Murphy, Principal

Julia Ward Howe School (& Sarah
J. Baker)
Dale Street
Roxbury, Massachusetts
　Catherine McDonagh, Principal

John F. Kennedy School
7 Bolster Street
Jamaica Plain, Massachusetts
　Sally Logue, Principal

MICHIGAN

Ann Arbor

*AN ENGLISH PROGRAM FOR
TRAINING SCHOOLS; 2,3,6

1627 Haven Hall
University of Michigan
　Daniel Fader, English Director
　Elton B. McNeil, Chief
　Consultant in Psychology

W. J. Makey Boys' Training
Schools
Whitmore Lake, Michigan
Leon Holman, Principal

Detroit

*PREPARING TEACHERS FOR
DISADVANTAGED CHILDREN:
THE MARCY-TROWBRIDGE
PROJECT; 6
Mercy College of Detroit
8200 West Outer Drive
Yvonne M. Lofthouse, Director
Lucille Beacom, Assistant
Director

*PREPARING TEACHERS FOR
DISADVANTAGED CHILDREN:
THE HUTCHINS JUNIOR HIGH
SCHOOL PROJECT; 6
Mercy College of Detroit
8200 West Outer Drive
Yvonne M. Lofthouse, Director
James Irwin, Assistant Director
James McCarthy, Assistant
Director

*PRE-TEACHING LABORATORY
EXPERIENCE WITH THE
DETROIT URBAN LEAGUE; 2,6
Mercy College of Detroit
8200 West Outer Drive
Sr. Thomas Mary, R.S.M.,
Director
Campbell School
Alexandrine Street
Dr. Parkllan, Principal

*CORKTOWN REMEDIAL
READING; 2,6
Mercy College of Detroit
8200 West Outer Drive
Sister Mary Columba, R.S.M.,
Director

JAMES COUZENS-MERCY
COLLEGE OF DETROIT
SPELLING PROJECT; 2,6
Mercy College of Detroit
8200 West Outer Drive
Paul M. Donahue, Director

SAMUEL BROWNELL, *Superintendent of
Schools*
CARL BYERLY, *Assistant
Superintendent*
CHARLES WOLFE, *Assistant
Superintendent*
PAUL RONKA, *Assistant
Superintendent*
CLARENCE WACHNER, *Director of
Language Education*

REMEDIAL EDUCATION FOR
ADULTS; 5
Detroit Board of Education
Schools Center, Building 2
5057 Woodward
Ray Ferrier, Director

*PRESCHOOL CHILD AND
PARENT EDUCATION
PROJECT; 1
1030 School Centers Building
5057 Woodward Avenue
Bert B. Pryor, Director

*ENGLISH S; 3
Room 922
Division of Language Education
Detroit Public Schools
Schools Center Building
Mrs. Ethel Tincher, Director

*THE DISADVANTAGED CHILD
AND THE LANGUAGE ARTS;
1,2,3,6
State Department of Public
Instruction
Lansing, Michigan
Michigan Language Arts
Curriculum Committee
Northern High School
9026 Woodward Avenue
A. T. Carty, Principal
R. I. Golden, English Department
Head

*GREAT CITIES SCHOOL
IMPROVEMENT PROJECT; 1,2,3
Detroit Public Schools Center
5057 Woodward Avenue
Detroit, Michigan
Dr. Louis Monacel

313

*MULTI-CULTURAL READERS; 2
Detroit Public Schools Center
5057 Woodward
Dr. Gertrude Whipple

*REACH; 3
Language Education Department
Detroit Public Schools
922 Schools Center Building
Clarence Wachner, Director
Henry Maloney, Junior High
School Supervisor

Pelham Junior High School
2001 Myrtle
Ray Morley, Principal

*ENGLISH LANGUAGE
LABORATORY (TAPES FOR
CHANGING SPEECH
PATTERNS); 3

40 Colorado Avenue
Highland Park, Michigan
Ruth I. Golden, Director
Mrs. Anne Shank, Assistant
Director

Northern High School

Ypsilanti

PAUL EMERICH, *Superintendent of
Schools*

PERRY PRESCHOOL PROJECT;
1

Ypsilanti Public Schools
300 West Forest
David P. Weikart, Director

MINNESOTA
Minneapolis

RUFUS PUTNAM, *Superintendent of
Schools*

RODNEY TILLMAN, *Assistant
Superintendent*

MABLE MELBY, *Supervisor of English*

MILDRED CARLSON, *Supervisor of
English*

*EXPERIMENTAL JUNIOR HIGH
SCHOOL; 3
1713–15 Plymouth Avenue North
John M. Mass, Principal

*CURRICULUM DEVELOPMENT
DEMONSTRATION PROJECT;
1,2
Elizabeth Hall School
1601 Aldrich North
Willard M. Ludford, Director
John Ott, Headstart Director

St. Paul

JUEL C. THOMPSON, *Superintendent
of Schools*

*MECHANIC ARTS HIGH
SCHOOL; 3

Central and Robert Streets
Charles Simmer, Principal
Robert C. Munns, Supervisor of
English

*MARSHALL JUNIOR HIGH
SCHOOL; 3

Grotto Street and Ashland Avenue
Jack Anderson, Principal

MISSISSIPPI
Philadelphia

*PRIMARY SUMMER PROGRAM
OF CHOCTAW INDIAN
AGENCY; 2,3,5

Bureau of Indian Affairs
Choctaw Indian Agency
R. J. Smith, Director

MISSOURI
Kansas City

JAMES A. HAZLETT, *Superintendent
of Schools*

ARTHUR W. GILBERT, *Assistant
Superintendent*

THOMAS MORRIS, *Consultant in
Secondary English*

314

*LINCOLN PLUS, MANUAL
PLUS, COMPENSATORY
EDUCATION; 1,2,3

JOHN A. CLAIR, Director
JUANITA YANCEY and STELLA MIN-
TURN, General Grade Consultants
Attucks, Banneker, Carver,
Humboldt, Phillips, Washington,
Woodland, Yates Schools

St. Louis

WILLIAM KOTTMEYER, *Superintendent*
SAMUEL SHEPARD, JR., *Assistant
Superintendent*

*OPERATION MOTIVATION; 2

Banneker School
2840 Lucas Avenue
Samuel Shepard, Jr., Director

Franklin Elementary School
814 North 19th Street
George L. Smith, Principal

Divoll Elementary School
2918 Dayton Street
Ernest Jones, Principal

Jefferson Elementary School
1301 Hogan Street
William C. Wyatt, Principal

Chouteau Elementary School
1306 South Ewing Avenue
Mrs. Era B. Perkins, Principal

NEW HAMPSHIRE

Hanover

ABC TEACHER INSTITUTE; 3,6
Dartmouth College
4 Parkhurst
Charles F. Dey, Director
Robert G. Tisdale, Associate
Director

NEW JERSEY

Hanover

HANOVER PARK HIGH
SCHOOL; 3
Hanover Park High School
Robert G. Watson, Assistant
Principal

Passaic

WOODROW WILSON JUNIOR
HIGH SCHOOL; 3

NEW MEXICO

Shiprock

SHIPROCK BOARDING
SCHOOL; 2
Bureau of Indian Affairs
Shiprock Subagency
Webster A. Schneck, Principal

NEW YORK

Buffalo

JOSEPH MANCH, *Superintendent of
Schools*
FRANK J. DRESSLER, *Assistant
Superintendent*
JAMES LANZ, *Director of English*

*CONTINUATION OF FORD
FOUNDATION PILOT
PROGRAM 1961; 2,6
Buffalo City Schools
712 City Hall
Jonah D. Margulis, Director
School 12
52 Ash Street
Helen Burns, Principal
School 46 Reading Center
389 Virginia Street
Eileen J. Hutchinson, Assistant
Principal

*CLOSED CIRCUIT TV FOR
MULTIPLE VIEWING OF
ENGLISH LESSONS; 3

315

Woodlawn Junior High School
450 Masten Avenue
William J. Fairlie, Principal

Ithaca

PROJECT LITERACY; 1,2,3,4,5,6
Cornell University
320 Wait Avenue
Harry Levin, Director

New York

BRIDGE PROJECT; 3,6
Department of Education
Queens College of the City
University of New York
Robert W. Edgar, Director
Albert J. Harris, Assistant
Director
Helen F. Storen, Assistant
Director

*MOBILIZATION FOR YOUTH;
1,2,3,5
271 East 4th Street
S. Alan Cohen, Director

Elementary Reading Clinic
P. S. 188 Manhattan
442 East Houston Street
Anna S. Harris, Coordinator of
Clinic
Abraham T. Tannenbaum,
Director of Education

School 12

Woodrow Wilson Junior High
School
Passaic, New Jersey

THE DIEBOLD GROUP, INC.
430 Park Avenue
John W. Blyth, Principal

*COMPARING READING
APPROACHES IN FIRST GRADE
TEACHING OF
DISADVANTAGED CHILDREN
(CRAFT); 2,6
The City University of New York
535 East 80 Street
Albert J. Harris, Director

Blanche L. Serwer, Assistant
Director
P. S. 160 Queens
109–59 Inwood Street
Jamaica, New York City, New York

*HARYOU ACT: AFTER SCHOOL
STUDY PROGRAM; 2,3
180 West 135th Street
New York, New York 10030
Mrs. Beryl James, Director

*GATEWAY ENGLISH: HUNTER
COLLEGE PROJECT ENGLISH
CURRICULUM CENTER; 3,6
Hunter College of the City
University of New York
695 Park Avenue
Marjorie B. Smiley, Director

Junior High School 120
18 East 120th Street
Alexander Rosenblatt, Principal

Junior High School 164
401 West 164 Street
Milton Levin, Principal

*BILLINGUAL READINESS
PROJECT; 1,2,4
Hunter College of the City
University of New York
695 Park Avenue
Mary Finocchiaro, Director
Paul King, Director

P. S. 145
150 West 105 Street
Carl Erdberg, Principal

P. S. 87
160 West 78 Street
Arthur Block, Principal

P. S. 191
210 West 61 Street
Stanley Becker, Principal

*INFORMATION RETRIEVAL
CENTER ON THE
DISADVANTAGED—PROJECT
BEACON; 6

Ferkauf Graduate School of
Education
Yeshiva University
150 West 56th Street
  Edmund W. Gordon, Director
  Doxey A. Wilkerson, Assistant
  Director

*INSTITUTE FOR
DEVELOPMENTAL STUDIES; 1
New York City Medical College
Department of Psychiatry
  Martin Deutsch, Director
  Caroline Saxe, Coordinator,
  Enrichment Staff

BERNARD E. DONOVAN, Superintendent
of Schools
TRUDA T. WEIL, Associate
Superintendent

*HIGHER HORIZONS; 2,3
Board of Education
110 Livingston Street
  Carmela Mercurio, Coordinator

P. S. 13, Manhattan
William Ettinger Junior High
School
106 Street and Madison Avenue
  Leonard Loeb, Principal

Morris High School
166th Street and Boston Road
  Paul Schweitzer, Principal

P. S. 262, Brooklyn
John H. McCooly School
500 Macon Street
  Wilbur Nordos, Principal

*PRE-KINDERGARTEN
CLASSES; 1
Board of Education
Bureau of Early Childhood
110 Livingston Street
  Rebecca A. Winton, Director

P. S. 123 Manhattan
301 West 140 Street
  Erwin C. Kaufman, Principal

P. S. 191 Manhattan
210 West 61 Street
  Stanley Becker, Principal

P. S. 199 Manhattan
270 West 70 Street
  Nathan Plung, Principal

*MORE EFFECTIVE SCHOOLS;
1,2
131 Livingston Street
  Mrs. Elizabeth C. O'Daly,
  Director
  Mrs. Elizabeth Cagan, Assistant
  Director
  Mrs. Hortense Jones, Assistant
  Director

Syracuse

FRANKLIN BARRY, Superintendent of
Schools

*URBAN TEACHER
PREPARATION PROGRAM; 2,3
305 Comstock Avenue
  Ernest J. Milner, Director
  Gerald Weinstein, Associate
  Director of Project

Madison Junior High School
Madison Avenue
  Joseph Bongo, Principal

NORTH CAROLINA

Chapel Hill

HOWARD E. THOMPSON,
Superintendent of Schools

GUY PHILLIPS JUNIOR HIGH
SCHOOL; 3
  Zora M. Rashkis, Chairman,
  Department of English

Charlotte

A. CRAIG PHILLIPS, Superintendent of
Schools
WILLIAM SELF, Assistant
Superintendent
JAMES SUBER, Supervisor of English

*COMPREHENSIVE SCHOOL
IMPROVEMENT PROJECT; 1,2
  Charlotte-Mecklenburg Instructional
  Services

317

7600 West Interstate Highway 85
John Phillips, Director
James Suber, Assistant Director

Lincoln Heights Elementary School
1900 Newcastle Street
O. N. Freeman, Principal

Raleigh

CHARLES F. CARROL, *State Superintendent of Schools*

J. E. MILLER, *Assistant State Superintendent*

MRS. JOAN P. NEWMAN, *State Supervisor of English*

J. O. SANDERSON, *Superintendent of Schools*

CONRAD HOOPER, *Assistant Superintendent*

*ITA (INITIAL TEACHING OF THE ALPHABET) CSIP; 2

Raleigh Public Schools
  Robert Pittillo, Director
Lucille Hunter School
1018 East Davie Street
  W. W. Hurdle, Principal

*COMPREHENSIVE SCHOOL IMPROVEMENT PROJECT; 1,2

Department of Public Instruction
Raleigh, North Carolina
  Woodrow Sugg, Director
South Nash Elementary School
Box 327
Spring Hope, North Carolina
  Kanawha Z. Chavis, Principal
Battle Elementary School
810 South Franklin Street
Rocky Mount, North Carolina
  Mrs. Katherine Nicholson, Principal
Lucille Hunter Elementary School
1018 East Davie Street
Raleigh, North Carolina
  W. W. Hurdle, Principal
Edgemont Elementary School
East Main Street
Durham, North Carolina
  W. W. Woody, Principal

Winston-Salem

*NORTH CAROLINA ADVANCEMENT SCHOOL; 2,3,6

North Carolina Advancement School
Gordon McAndrew, Director

OHIO

Cincinnati

WENDELL H. PIERCE, *Superintendent of Schools*

ROBERT P. CURRY, *Associate Superintendent*

MARJORIE L. ROGERS, *Supervisor of Library*

*ELEMENTARY LIBRARY; 2

Cincinnati Board of Education
608 East McMillan Street
  Althea Beery, Director
Washington Park School
113 West Fourteenth Street
  William J. Ciarniello, Principal

*PRE-KINDERGARTEN EDUCATION PROGRAM; 1

Cincinnati Board of Education
608 East McMillan Street
  Lawrence C. Hawkins, Director
  Mrs. Jane F. Pope, Assistant Director
Hays School
1035 Mound Street
  Mrs. Vivian J. Beamon, Principal
Millvale School
3277 Beekman Street
  Mrs. Grace T. Williams, Principal
Herberle School
2015 Freeman Avenue
  Albert J. Isler, Principal
Sands School
940 Poplar Street
  Alonzo Saunders, Principal

*TUTORIAL PROGRAM; 2

Cincinnati Board of Education
608 East McMillan Street
  James N. Jacobs, Director

318

Windsor School
937 Windsor Avenue
Coy Hale, Principal

*CONTINUATION EDUCATION;
4,5,6

Cincinnati Public Schools
608 East McMillan Street
Robert Finch, Director
Ruth Goering, Assistant Director

Stow Adult Center
7th Street
Theodore S. Genther, Principal

*REMEDIAL READING
PROJECT; 2

Cincinnati Public Schools
608 East McMillan
Althea Beery, Director
Anna M. Evans, Assistant
Director

Hays School

*PROGRAMS IN READING
IMPROVEMENT,
SUPPLEMENTAL ENGLISH; 3

Cincinnati Public Schools
608 West McMillan Street
Mary Louise Schroth, Supervisor

Heinold Junior High School
2240 Baltimore Avenue
Robert Wagner, Principal

Robert A. Taft Senior High School
420 Lincoln Park Drive
Walter Zach, Principal

Porter Junior High School
1030 Cutter Street
Martha Leeds, Principal

*TALENT DEVELOPMENT
(PILOT PROJECT ON
LANGUAGE DEVELOPMENT); 2

Center for School Experimentation
College of Education
The Ohio State University
Columbus, Ohio
Alexander Frazier, Director

North Avondale School
615 Clinton Springs

Cincinnati, Ohio
Luise Reszhe, Principal

Cleveland

PAUL W. BRIGGS, *Superintendent of
Schools*

ALVA R. DITTRICK, *Deputy
Superintendent*

VERDA EVANS, *Directing Supervisor*

*PACE, ELEMENTARY SCHOOL
LIBRARY PROGRAM; 1,2,5,6

518 The Arcade
420 Superior Ave.
R. B. Binswanger, Executive
Director

*COMMUNITY ACTION FOR
YOUTH; 2,3

1837 E. 79 St.

Ray Lewis, Director
James Misch, Assistant Director
James Tanner

East High School
1380 E. 82 St.
J. R. Klein, Principal

Addison Junior High School
1725 E. 79 St.
Joseph Dinunzio, Principal

Wade Park Elementary School
7600 Wade Park Avenue
Mrs. Margaret A. Prewitt,
Principal

Kent

PROJECT HEADSTART
ORIENTATION WORKSHOP,
June 20–26, 1965; 1,6

104 Merrill Hall
Kent State University
Roger T. Beitler, Director
Leah Houser, Asst. Director

OREGON

Eugene

*LANE COUNTY YOUTH
PROJECT; 2,3

1901 Garden Ave.
Harold McAbee, Chief of

Educational Programs
Erwin Juilfs, Director of
Secondary Education

Ida Patterson Elementary School
Glendora Burbank, Principal

Woodrow Wilson Junior High
School
William I. Williams, Principal

South Eugene High School
Clifford Moffitt, Principal

PENNSYLVANIA

Bethlehem

CHARLES E. CHAFFEE, *Superintendent
of Schools*

ITA PROGRAM IN FIRST
GRADE; 2

Lehigh University
Albert Mazurkiewitz, Director
Rebecca W. Stewart, Codirector

Manvine School
1400 Lebanon St.
Michael Loupes, Principal

Pacher School
940 E. Fourth Street
Jerome Quarry, Principal

Washington School
1720 E. Fourth Street
David Alexy, Principal

Chester

*GREATER CHESTER
MOVEMENT; 1

1700 West 3rd Street
Terry Dellmuth, Director

Harrisburg

EVERETT A. McDONALD,
Superintendent of Schools

RUTH E. ROBERTS, *Local Project
Coordinator*

*PRESCHOOL AND PRIMARY
EDUCATION PROJECT; 1,2

Dept. of Public Instruction
Education Building, Room 218

Allan S. Hartman, Director
Ernest J. Rookey, Assistant
Director
Harold E. Sadofsky, Assistant
Director

Lacey Park School
Van Horn Drive
Warminster, Pa.
Charles C. Loughery, Principal

Philadelphia

C. TAYLOR WHITTIER, *Superintendent
of Schools*

DAVID A. HOROWITZ, *Associate
Superintendent of Curriculum*

*GREAT CITIES SCHOOL
IMPROVEMENT PROGRAM;
2,3,6

Curriculum Office, Rm. 202
Board of Education
Administration Bldg.
21st and Parkway
David A. Horowitz, Director
George Green, Coordinator
(Director)

Dunbar School
12th St. North of Columbia Ave.
Mark Levin, Principal

Ludlow School
6th and Master Streets
Bernard Dubrow, Acting
Principal

John Wanamaker Jr. High School
11th St. and Columbia Avenue
Wm. Lucas, Acting Principal

*EXPERIMENTAL NURSERY
SCHOOL PROGRAM; 1

College of Education
Temple University
Ritter Hall
13th and Montgomery Sts.
Gabrielle J. Faddis, Director
E. Kuno Beller, Research
Director

Paul Laurence Dunbar School
Kenderton School
15th and Ontario Sts.
F. Robert Hagerty, Principal

320

Gen. John F. Reynolds School
24th and Jefferson Streets
Franklyn N. Rider, Principal

State College

BRUCE R. BRUMMITT, *Superintendent of Schools*

WILLIAM E. BABCOCK, *Director of Curriculum*

NORMAN LAMPMAN, *Supervisor of English*

*SLOW ACHIEVER ENGLISH PROGRAM; 3
114 W. Foster Ave.
Junior High School
Westerly Parkway
Richard Jones, Principal

RHODE ISLAND

Providence

*BASIC EDUCATION; 5
Department of Education
Hayes St.
Edward J. Medeiros, Director
Oscar F. Miller, Assistant Director
Samuel W. Bridgham Jr. High School
359 Carpenter St.
Kenneth Kane, Principal

SOUTH CAROLINA

Columbia

GUY L. VARN, *Superintendent of Schools*

C. E. KITCHENS, *Assistant Superintendent*

*READING PROJECT; 3
1607 Laurel
Charlie G. Williams, Director
W. G. Sanders, Assistant Director
C. H. Johnson High School
2200 Barhamville Road
C. J. Johnson, Principal

TENNESSEE

Chattanooga

B. E. CARMICHAEL, *Superintendent of Schools*

AVONDALE PROJECT; 3
2302 Ocoee St.
William F. Smith, Director

*CHATTANOOGA AREA LITERACY MOVEMENT, INC.; 5
Siskin Memorial Building
526 Vine St.
Mrs. Boyd Jacoway, Executive Secretary
Elizabeth Abernathy, President of Board of Directors

Murfreesboro

EARLY TRAINING PROJECT; 1
Murfreesboro Public School Program
Susan Gray, Director

TEXAS

Austin–San Antonio

*USOE COOPERATIVE RESEARCH PROJECT # 2648, READING INSTRUCTION FOR SPANISH-SPEAKING SCHOOL BEGINNERS; 2,3,6
The University of Texas
Sutton Hall 434
Thomas D. Horn, Director
Mrs. Elizabeth Ott, Assistant Director
Navarro School
San Antonio, Texas
Mrs. Lea Young, Principal
Johnson School
San Antonio, Texas
Mrs. Irma Wisdom, Principal
Carvaial School
San Antonio, Texas
Dora Mabrito, Principal

Houston

JOHN W. McFARLAND, *Superintendent of Schools*

321

EDWIN D. MARTIN, *Deputy Superintendent of Schools*

MRS. JOZIE MOCK, *Supervisor of English*

MRS. RUTH REEVES, *Supervisor of English*

*TALENT PRESERVATION PROJECT; 3

Houston Independent School District
1300 Capitol
   Jozie Mock, Director

Stonewall Jackson Junior High School
5100 Polk Avenue
   Harry H. McCurdy, Principal

Jane Long Junior High School
6501 Bellain Boulevard
   Mrs. Lela McCurdy, Principal

William E. Miller Junior High School
1960 Cleburne
   Robert M. Dawson, Principal

George Washington Junior High School
4701 Dickson
   Chester M. Card, Principal

James S. Hogg Junior High School
1100 Merrill
   Leslie R. Center, Principal

Frank M. Black Junior High School
1400 Lamonte Street
   J. Hubert Barr, Principal

Frances Harper Junior High School
3203 Center
   Wendell P. Terrell, Principal
   Mrs. Mary A. Wilson, Assistant Principal

UTAH
Brigham City

WILMA VICTOR, *Superintendent of Schools*

MRS. MARJORIE CHILDS, *Education Specialist*

ENGLISH AS A SECOND LANGUAGE; 2,3,6

Bureau of Indian Affairs
Intermountain School
P. O. Box 345
   L. W. Capps, Principal

WASHINGTON
Seattle

ERNEST W. CAMPBELL, *Superintendent of Schools*

JACK GREAVES, *Assistant Superintendent*

HELEN OLSON, *Supervisor of English*

*READING EMPHASIS; 3
Washington Junior High School
2101 South Jackson
   Mrs. Helen Elicker, Director
   Mrs. Isabelle Moe, Director

Washington Junior High School
2101 South Jackson
   Frank Fidler, Principal

WISCONSIN
Milwaukee

HAROLD S. VINCENT, *Superintendent of Schools*

DWIGHT TEEL, *Assistant Superintendent for Instruction and Curriculum*

*ORIENTATION CENTER PROGRAM; 2,3

Milwaukee Public Schools
5225 W. Vliet St.
   Clemens C. Zebrowski, Acting Coordinator

Victor L. Berger School
3275 N. 3rd St.
   Earl F. Powell, Principal

322

Henry L. Palmer School	**Welles Street Junior** High School
1900 North First St.	830 North 19th St.
Margaret Borkowski, Principal	John Schertzl, Principal
Fifth St. School	North Division High School
2770 North Fifth St.	1121 West Center St.
Gladys Caughlin, Principal	Robert S. Brandel, Principal

Observers from the Task Force also attended six teacher institutes. In order of occurrence, these were:

DOMINICAN COLLEGE, Racine, Wisconsin, dealing with preschool and elementary education in the Inner City. June 14–August 13. Sister Rose Albert, Director.

BOWLING GREEN STATE UNIVERSITY, Bowling Green, Ohio, dealing with urban education, grades 6–8. June 21–August 6. F. James Rylak, Director.

WAYNE STATE UNIVERSITY, Detroit, Michigan, dealing with urban education, grades 7–10. June 28–August 21. William E. Hoth, Director.

PENNSYLVANIA STATE UNIVERSITY, University Park, Pennsylvania, dealing with rural secondary education, July 5–August 13. Edward R. Fagan, Director.

INDIANA UNIVERSITY, Bloomington, Indiana, for teachers from predominantly Negro colleges. Willam A. Madden, Director.

UNIVERSITY OF NORTH CAROLINA. Summer Civil Rights Institute at North Carolina Advancement School, Winston-Salem. June 2–August 6.

Members and Consultants of the NCTE Task Force

RICHARD CORBIN is President of the National Council of Teachers of English (1964–65) and chairman of the English Department of Hunter College High School.

MURIEL CROSBY is First Vice President of the National Council of Teachers of English (1964–65), Assistant Superintendent for Educational Programs of the Wilmington Public Schools, editor of *Reading Ladders for Human Relations,* and author of *Adventure in Human Relations.*

PAUL D. ALLEN, now an instructor in the College of Education at Wayne State University, was a fifth grade teacher at the Mary C. I. Williams School in Wilmington, Delaware, during his work on the Task Force.

ROGER K. APPLEBEE is a lecturer in the Department of English, University of Illinois, and Associate Director of the National Study of High School English Programs, a study cosponsored by the National Council of Teachers of English.

ROBERT F. BARNES, Assistant Professor of Agricultural Education, University of California at Davis, was a member of the Department of Education, Ohio State University and director of a study of the problems of adult basic education, in addition to working on the Task Force.

CARL E. BEREITER is director of an experimental preschool for disadvantaged children and an Associate Professor of Experimental Psychology, University of Illinois.

BERNICE M. CHRISTENSON is Curriculum Supervisor of Elementary English, Los Angeles Public Schools.

WILLIAM M. DALLAM is Curriculum Planning Specialist for the Pennsylvania State Department of Public Instruction, Harrisburg, Pennsylvania.

Roger D. Gehlbach was a Staff Assistant at the National Council of Teachers of English.

Robert F. Hogan is Associate Executive Secretary of the National Council of Teachers of English.

Tom R. Hopkins is an Education Specialist for the U. S. Bureau of Indian Affairs Field Technical Unit.

Arno Jewett is Chairman of English and Foreign Languages, Bureau of Research, United States Office of Education. He was director of a recent national conference on improving the English skills of the disadvantaged and coauthor of *English for the Academically Talented Student*.

Samuel A. Kirk is the Director of the Institute for Research on Exceptional Children at the University of Illinois. The author of *The Early Education of the Mentally Retarded* and other books, he has served as a consultant to various federal agencies. He was the recipient of the first International Award for Professional Service in Mental Retardation of the Joseph P. Kennedy, Jr., Foundation and is a former president of the International Council on Exceptional Children.

Robert J. Lacampagne is Director of Special Projects at the National Council of Teachers of English.

San-su C. Lin is a Professor of English at Southern University and the director of a three-year project on the teaching of English to students handicapped by a local dialect. She is the author of *Pattern Practice in the Teaching of Standard English to Students with a Non-Standard Dialect*.

Walter Loban is Professor of Education, University of California, Berkeley, and Director of a twelve-year longitudinal study of children's language development. He is author of *The Language of Elementary School Children* and coauthor of *Teaching Language and Literature*.

Allan Muskopf is Assistant Professor of Education and Director of the Reading-Study Center of the Department of Education, Wisconsin State University, Eau Claire, Wisconsin.

LEE A. PEDERSON is a specialist in social linguistics and Assistant Professor of English at the University of Minnesota.

VIRGINIA M. REID is Chairman of the Elementary Section of the National Council of Teachers of English (1963–65) and Supervisor of Elementary Education, Oakland Public Schools, California.

FRANK E. ROSS is Chairman of the Secondary Section of the National Council of Teachers of English (1964–66) and Director of English Education, Oakland County Schools, Pontiac, Michigan.

JANET B. SAWYER is an Associate Professor of Linguistics at California State College at Long Beach and coauthor of *From Speech to Writing: An Applied Grammar*. She is a specialist on linguistics and the teaching of English as a second language.

WILLIAM M. SEE is Chairman of the English Department of Jefferson High School in Portland, Oregon, and a past president of the Oregon Council of Teachers of English.

ROGER W. SHUY is an Associate Professor of English and Linguistics at Michigan State University and editor of *Social Dialects and Language Learning,* a publication of the National Council of Teachers of English.

MARJORIE B. SMILEY is a Professor of Education at Hunter College and Director of the Project English Curriculum Center for teaching English to the disadvantaged.

JAMES R. SQUIRE is Executive Secretary of the National Council of Teachers of English and Professor of English at the University of Illinois.

SOL TAX is a Professor of Anthropology and Dean of the University Extension at the University of Chicago. With much experience in cross-cultural education, he is Director of the Carnegie Cross-Cultural Education Project, a project designed to study and strengthen educational programs for the American Indian.

ETHEL C. TINCHER is Director of the Department of Educational Broadcasting of the Detroit Public Schools and coauthor of guides for radio and television teaching.

DARWIN T. TURNER is President of the Piedmont Affiliate of the National Council of Teachers of English and chairman of the English Department at North Carolina Agricultural and Technical College. He is past president of the College Language Association.

ANDREW J. VISCOVICH is Coordinator of Special Urban Educational Services of the Oakland Public Schools.

MARY YORK is Supervisor of the Division of Curriculum and Educational Research of the St. Louis Public Schools.